Living Patiently

Living Patiently

A Devotional Study
of the
Book of Job

by
J. ALLEN BLAIR

LOIZEAUX BROTHERS
Neptune, New Jersey

FIRST EDITION, JULY 1966
THIRD PRINTING, MARCH 1970
FIRST PAPER EDITION, SEPTEMBER 1976

ISBN 0-87213-051-7

Library of Congress Catalog Card Number: 66-25720

PRINTED IN THE UNITED STATES OF AMERICA

Dedicated
to
All the faithful saints of God
who down through the years
have worked, prayed, and given
that the Gospel of Christ
might be propagated by means of the
Glad Tidings radio and literature ministry

With grateful acknowledgment to Mrs. Lois Couch
for her valuable editorial assistance

CONTENTS

	Page:
Introduction	9
Job 1:1-10	11
Job 1:6-12; 2:1-10	21
Job 1:13-22; 2:7-10; 3:1-26	32
Job 4:1-21; 5:1-27	42
Job 6:1-30; 7:1-21	51
Job 8:1-22	59
Job 9:1-39; 10:1-22	69
Job 11:1-20	79
Job 12:1-25	89
Job 13:1-28	99
Job 14:1-22	110
Job 15:1-35	120
Job 16:1-22	130
Job 17:1-16	140
Job 18:1-21	149
Job 19:1-29	158
Job 20:1-29	169
Job 21:1-34	178
Job 22:1-30	187
Job 23:1-17	197

8 CONTENTS

Job 24:1-25   207

Job 25:1-6   215

Job 26:1-14   219

Job 27:1-23   225

Job 28:1-28   235

Job 29:1-25   245

Job 30:1-31   255

Job 31:1-40   264

Job 32:1-22   274

Job 33:1-33   284

Job 34:1-37   293

Job 35:1-16   303

Job 36:1-33   312

Job 37:1-24   322

Job 38:1-41   332

Job 39:1-30   341

Job 40:1-24   351

Job 41:1-34   360

Job 42:1-17   370

INTRODUCTION

"YE HAVE HEARD of the patience of Job" (James 5:11). Yes, from early childhood many of us have heard the phrase time and time again, "The patience of Job." Where did he get all his patience? Did he have some special entree into this virtue that the rest of us know nothing about? No, Job was just a frail, stumbling human with all the deficiencies that mark believers. But there was one thing he knew how to do: he knew how to lean on God. It is true that he wavered when the load of care became almost unbearable, but the Lord never failed, not even once.

Job provides a living example of God's matchless care and provision for His saints. Who of us is without trials or hardships of some kind? The circumstances may differ from Job's but the sorrow and anxiety are the same. But more than this, the Lord is the same. As He undertook so overwhelmingly for Job, we may trust Him to do the same for us. It is for this reason that living patiently is not only a requisite for happiness but a grand privilege for all who know the Lord. Therefore, "Let us run *with patience* the race that is set before us, Looking unto Jesus the author and finisher of our faith" (Hebrews 12:1-2).

JOB 1:1-10

PROBABLY THE OLDEST BOOK in the world is the book of Job, which is believed to have been put into writing by Moses. Though it is not quite certain as to the time when the events of the book transpired, many seem to think that it was during Abraham's day. Doubtless it was no later, for there is no mention of Israel, the Tabernacle, the Temple, the law, or anything that would suggest a later date.

The theme of the book seems to be, "The child of God facing trials." The Lord uses Job as an object lesson of suffering for the people of God of every generation. It is for this reason that true believers find Job to be an extremely practical and helpful book, filled with encouragement for the suffering and sorrowful saint.

It should be noted also that Job was a real person. He was not a myth, as some have claimed. If you will turn to Ezekiel, the 14th chapter, and read verses 14 and 20, you will find that Job is mentioned by the Lord Jehovah along with Noah and Daniel. It is taken for granted in these passages that he was a living human being.

11

Looking into the first chapter, we notice four things relative to the character of God's servant: his integrity (verses 1 and 8); his wealth (verse 3); his wisdom (verse 5); and his protection (verses 9 and 10).

Consider his integrity as it is portrayed in verses 1 and 8: "There was a man in the Land of Uz, whose name was Job; and that man was perfect and upright, and one that feared God, and eschewed evil. . . . And the Lord said unto Satan, Hast thou considered My servant Job, that there is none like him in the earth, a perfect and an upright man, one that feareth God, and escheweth evil?"

From these verses we see that Job was all that a human could be in respect to holiness and character. He was morally upright, fearing God and abstaining from evil. In Psalm 4:4 God says, "Stand in awe, and sin not." Job obeyed this implicitly. He reverenced God with a holy fear, and sought to walk in the way of the Lord, abstaining from evil. The word "perfect" as it is used here does not mean sinlessness, but rather that Job was a man of integrity. The Bible declares in Ecclesiastes 7:20 that "There is not a just man upon earth, that doeth good, and sinneth not." Job is a type of the believer who has been born again by the Spirit of God, redeemed by the blood of Christ. No believer possesses any holiness of his own; it is the gift of God. In Romans 13:14 we read, "Put ye on the Lord Jesus Christ, and make not provision for the flesh, to fulfil the lusts thereof." It is Christ who enables us to overcome the lusts of the flesh and to walk well pleasing before God.

One of the interesting things about Job 1:1 and 8 is that this is not Job's testimony of himself, but God's. So often even Christians have a good opinion of themselves. With superficial piety we might think of ourselves as Job is described in these two verses. But our description of ourselves is usually faulty. The Lord's is always true. We read in 1 Samuel 16:7, "For the LORD seeth not as man seeth; for man looketh on the outward appearance, but the LORD looketh on the heart." God sees us as

we are and He knows our true character. Indeed, Job must
have been a man of integrity and uprightness to have God say
so much in his favor.

In Psalm 44:21 we read of our Lord that "He knoweth the
secrets of the heart." He sees us as we are. We may be able to
fool our friends and neighbors, and even dearest loved ones,
but we cannot fool God. I wonder what His description of you
would be. I wonder what His description of me would be. Oh,
how needful that we search out our hearts before God, and, if
there is known sin, that we confess it immediately, that we who
profess to be followers of Jesus Christ might be men and women
of integrity and uprightness, fearing God and walking in the
paths of righteousness and holiness for His glory.

It was Charles Haddon Spurgeon who said, "A Christian
should be a striking likeness of Jesus Christ. You have read
lives of Christ, beautifully and eloquently written; but the best
life of Christ is His living biography, written out in the words
and actions of His people. If we were what we profess to be and
what we should be, we would be pictures of Christ, yea, such
striking likenesses of Him that the world would not have to
hold us up by the hour and say, 'Well, it seems somewhat of a
likeness.' But they would, when they once beheld us, exclaim,
'He has been with Jesus; he has been taught of Him; he is like
Him; he has caught the very idea of the holy man of Nazareth,
and he works it out in his life and everyday action.' " The Bible
leaves no room for a superficial, hypocritical kind of piety. Our
God is a God of truth and holiness. How essential that you and
I, who have claimed Him as Lord and who profess to be His
servants, be fully controlled and mastered by Christ our Lord.

Let me ask, do you really know the Lord or do you merely
think you do? I find so many who, when asked if they have
received Christ, reply, "I think so." The Bible would have you
be sure of your salvation. Above all else, you should be sure of
salvation. I do not think anything could be any clearer than
1 John 5:12, "He that hath the Son hath life; and he that hath

not the Son of God hath not life." Do you have the Son? I mean by that, have you definitely asked Jesus Christ to come into your life? If you have, and if you really meant it, if you were sincere, then you have life, eternal life, never to perish, with the assurance of someday seeing Christ face to face to spend eternity with Him. If you do not have the Son, if you have not definitely received Him into your heart, the Scriptures are clear: you do not have life, you are still under the condemnation of God, and when you die you must be eternally separated from Him to suffer the torments of hell. Why choose death when you may have life? Let God live through you by receiving Him into your heart. Then, after receiving Him, you, like Job, will be enabled to be a man or woman of integrity and uprightness. It will not be difficult to be honest, kind, thoughtful, and loving. It will be Christ living through you.

In verse 3, we read of Job's wealth: "His substance also was seven thousand sheep, and three thousand camels, and five hundred yoke of oxen, and five hundred she asses, and a very great household; so that this man was the greatest of all the men of the east." It would seem that Job was the wealthiest man living in his day. Not always is it the case that holy men are rich. God provided a premium for Job, and it may be, as we have seen so often in the Old Testament, that he was rewarded with material things for his obedient and holy life.

God does not permit all of His children to become rich. Not all of us know how to handle wealth. I believe it is for this reason that God keeps many of us poor. Riches can often be a stumbling block to one's growth in grace. We are warned in Psalm 62:10, "If riches increase, set not your heart upon them." How many there are who have been deceived by "uncertain riches," uncertain in the sense that they are transitory. Is it not true that riches often turn our eyes from the really important things of life? There is a tendency when riches increase to set our heart on them rather than on Christ. In Mark 10:25 God says, "It is easier for a camel to go through the eye of a needle, than for a rich man to enter the kingdom of God." Then in 1 Timothy 6:10 God says further, "For the love of money is the root of all evil." Indeed it is. Thus the Lord does not entrust many of His people with riches.

It is far better to have spiritual riches than material. All who are in Christ and living in fellowship with Him are blessed with unlimited spiritual riches. In Ephesians 1:3 we read, "Blessed be the God and Father of our Lord Jesus Christ, who hath blessed us with all spiritual blessings in heavenly places in Christ." What manifold spiritual blessings we possess through our Lord: the privilege and power of prayer, the joy of searching the Scriptures to find inspiration, encouragement, and help, the presence of the indwelling Holy Spirit, and many, many more. The spiritual blessings are innumerable.

As we delve further in the study of the book of Job, we shall find that though God's servant loses all of his material riches, he does not lose the spiritual. Though everything is shattered before his eyes, he still has the strength and help of God in his life. Many of us have been through this same experience. Material things passed away, but the Lord did not forsake us. We found it to be true, as we see in Proverbs 15:16, "Better is little with the fear of the LORD than great treasure and trouble therewith."

There may have been a time when you had a hold on God. But as wealth increased you became more occupied with the temporal and mundane things. Gradually you forgot about the most important things of life. The result has been that you have drifted far from the Lord. Money has been the snare Satan has used to turn your eyes from God.

One time when a minister went to the pulpit to preach, he found a note which read, "Please request the prayers of our congregation for a man who is growing rich." Indeed, one who is increasing in wealth is in need of prayer, because very often this can be a deterring influence rather than a means for good.

But notice, too, Job's wisdom in verse 5: "And it was so,

when the days of their feasting were gone about, that Job sent and sanctified them, and rose up early in the morning, and offered burnt offerings according to the number of them all: for Job said, It may be that my sons have sinned, and cursed God in their hearts. Thus did Job continually." I see three things here: first, Job recognized the power of sin; secondly, he had a spiritual concern for his children; and thirdly, he was regular in his worship.

All of us need to recognize the power of sin as did Job. He was fearful that there was sin in the lives of his sons. He knew well the sorrowful results of sin. God says in Proverbs 4:19, "The way of the wicked is as darkness." Job did not want his children walking in darkness. He had a spiritual concern for them. He interceded for them. He prayed that they might walk with the Lord. After our children reach a certain age it becomes more and more difficult to tell them what to do. Sometimes we can say very little. We must entrust them to the Lord. But prior to this time there must be the holy example and influence in the home. Job wanted to be the right kind of father. I am not so sure his wife was the right kind of mother. Nevertheless, Job wanted to do his part in rearing his children properly. In Mark 9:42 we read, "And whosoever shall offend one of these little ones that believe in Me, it is better for him that a millstone were hanged about his neck, and he were cast into the sea."

There is no greater offense one can commit before his children than to set an unholy example. God pronounces judgment on such parents. If you know the Lord, you have an obligation before God to rear your children in the way of the Lord. Job was a good example because he was a man who gave due attention to God before his children. Not only that; he interceded continually for them. The word "continually" means that Job's worship was not spasmodic, up and down, today and not tomorrow. Daily he interceded and offered burnt offerings for his children. He was so concerned that they walk in the way of the Lord that he prayed and offered sacrifices daily for them. This reminds me of David, of whom we read in Psalm 55:17, "Evening, and morning, and at noon, will I pray, and cry aloud." How wonderful to see David and Job as men who believed in prayer, who realized that their power was in prayer.

Of course, to pray effectively we must be in a right relationship to God. If there is unconfessed sin in the heart and life, the Lord will not hear. If there are idols of any kind, such as the business, the club, or even our loved ones, which crowd God out of our life, prayer will be ineffectual. Job was a man of prayer. He reared his children well. What an example for you and for me. Are you the kind of parent God can honor? Do you have Christ in your heart and Christ in your home? Do you have family worship in the home? Do you gather around the Word daily and read it to the children? Do you teach them to pray? Do not miss out on the really important things of life. If you are having trouble in the home, or trouble with your children, it may be that there is trouble in your own heart. Maybe you have never received Christ into your life. You need Him, for only He can provide the solution for your greatest problem, the problem of your heart.

God says in His Word in Proverbs 22:6, "Train up a child in the way he should go: and when he is old, he will not depart from it." Here is a marvelous promise from the Lord. If we who know Christ are faithful in training up our children in God's way, the divine promise is that they will never drift away, they will never depart. But how many parents there are who have little concern for the spiritual welfare of their children.

Two proud young parents were showing the minister their little first-born. Very thoughtfully the young mother said, "I don't know whether I know enough about a baby to raise him or not." The young husband laughed, "She says that because she didn't get a book of instructions with him." Of course, he was mistaken. There is a book of instructions given. God's Book, the Bible, is the book of instructions that should be studied as never before when a little child comes, that he might be reared in the way of the Lord. Praise God for a man like Job who was concerned about his children.

We see one more thing about God's servant in chapter 1— His protection (verses 9-10): "Then Satan answered the LORD, and said, Doth Job fear God for nought? Hast not Thou made a hedge about him, and about his house, and about all that he hath on every side? Thou hast blessed the work of his hands, and his substance is increased in the land." Consider three circles of defense: God put a hedge around Job personally, around his family, and around all of his possessions. Because of this we can say that whatever came into the life of Job came only by God's permissive will.

The Lord cares for His own and protects them. In Psalm 125:2 we read, "As the mountains are round about Jerusalem, so the LORD is round about His people from henceforth even for ever." Sometimes we think we are alone in our calamity, but God is still with us. We cannot always see the protection God has established around us, but you may be sure the devil can. Satan acknowledged in verse 10 the fact that God had put a hedge around Job, his family, and his possessions. He further gives God the credit for blessing Job with his fruitful increase in land, property, and wealth. We read in Psalm 34:7, "The angel of the LORD encampeth round about them that fear Him, and delivereth them." Satan knows that. Further he knows he can do only what God permits him to do. How important then that we trust wholly in the Lord. Whatever the circumstances, whatever the need, remember, we have an unfailing God. David said in Psalm 16:8, "I have set the LORD always before me: because He is at my right hand, I shall not be moved." Have you set the Lord before you, or is your trouble set before you? Your sickness? Your bereavement? Your heartbreak? Are these what you have set before you?

Recall the occasion when Isaiah went up into the temple. He went with a heavy heart because of all of his problems. But he declared, "I saw the LORD." The Lord was set before him. He did not see his problems; he saw the Lord.

A veteran missionary used to have a card on the wall of one of his rooms which read, "Can you trust the Lord?" That was a heart-warming challenge. However, as one went into the next room, on the other side of the same wall was another card which read, "Can the Lord trust you?" That was something deeper and struck a challenge to the depths of the heart. We know that we can trust the Lord. Look back over your past. Has He ever failed you? Of course not. All right then, can He trust you to trust Him for the future?

Do you think you could trust God for the next minute? You do? What about the next hour? If you can trust Him for a minute, you can trust Him for twenty-four hours, thirty days, a year. You can trust Him until you meet Him in eternity. Remember, as He protected Job, He is protecting you today. You may not be able to realize this because you cannot see the protection. But God has set a hedge about you. Do you have fears? Are you unhappy? Remind yourself of the great God you possess in Christ. If you have taken Christ into your heart and life, you have nothing to fear. We are told in the Bible that a little sparrow cannot fall without the Father. How can we fail to trust the God who personally is aware of the death of a sparrow? Do not limit God by your little faith. Recognize Him as He is, the all-powerful, almighty, absolute God, able to supply your needs, able to lead you out of your problems and perplexities if only you will let Him do it.

The real question is this: do you know Him personally, intimately, as your Saviour and Lord? This is of foremost importance. God helps only those who will let Him. He forces Himself on no one. The issue of greatest importance is to receive Jesus Christ into your heart and life. Have you ever definitely received Him? If you want His protection, you must know Him as your Saviour and Lord. In Isaiah 43:11 God says, "I, even I, am the LORD; and beside Me there is no saviour."

As I write these lines, I am sitting in a room filled with air. Air is the gift of God. To live I must accept this gift. If I refuse to accept it, I will die. Freely I inhale the gift God has provided that keeps me alive. The same is true with the gift of eternal life. I can refuse to receive Christ into my life and die; or I can believe on Him as the Son of the Living God and receive Him as my Saviour and live. Do not spurn the greatest gift God has given to men—the gift of His Son. Do not turn your face from the Christ who died on the cross that you might have eternal life. You have been trying to weather the storm alone. No wonder you have failed. Turn to Christ today. Let Him lift your burden. Let Him heal your broken heart. He is an unfailing Saviour.

JOB 1:6-12; 2:1-10

THE BIBLE says Job was "perfect and upright, and one that feared God, and eschewed evil." He was a man of integrity who sought to please God in all that he did. He was a very wealthy man, and not only that, but one who evidenced wisdom in facing the reality of sin.

Job was soon confronted with a mighty enemy. And be sure, his enemy is yours and mine. In the first chapter, verses 6 to 12, and in chapter 2, verses 1 through 10, the enemy is portrayed. Thus as we move into the next episode in the story of Job, we see him on the battleground with the worst of all enemies. Keep in mind that God is holding Job up before us as an object lesson; that, as we study this book, we shall see God's servant as representative of all of the Lord's people. In Romans 15:4 we read, "For whatsoever things were written aforetime were written for our learning, that we through patience and comfort of the scriptures might have hope." Consequently, as we see Job in his conflict with the wicked one, let us not overlook the lesson God has for us.

None of us are excluded from the devil's trickery. But praise the Lord, we have One who is stronger than the devil, who can give deliverance. In 1 Corinthians 10:13 we read, "There hath no temptation taken you but such as is common to man: but God is faithful, who will not suffer you to be tempted above that ye are able; but will with the temptation also make a way to escape, that ye may be able to bear it." Whatever the temptation that comes our way, God will provide a way of escape if we trust Him. Be sure, the Lord is the believer's only means of escape. Job's integrity, wealth, and wisdom were insufficient to cope with the mighty enemy. It was his reliance on the Lord that gave victory.

The devil is a real personality. There are many who think we mean by the devil, a mere evil force. The Bible does not teach this. Note in the first chapter of Job, verse 6, "Satan *came*"; then verse 7, "Satan *answered*"; and also in this same verse, we read of Satan "*going* to and fro in the earth and *walking* up and down in it." In verse 8, God asked Satan if he had "*considered*" His servant Job. In verse 12 we read that Satan "*went forth* from the presence of the Lord." All these expressions make sense only when used of a definite, distinct personality.

These few instances I have cited could be multiplied hundreds upon hundreds of times if we were to examine other passages of Scripture. For example, here is just one, John 13:2: "The devil having now put into the heart of Judas Iscariot, Simon's son, to betray Him." Judas' wicked act was motivated by a wicked mind, the mind of the devil. The devil's single ambition is to turn you and me away from God and all that is good. To be sure, he is not as he has been pictured and characterized by many, with horns and a spiked tail. He appears in many ways. He is very wise and clever, much wiser than we, and so subtle. Some may laugh at such an idea, but of course this does not alter the case.

There was a young man who had been reared in a Bible-believing church and who later went off to a large seminary noted for its liberalism. When he had completed his ministerial training, he returned home and preached in the local church. He preached on the subject of the devil. He advised the congregation that he had made a special study of physiology and psychology and found that iniquity originates in diseased glands in the neck.

"Get those glands straightened out," he said, "and you won't be bothered with the devil any more." That is a pretty good one, is it not? "The devil originates in a man's neck." I wish the problem were that simple. But those of us who have been encountered by the devil know the problem we have on our hands.

There is only one devil, but he is assisted by legions of fallen angels. And do you know, the devil is being worshiped right here in our own country? I am not thinking about the heathen darkness of the mission field. There are people in America today actively organized into "Lucifer cults" for the spreading of devil worship. The "Satanists," as they are called, flourish in New York City, Washington, D.C., and other centers of population and influence. This devil-worshiping cult includes people of wealth and political power. It reaches the young also. One such cult of diabolism, membered by high school pupils of fifteen and younger, was exposed by Nassau County authorities of Long Island.

In *Christian Victory* an article on the devil cult in Washington, D.C., reported: "Their shrine is a penthouse in a sedate and expensive apartment house, whose correctly attired doormen have no idea that the beautifully gowned women and the handsomely dressed men they assist from their limousines two or three evenings a week ride to the tall roof in the elevator and convert themselves into semi-savages, discarding all that civilization has given them and abandoning themselves to an orgiastic ritual in the worship of the cloven-hoofed one." The "high priestess" of the cult is a wealthy divorcee who has traveled widely in the Orient. "Before an altar raised to Satan, the high priestess leads her disciples in reciting the allegiance: 'Satan is our master. He is our lord, and we are his disciples.' " The pledge continues: "O Satan, our master, our lord, we thy disciples worship thee. We pledge ourselves to the performance of every evil thou hast ever conceived, promising to shun every act that might be construed as good, we will follow faithfully thy thirteen commandments and will carry out each instruction contained in the seven books of deadly sin. This we promise, O Satan, our master, our lord."

Indeed, the Scripture is true: "But if our gospel be hid, it is hid to them that are lost: In whom the god of this world hath blinded the minds of them which believe not, lest the light of the glorious gospel of Christ, who is the image of God, should shine unto them" (2 Corinthians 4:3-4). Satan is the god of this world. He has blinded the minds of many, and he is blinding the minds of many in our day. Maybe he has blinded you to the glorious gospel of Christ. Possibly you have been blinded in your sins. Oh, recognize Satan's power and, at the same time, his false promises which lead only to destruction. Wholly lean on Christ and trust Him for constant deliverance from the devil's delusive and destructive power.

Where did the devil come from, anyway? Just as surely as we have problems in determining the origin of sin, we have problems also as we consider the devil's beginning. God has not given us all the answers. There are many mysteries involved in the subjects of sin and the devil. But we are assured from the Bible that "those things which are revealed belong unto us" (Deuteronomy 29:29). Thus looking into Isaiah 14 we get some insight as to the devil's beginning. Doubtless he had been an angel of great honor and authority, perhaps as Michael, the archangel. He was one of the myriads of ministering spirits, created to obey and serve God. But in Isaiah 14:12-17 we see the devil rebelling against the rule of God. The Lord says, "How art thou fallen from heaven, O Lucifer, son of the morning! how art thou cut down to the ground, which didst weaken the nations!" Then God tells us how the devil fell: "For thou hast said in thine heart, I will ascend into heaven, I will exalt my throne above the stars of God: I will sit also upon the mount of the congregation, in the sides of the north: I will ascend above the heights of the clouds; I will be like the most High." But the Lord said, "Yet thou shalt be brought down to hell, to the sides of the pit." The devil was thrust from his high and lofty position, and since that time has continued in open revolt against God.

His domain is earth and the first heaven. He is the god of this world. But lest we think him to be more than he really is, remember all that he does is limited by the permissive will of God. The Lord Jehovah could destroy the devil immediately, but God uses him to fulfill even divine purposes. Job 1:11 gives some insight into this fact: "But put forth Thine hand now, and touch all that he hath, and he will curse Thee to Thy face." This seems to be the devil's chief occupation—to put God and man at variance one with another. He is always stirring up trouble between God and man. The Bible gives us scores of examples. Adam and Eve were doing well until the devil came along and insinuated that God did not really mean what He said. In the same manner, he sowed the seeds of discord and unbelief in the hearts of Cain, Saul, Judas; and can we not say he has done it to you and me on many occasions? He creates doubt within our hearts and minds, causing us to disbelieve and distrust God.

One would think that the more knowledge the believer receives from the Word of God and the stronger he gets in the things of the Lord, the less susceptible he would be to the devil's lies. But just the opposite seems to be true. The devil strikes all the harder at those who are walking with God. We see this in the life of Job. Here is a man walking with God, living for Him, and reverencing Him in every respect. Suddenly the devil appears on the scene and tries to destroy Job's reliance on the Lord. Thus I am confident I am correct in saying that the closer one gets to God, the hotter the battle becomes with the devil. Somebody has said, "No sooner is a temple built to God but the devil builds a chapel nearby."

Never was this so true as seen in the life of our Lord. He began His public ministry and immediately the devil confronted Him, and three times sought to ruin the life, work, and character of the Son of God. What a warning to you and me! If the devil was fool enough and brazen enough to attack the Son of the Living God with the intention of ruining Him, what do you think he will do to us? Need I remind you that he is powerful, extremely powerful?

To illustrate his great power, let us look at a few verses found in the Word. In John 8:44 Jesus said of some of the wicked men of His day, "Ye are of your father the devil." That means that they were controlled by the devil. He controls men. He also tempts men, as seen in John 13:2. Here we have the occasion of the devil putting the seeds of betrayal into Judas' heart. Judas did not have to betray Christ. He chose to do it. He responded to the devil's temptation and yielded. Further we see that the devil sifts men. In Luke 22:31 Jesus said to Peter, "Satan hath desired to have you, that he may sift you as wheat." He overcomes men. Look at 2 Corinthians 2:11 where Paul warns us by saying, "Lest Satan should get an advantage of us." He devours men. Peter tells us that the devil "walketh about, seeking whom he may devour" (1 Peter 5:8). Paul informs us that he hinders men, according to 1 Thessalonians 2:18. The apostle assured the Thessalonian believers that he would have come to them for a visit, but "Satan hindered." In Revelation 12:10 we see that the devil is "the accuser." This means that he falsely accuses men. From Revelation 20:10 we see that he is the great deceiver.

We should realize also that the devil has two mighty weapons which he uses constantly in the display of his power. He uses the elements—wind, rain, and snow; and he uses the hearts of ungodly men and women. These are his two arsenals. In the first chapter of Job he used the Sabeans and the Chaldeans, along with fire and wind, to bring destruction, to kill Job's children, and to rob him of his wealth. Read about this in Job 1:13-19 and notice how clever the devil is to put the blame on God. He put it in the heart of the servant to say, "The fire of God is fallen from heaven." Indeed, he is very clever.

Though the devil is mighty, he is also limited in his power. Look at verse 12, "And the Lord said unto Satan, Behold, all that he hath is in thy power; only upon himself put not forth thine hand." Here is the enemy's defeat. In the Lord he is always defeated. We are told in Isaiah 59:19, "When the enemy shall come in like a flood, the Spirit of the Lord shall lift up a standard against him." In Christ we can overcome the wicked one. James 4:7 says, "Submit yourselves therefore to God. Resist the devil, and he will flee from you." What is the secret of victory? The first word provides the answer—"submit." "Submit yourselves therefore to God." You and I are no match for the wicked one. We need the power of God in our lives. He is the only one who can give the victory. If you have not yet received Christ into your life, you are powerless before this powerful foe. To you I say, let the Lord enter your heart now. For be assured, if the Lord is not in your heart, the devil is. Let Christ have the place He should have, the place He desires to have: the rulership, the lordship of your life. He will give you strength over temptation. He will guide you and lead you if you will let Him do it.

Having considered the character of God's servant and the enemy of God's servant, let us proceed further by thinking about the testings of God's servant. Even the name of Job suggests testings, for it means "persecuted." Certainly his experiences in life proved the divine choice of his name.

As it was true in Job's suffering, so it is true of most suffering; it often provokes the question, "Why?" Often when we are confronted with some severe suffering we ask, "Why must this happen to me? Why must I suffer so? What have I done that I should bear this trial?" To be sure, we have no right to interrogate God about anything. We are the creatures; He is the Creator. He is sovereign. We are the clay in the Potter's hand. But there is always the tendency on the part of weak flesh to question God's providence.

Christ is the only one who had any authority to ask why. He did this only once during all of His earthly ministry. While on the cross He cried out in deepest agony, "My God, *why* hast Thou forsaken Me?" Christ had a perfect right to ask God why, because He was completely forsaken. The Father turned His face from His only begotten Son, that He need never turn His face from you or me. We are never alone in our suffering. The face of God is turned toward us at all times, and He is always ready to help us. It is for this reason that we need never worry. When prone to pity yourself or to ask God why, console yourself with Hebrews 12:6 and 11: "For whom the Lord loveth He chasteneth, and scourgeth every son whom He receiveth. . . . Now no chastening for the present seemeth to be joyous, but grievous: nevertheless afterward it yieldeth the peaceable fruit of righteousness unto them which are exercised thereby." From these words we are assured that all suffering is purposeful. Thus the child of God may know that he is the Lord's possession and that truly "All things work together for good to them that love God, to them who are the called according to His purpose" (Romans 8:28).

The Lord gives us some light as to the reason for Job's suffering. Examining verses 9 through 11 in the first chapter of Job, we notice that there are two cross purposes at work: the divine and the satanic. "Then Satan answered the LORD, and said, Doth Job fear God for nought? Hast not Thou made an hedge about him, and about his house, and about all that he hath on every side? Thou hast blessed the work of his hands, and his substance is increased in the land. But put forth Thine hand now, and touch all that he hath, and he will curse Thee to Thy face." The devil's philosophy as given here is that, if a man's possessions are taken from him, he will curse and despise God. For many, this is true. There have been numerous instances where unsaved people lost their earthly possessions and blamed God for the tragedy. Such an attitude is diabolical. The devil deceives men into cursing God in times of material loss. The reason is, of course, that usually these people worship their possessions as their god. Jesus warned in Luke 12:15, "Beware of covetousness: for a man's life consisteth not in the abundance of the things which he possesseth." Many people think that real living is found in possessions. Thus they center everything they have in what the eye can see. If these things vanish, everything else goes, as well.

How different it is for the child of God, that is, the one who has been born of the Spirit and who possesses new life in Christ. He realizes that whatever happens, the Lord is still on the throne, that even though the devil may be at work, God has the upper hand.

> God's grace—thorns—ah, what forms they take!
> What piercing, smarting pain they make!
> And yet, each one in love is sent,
> And always just for blessing meant.
> And so, whate'er thy thorn may be
> From God accept it willingly;
> But reckon Christ—His life—the power
> To keep, in thy most trying hour.

After the devil stated his philosophy before God, "The Lord said unto Satan, Behold, all that he hath is in thy power; only upon himself put not forth thine hand." What God is saying here is, "I will prove to you, Satan, that your philosophy is a lie. You may take everything Job has from him, and you will see that he will not curse Me. And furthermore, you may not touch his life." The devil can go only as far as God permits. Thus already we see the Divine Hand at work in Job's suffering.

Why the Lord permits the devil to tempt His own we shall not fully understand in this life. But in spite of this we know that God's purposes are perfect. Those of us who love the Lord need not question His purposes. It is for this reason that we can praise Him for whatever He sends.

A friend was summoned to the bedside of his aged mother, who was more than eighty years of age. She was stricken with what they feared would prove to be her fatal illness. While her children were gathered in the room, her pastor came, and as he was about to lead them in prayer he turned to the aged saint and asked her what selection of Scripture he should read. She said, "Make your own selection, but let it be of praise." The weakness of old age was on her and the pain of sickness, but there was no gloom. It was light at eventide: "Let it be of praise."

This is the way the true believer can look at any trial of life. He knows that God will not fail, that somehow, some way, the Lord will undertake, even as He did for Job. Later Job says in the midst of his trials, "Though He slay me, yet will I trust in Him." He knew God would not fail. You may be sure that He will not fail you today. Things may look very, very bad. All may be overcast with gloom and sadness. But cheer up, saint of God. The light will shine soon. The Lord will undertake. Trust Him.

Perhaps in your affliction God is trying to speak to your heart. It may be that you do not know Him as your Lord. Even now He is trying to draw you to Himself. Christ knows all about suffering. He went to the cross for you. He wants to deliver you from your load of sin and the cares of this life. Why not turn to Him just now and trust Him as your Saviour and Lord? You may be sure that His grace will be sufficient for your need, whatever it may be. Our God wants you to come to Him.

JOB 1:13-22; 2:7-10; 3:1-26

GOD'S SERVANT, JOB, suffered severely. The devil in performing his diabolical work struck Job awfully hard. Probably no one has suffered more, in such a short period of time, than Job. Consider his losses. First of all, in chapter 1:13-17, we see the loss of his property and servants. Satan worked in two ways, through ungodly men and by means of the elements. As the result, Job's 7,000 sheep, 3,000 camels, 500 yoke of oxen, and 500 she-donkeys were all stolen or burned up, along with his many servants. In one day he was completely bankrupt. Think of this for a moment. Try to imagine everything you own being snatched from you in one day. Can you conceive of yourself in such circumstances? What do you think your attitude would be toward God?

Let us go on; we do not stop here. Job's loss of property and possessions was bad enough, but notice verse 19: "And, behold, there came a great wind from the wilderness, and smote the four corners of the house, and it fell upon the young men, and they are dead." "Young men" as used here is literally "young people." Every one of Job's seven sons and three daughters were killed by means of a tornado. Add this to the loss of his property and servants. What a catastrophe! What sorrow! But there is still more to come.

In verse 7 of chapter 2 we read, "So went Satan forth from the presence of the LORD, and smote Job with sore boils from the sole of his foot unto his crown." The "boils" were "burning ulcers." This affliction seems to have been a form of leprosy. Every inch of Job's body was inflamed. His feet were swollen twice their size. He was in physical pain night and day.

Next, we read of Job's loss of position in Job 2:8, "And he took him a potsherd to scrape himself withal; and he sat down among the ashes." The potsherd was used to scratch one's body. There must have been constant itching along with the inflammation. Job sat down among the ashes in extreme mourning, utterly cast out. Here was one of the greatest of the men of the East who became one of the lowest of the men of the East in a matter of hours.

Job was without needed encouragement. All of us are thankful for friends. Most of us have at least one or two dear friends to whom we can turn in times of sorrow for comfort and help. Job went to the one who should have been his greatest help in his calamity, his wife. But look at the advice she gave: "Then said his wife unto him, Dost thou still retain thine integrity? curse God, and die." What advice, coming from one's wife! If anyone should have been sympathetic and kind to Job at such a time, it should have been his wife. But she proved herself to be just one more disappointment added to Job's long list of woeful experiences.

Job's wife suggests to me the carnal Christian who speaks well of God when all is going smoothly, but when adversities come he forgets all about the Lord's unfailing grace. Job, on the other hand, represents the spiritual man who believed God whatever the cost. Which class are you in today? Are you a fair-weather Christian who trusts the Lord only when you have everything?

David said in Psalm 16:8, "I have set the LORD always before me: because He is at my right hand, I shall not be moved." This seems to be the attitude of Job, does it not? In spite of his suffering, he knew the Lord was still with him. He knew God would find a way of escape. The Bible says in 1 Corinthians 10:13, "There hath no temptation taken you but such as is common to man: but God is faithful." Did you get those three words? "God is faithful." Certainly He is! He always is. "God is faithful, who will not suffer you to be tempted above that ye are able; but will with the temptation also make a way to escape, that ye may be able to bear it."

Sometimes we think we have more trouble than we can stand. Never, if you are a child of God! The Lord knows how much you can take. He never overloads any of us. He permits only what we can bear. Probably Job could bear more than most of us. But God knew that; He made him that way. He did not overload Job, even though Job probably thought so, and surely we can understand why he thought so. But God always cares for His own. Thus we must trust Him. Maybe you are saying, "Well, I trust Him." Do you really? Let me ask, do you ever worry about anything? Are you guilty of this miserable evil? Worry is sin because worry doubts God. All worry doubts Him.

I am reminded of three elderly ladies who were talking of their experiences. One said, "I have had lots of troubles. I've lain awake nights with them, but those that worried me most never happened."

"My husband," said another, "used to say I carried three bags of trouble: those I had, those I used to have, and those I expected to have."

The third lady chuckled a bit and said, "Right now I can't seem to remember my troubles. The good Lord told me to cast all my cares on Him, and He gave me strength for each day's work and helped me over the hard places. At night, by the time I've finished thanking Him for His goodness, I'm always so tired I just fall asleep."

God would have us be like this, casting all our care upon Him, assured that He cares for us. What are you troubled about today? Trust the Lord! Your calamity is certainly no worse than Job's. He lost his possessions, his children, his health, his position, and lacked needed encouragement. But he did not lose his God who undertook for him. The Lord can undertake for you. Will you believe Him for your present need?

In the hour of trial we always get a better insight into our spiritual life than can be realized in seasons of prosperity. As one faces trial, his true spiritual depth can be determined. I have seen people who were faithful in church attendance week after week, who gave every evidence of being true followers of our Lord; yet these same friends went all to pieces when confronted with adversity and suffering. One wonders if they have ever had a real encounter with Christ. The true believer ought to be able to say with David, "I will love Thee, O LORD, my strength. The LORD is my rock, and my fortress, and my deliverer; my God, my strength, in whom I will trust; my buckler, and the horn of my salvation, and my high tower" (Psalm 18: 1-2). Anyone can be happy and glad when everything is going well. The real test of faith comes in the hour of the storm. How do you react when trouble comes? Do you go all to pieces or do you go to your knees and say, "Dear Lord, I know You will not fail. I know a way will be provided." In Colossians 3:3 we read, "Your life is hid with Christ in God." What greater refuge do we need than that? "Your life is hid with Christ in God." Ah, child of God, you are secure. You belong to Him, the Lord Jesus, who gave His life's blood for you. He will not forsake you. Job believed God. We too must believe Him.

Suffering is never in vain. Notice the effect it had on Job. "Then Job arose, and rent his mantle, and shaved his head, and fell down upon the ground and worshipped" (Job 1:20). This followed immediately after the loss of all his property and all his children. He did not curse God as Satan said he would; he worshiped God. Do you see what I mean? Here is an important test of one's spirituality. What will he do in his afflictions? Where will he go for help? Job went to the Lord immediately.

What do you think he did when he worshiped God? Doubtless he rededicated himself to the Lord, with the confidence in his heart that God would undertake. He worshiped. He revered God. He praised the Lord. I tell you, this was a great victory in Job's heart. The devil could not be defeated worse than he was at this moment when Job worshiped the Lord. Isaiah declared, "Thou wilt keep him in perfect peace, whose mind is stayed on Thee" (Isaiah 26:3). How wonderful is this peace! How comforting! Indeed, God gave His peace to Job at this moment.

In verse 21 of chapter 1, Job said, "Naked came I out of my mother's womb, and naked shall I return thither: the LORD gave, and the LORD hath taken away; blessed be the name of the LORD." For many generations, these memorable words have been quoted in funeral services to comfort distressed hearts. They were spoken by a man who knew what death really was. He had lost ten of his children. But behind the Sabeans, behind the Chaldeans, behind the tornado, Job saw the hand of God in all of this. He knew with perfect confidence that God could never make a mistake. In the midst of his calamity he could bless the name of the Lord. How could he do it? Look at the first verse of the book again, "Job was perfect and upright, and one that feared God, and eschewed evil." He was a man of integrity who had a hold on the Lord. His complete confidence and trust was in the living God. When you and I really know Christ as our Redeemer and Lord, we, too, can bless God in the face of any affliction. In the Sermon on the Mount Jesus said, "Blessed are they that mourn: for they shall be comforted" (Matthew 5:4). This is true. The Lord always comforts us in the hour of death. He comforted Job. He never fails.

It is interesting to note further that Job did not sin in the midst of his affliction. "In all this Job sinned not, nor charged God foolishly" (1:22). Many people do sin when trouble comes. They get drunk or go out and have their fling. How foolish! How ridiculous! They only add more woes to their misery. Job was a wise man. He did not sin in his affliction. He trusted God.

In chapter 2, verse 10, Job in replying to his wife gave this wonderful testimony, "Shall we receive good at the hand of God, and shall we not receive evil?" He meant "evil" in the sense of adversity or that which is displeasing, not evil in the sense of sinfulness. What he said was, "Can we expect to have good things in life only; must we not expect to have adversity as well? Is this not part of the life which we live? Are we not children of Adam, and has not suffering come upon us because of the fall? Thus be reasonable." Job said to his wife, "We must face things as they are. Suffering is no sign that God has forsaken us." This is so true. God is not forsaking us in trial. Usually He is preparing us for something greater. He is making us more useful.

About eight years after a certain blacksmith had given his heart to God, he was approached by an intelligent unbeliever with several questions.

"Why is it that you have so much trouble? I have been watching you since you became a Christian. You seem to have twice as many trials and accidents as you had before. I thought when a man gave himself to God his troubles were over."

"You see this piece of steel?" with a thoughtful but glowing face the blacksmith replied. "It is for the springs of a wagon, but it needs to be tempered. In order to do this I heat it red hot and then cool it with water. If I find it will take a temper, I heat it again, and then hammer and bend it and shape it so that it will be suitable for the wagon." He paused a moment, and his listener nodded.

"God saves us for something more than to have a good time," the blacksmith continued. "At least, that is the way I see it. We have the good time, all right, for the smile of God means Heaven. But He wants us for service just as I want this piece of steel, and He puts the temper of Christ in us by the testings and trials which come our way. He also supplies the strength to meet these testings." This is precisely what God is doing in you and me, putting temper in us that we might be usable. Thus we must expect adversity.

In chapter 2, verse 10, we read, "in all this did not Job sin with his lips." In times of suffering we need to ask God to guard our lips. Satan tempts us to say the wrong thing that will injure the cause of Christ and usually prove harmful to others. Job was very careful about what he said. Here was a man destitute of everything except faith in his wonderful God. Though tempted sore, he "did not sin with his lips."

Maybe you are burdened down with some trial of life at this moment. Consider these important lessons from Job. Read over the first two chapters of the book to reassure yourself. Claim the blessing He has for you in these two wonderful chapters of instruction and help.

Thus far we have seen the character of God's servant, the enemy of God's servant, the testings of God's servant, and now we begin the consideration of the comforters of God's servant. For many chapters in the book of Job we shall be examining the battle of words between Job and his comforters.

The battle was touched off when Job cursed the day of his birth. We read in chapter 3, verses 1-3, "After this opened Job his mouth, and cursed his day. And Job spake, and said, Let the day perish wherein I was born, and the night in which it was said, There is a man child conceived." Job comes awfully close to Satan's prediction recorded in chapter 1, verse 11, where Satan said to God, "Put forth Thine hand now, and touch all that he hath, and he will curse Thee to Thy face." Yes, Job came close to yielding, but praise God, he did not go all the way. He cursed the day of his birth, but he did not curse God.

Somehow, even in the severest trials of life God gives sustaining grace. Here was a man who in all probability had suffered more or as much as anyone, and yet the Lord restrained him from fulfilling the devil's prediction.

Job wanted to die. I think most of us can understand his situation. Some of God's people have wanted to die with even less suffering. Of course, Job's desire at this point was not commendable, but I am sure all of us understand well the weakness of frail flesh, especially in the time of testings.

In chapter 3, verses 11, 12, and 23, Job asks the question, "Why?" five times. This is the usual result of suffering, though it is not necessary. We should never ask God, "Why?" To do so doubts God's providence and wisdom. We need never fear nor falter, for the Lord makes no mistakes. Sometimes it would seem as though we are completely forsaken, but this could never be. God says in Deuteronomy 33:25, "As thy days, so shall thy strength be." It is not necessary that we know why God permits a certain trial. The important fact is that we know that He will give us the strength to bear this trial if we trust Him for it.

The story is told of a young theological student who one day came to the great preacher C. H. Spurgeon, telling him the Bible contained some verses which he did not understand and about which he was very much worried. To this Spurgeon replied, "Young man, allow me to give you this word of advice. You must expect to let God know some things which you do not understand."

The same could be said of the many mysteries involved in the believer's sufferings. We need not know why. As long as God knows, that is all that matters. We may rest in the truth that God loves those who are His blood-bought children. Also, we may be sure that the Lord will either lead us out of our affliction or give us the grace to bear it. He never forsakes His own. He is mindful of our calamity, and because of that He will provide help. David said in Psalm 27:1, "The LORD is my light and my salvation; whom shall I fear? the LORD is the strength of my life; of whom shall I be afraid?" This is enough. We need no more. Must I have an answer to my questions? Of course not. "The Lord is my light and my salvation." He will care for every need. I am to trust Him and believe Him wholeheartedly, without doubting.

Thus we see Job, a man of moral integrity and uprightness, who had abstained from evil, beginning to waver under the load of his care. Please do not misunderstand; I am not being critical of Job. When we consider the extent of his trials, and how we have complained with far less suffering, we cannot be hard on Job. But the thing I am trying to present is that which I believe God would have us learn: that Job is an object lesson for you and for me, that we might know better how to face our trials in the strength of the Lord.

Something else is seen in Job's moments of weakening. Do you recall what was said in chapter 2, verse 10? Look at the last phrase, "In all this did not Job sin with his lips." Not long after this was said of Job, he sinned with his lips. He cursed the day of his birth, he complained, he questioned the providence of God. This provides an important reminder for each one of us to beware of uncontrolled lips in times of adversity. When all is going well, when there is no pressure, it is not too difficult to guard our lips. But under the strain and stress of trials it is easy to say the wrong thing. Oh, that we might permit the Lord to control our words, especially during times of adversity. We should pray as did the Psalmist in Psalm 19:14, "Let the words of my mouth, and the meditation of my heart, be acceptable in Thy sight, O LORD, my strength, and my redeemer."

There is just one more thing I want to share with you before concluding this chapter. Have you ever heard anyone curse the day of his birth? Have you ever said something like this: "I wish I had never been born"? Going through some season of sorrow or testing, were you sorry you had ever seen this world? I suppose many of us are guilty. But I will tell you one thing:

though I have known some to curse the day of their first birth, I have never known anyone to curse the day of his second birth. Have you? I am sure you have not. No, one who has been born again by the Holy Spirit would never curse the day he came to Christ. In fact, can we not agree that this is the most important experience in life? Nothing could be any greater than to come to Jesus Christ and have all sin completely forgiven, to begin life anew. No one would be fool enough to curse this day. But, regrettably, many are foolish enough to neglect this day.

Maybe you have never yet turned to God and claimed Christ as your Saviour and Lord. You do not know what you are missing. You may have money and all that money can buy, but be assured, there is one thing money cannot buy. Money cannot buy happiness, and you cannot have happiness in this life without Jesus Christ. God says in 1 Peter 1:23, "Being born again, not of corruptible seed, but of incorruptible, by the word of God, which liveth and abideth forever." Have you been born again by the Word of God? What does this mean? The Word of God, the Bible, tells us that Christ died for our sins and rose again. We are told further that the moment we believe on the Lord Jesus Christ we are eternally saved; we are reborn spiritually—we are born again. This, I say, is the most important step a person can take in life. If you have never really trusted Christ by receiving Him into your heart, I hope you will do so immediately.

JOB 4:1-21; 5:1-27

MOST OF THE BOOK OF JOB is a battle of words between Job and his three comforters. It all began when Job cursed the day he was born and asked God why he had to suffer so. Suddenly Eliphaz stepped to the front and gave his first speech. He began very tenderly by saying, "If we assay to commune with thee, wilt thou be grieved?" In other words, he asked if he might offer some advice to Job during his time of intense suffering. Certainly there is nothing wrong in one's offering advice to another in times of trial, but it is important that the one who does so should be in a position to proffer advice. He should be one who knows the Lord and is in fellowship with Him. He should be qualified spiritually. Mere human wisdom, though consoling to some degree, can have no worth-while effect.

The man or the woman who helps most in times of need is the one who has a prayer life. You may be sure such a one will give lasting words of wisdom, God's wisdom. The Bible says in James 1:5, "If any of you lack wisdom, let him ask of God, that giveth to all men liberally, and upbraideth not; and it shall be given him." Oftentimes God gives us this promised wisdom

42

through His people who are living in constant fellowship with Him.

Few of us seem to capitalize upon the mighty privilege that is ours in prayer. We would be less disturbed and fearful if we would pray more. Even when we do pray, so often we are not in dead earnest. Can you sense something of the burden of prayer that was in the heart of David as he cried out to the Lord, "Give ear to my words, O LORD; consider my meditation. Hearken unto the voice of my cry, my King and my God: for unto Thee will I pray" (Psalm 5:1-2). These words suggest to me that David came to the realization that there was only one source of help. He believed with all his heart that God would hear and undertake. Oh, that you and I could pray in this same manner.

We are told that "The effectual fervent prayer of a righteous man availeth much" (James 5:16). It is "the effectual fervent prayer" coming from the heart of a man or a woman right with God that "availeth much." Immediately after this statement, James gives us an example of a righteous man who experienced the power of prayer. "Elias was a man subject to like passions as we are, and he prayed earnestly that it might not rain: and it rained not on the earth by the space of three years and six months. And he prayed again, and the heaven gave rain, and the earth brought forth her fruit" (James 5:17-18). Beloved in Christ, do you know of anyone in your circle of friends who prays like this? The power Elijah experienced is for you and for me as well. Jacob evidenced this same concern as he wrestled with his heavenly visitor, saying, "I will not let Thee go, except Thou bless me" (Genesis 32:26). Most of us give up too soon in prayer, proving our lack of real belief and hope in God.

George Mueller, the prince of intercessors with God, began to pray for a group of five personal friends. After five years one of them came to Christ. In ten years, two more of them found peace in the same Saviour. He prayed on for twenty-five years, and the fourth man was saved. For the fifth he prayed until the time of his death, and this friend, too, came to Christ a few months afterwards. For this latter friend, Mr. Mueller had prayed almost fifty-two years.

When we behold such perseverance in prayer as this, we realize that we have scarcely touched the fringe of real importunity in our own prayer life. Do not permit Satan to rob you of precious time in the presence of God. He will do everything in his power to keep you busy in an effort to prevent you from going to your knees. Do not be deceived by his wicked machinations. Call upon God many times throughout the day. Enter into David's experience, "Evening, and morning, and at noon, will I pray, and cry aloud: and He shall hear my voice" (Psalm 55:17).

It appears that Job's comforters were of little help to God's servant because their own experience with the Lord was so shallow. In Proverbs 9:10 we read that "The fear of the LORD is the beginning of wisdom." From what is seen in the book of Job, the three comforters had little fear for God. Their hearts were cold.

It is the man who is living in vital fellowship with the Lord who can best help struggling and needy humanity. One with a cold heart, even though he may profess to be a follower of God, is helpless in attempting to warm the heart of another. So many in our churches today possess cold hearts. Some of them were being used of God at one time, but they have drifted, neglecting to spend necessary time with the Lord. They have permitted their lives to become cluttered with things of little value. To them God says, "I know thy works, that thou art neither cold nor hot: I would thou wert cold or hot" (Revelation 3:15). Let me ask you, is your heart burning for God? Unless it is, you will be of little use to God and to your fellow man. Someone has said, "There is no sunlight in the life when there are no sky lights in the soul." Unless a man is walking in fellowship with the Lord, he is wasting his time trying to do a spiritual work for others.

We are living in an age when everybody wants something for nothing. Regrettably, they carry this same attitude over into their Christian experience. Most assuredly, salvation is free. No one can become a Christian any other way than by the grace of God. But after one makes this decision to follow Christ, there is a price to be paid. We should be reminded that good things cost. Valuable possessions are high-priced. What is cheaply acquired is apt to be of inferior quality. The type of life that follows the course of least resistance, that drifts with the current instead of rowing against it, is too often in evidence, and the sad consequences are apparent.

To be a Christian costs the renunciation of the forces that pull down and alliance with those that lift up. Christian discipleship must meet the standards set up by Christ instead of any that man may set up. He declared that a tremendous cost must be involved if any one will be His follower. The will must be yielded to Him. Life must be made anew by Him. It cost Jesus His all to be able to offer discipleship to all who would follow Him. Here is what He says regarding His disciples: "Whosoever he be of you that forsaketh not all that he hath, he cannot be My disciple" (Luke 14:33). This is not a cheap, inferior kind of experience. It demands our all. To be sure, if Christ has your all, you will be a blessing to all those around you. You will then be in a position to help those who so greatly need your help. Eliphaz was not this kind of man, but nevertheless, he does his best to volunteer comfort.

First Eliphaz offers comfort by means of commendation. He says to Job, "Behold, thou hast instructed many, and thou hast strengthened the weak hands. Thy words have upholden him that was falling, and thou hast strengthened the feeble knees." This was as if to say to Job, "You have helped other people. Now that you are suffering, you have nothing to fear." Eliphaz suggests that someone will help Job because he helped others.

Next he offers comfort on the ground of God's dealings with

humans. "Remember, I pray thee, who ever perished, being innocent? or where were the righteous cut off? Even as I have seen, they that plow iniquity, and sow wickedness, reap the same. By the blast of God they perish, and by the breath of His nostrils are they consumed." Eliphaz argues that, if a man is innocent, if he is righteous, God will take care of him. On the other hand, if he has lived for the flesh and sown iniquity, he must suffer punishment. Since Job has been a moral and an upright man, he had nothing to fear. At least, this was the essence of the advice the comforter was giving.

Further, Eliphaz trys to offer comfort by reminding Job of divine providence. "Although affliction cometh not forth of the dust, neither doth trouble spring out of the ground" (5:6). The testings of life are not by chance. They do not merely happen. They are to be expected. Of course, what Eliphaz says here is true. Anyone who is at all familiar with the Bible will realize that this truth appears in the Scriptures frequently. Some people get all excited when trouble comes, as though such a thing is unusual. The Bible teaches that it is normal and natural. The Apostle Peter says, "Beloved, think it not strange concerning the fiery trial which is to try you, as though some strange thing happened unto you" (1 Peter 4:12). We are not to be surprised when trials come. Rather, they are to be expected in the providence of God.

We need not be surprised, because these trials are no surprise to God. He knows all about them. I like those words recorded in Matthew 6:32, "Your heavenly Father knoweth that ye have need of all these things." Of course, if our Heavenly Father did not know about our afflictions, we should have reason to be discouraged and frightened. But what a great comfort it is to realize that nothing is hidden from Him, that He understands our condition and circumstances thoroughly. Even more than that, He realizes just how hard it is for us to bear up under it all. But the very fact that He knows all about our difficulties and problems should be enough to make us strong.

Perhaps you say, well, if He knows, why doesn't He change things? Why doesn't He do something to relieve my suffering? Child of God, this is precisely where you must walk by faith and not by sight. Surely He could change all of this if He wanted to. And you may rest in the fact that, if it were for your good, He would change these things. The fact that you are not receiving immediate relief from your suffering strongly suggests that there is some mission God wants that suffering to work in you, some lesson you need to learn while enduring it, some new power of usefulness and service which He would have you gain through your trial. Consequently, accept your trial from the hand of God. Do not be surprised. Do not be alarmed. This is not an accident; it is the result of divine providence.

Eliphaz continues by saying, "Yet man is born unto trouble, as the sparks fly upward" (5:7). Trouble is a part of life. It came into the world as the result of Adam's sin. As the sparks fly upward from a flame, just so we can be certain of trouble.

But Eliphaz does not stop here. He proceeds by telling Job what to do with his troubles. "I would seek unto God, and unto God would I commit my cause." This seems easy for Eliphaz to say, but had he been in Job's shoes, I wonder what he would have done? It is not too difficult to say what we would do when all is going well, but it is quite different when we are in the midst of calamity.

Nevertheless, in this instance Eliphaz was right. Our only hope, our only refuge, in seasons of trial is to get near to the heart of God. In Lamentations 3:32 we read, "But though He cause grief, yet will He have compassion according to the multitude of His mercies." Though God oftentimes sends trials for our welfare, He also provides the needed help and care. And is it not true that, during our seasons of affliction, He becomes even more real and precious to us.

A young English minister took a walk one afternoon. He came to a limestone gorge about two and one-half miles long. He was enjoying the scenery as he passed through the gorge and did not notice the storm clouds gathering overhead. Finally he looked up and saw the dark overcast sky. He turned and hastened toward home. The storm, however, overtook him. The rain began to fall in torrents. The young minister found shelter in the cleft of a great limestone rock. As he stood there in the place of shelter, he watched the rain descend. The thunder roared, and he saw the lightning flash. He was deeply impressed. He took a pencil and piece of paper from his pocket and wrote these words: "Rock of Ages, cleft for me, Let me hide myself in Thee." This experience was the inspiration that led Augustus M. Toplady to write our great hymn of faith, hope, and love. How beautifully the hymn sets forth our trust in Christ who once offered Himself that we might take shelter in Him.

It may be that in your hour of trial God wants you to draw near to Him. You may have become occupied with things that will soon pass away. The Lord wants you to enter into a fresh experience, that your life may be more effective for Him. Do not look at your trial as a heavy burden. Claim it as a blessing and use it for the glory of God. I know it is hard to recognize trials as blessings, but nevertheless, that is what they are. In Psalm 55:22 God says, "Cast thy burden upon the LORD, and He shall sustain thee: He shall never suffer the righteous to be moved." This word "burden" is interesting in the Hebrew because it is really the word for "gift." Thus instead of reading the verse, "Cast thy *burden* upon the LORD," it should be read, "Cast thy *gift* upon the Lord." Your burden is God's gift. It does not matter how it came, it is God's gift to you. We may be sure that all of God's gifts are good. This is not to suggest that your disease is good, or that your pain is good. Look beyond this to the mercy of God and realize that this entire experience, arranged under the providential care of God, is for your wel-

fare and God's glory. Thus you may fully rest in the Lord,
knowing that His grace will be sufficient and that in His own
time He will provide your every need.

In continuing his advice, Eliphaz speaks of God's divine
blessing, "Behold, happy is the man whom God correcteth:
therefore despise not thou the chastening of the Almighty"
(5:17). Indeed, these are words well spoken. Sprinkled in
with his humanism, Eliphaz has some good scriptural advice.
Surely there is blessing in chastening, for in it we know God's
love is being revealed. This is what we read in Hebrews 12:6,
"Whom the Lord loveth He chasteneth."

Next Eliphaz tries to offer comfort by reminding Job of God's
divine power. "He shall deliver thee in six troubles: yea, in
seven there shall no evil touch thee" (5:19). Here is another
worth-while truth. It makes no difference how great the sorrow
we may face, God will always provide the solution. This He
can do because He is the all-powerful One.

Once the passengers of a vessel steaming along the St. Law-
rence River were very angry because, in spite of the fact that a
heavy fog was encircling the boat, full speed ahead was main-
tained. At last they went to the first mate and complained.

"Oh, don't be afraid," the mate replied with a smile, "the
fog lies low and the captain is high above it and can see where
we are going." Likewise, you may rest in the fact that God has
the situation under control. He is not limited in His perception.
He can see the end from the beginning. Even more than that,
He can provide the solution because of His mighty power.

It is always well for us to look into the past in the time of trial
and consider how God delivered us. In Psalm 34:19 we read,
"Many are the afflictions of the righteous: but the LORD delivereth him out of them all." You may have many troubles,
but God will provide deliverance, for He delivers His own "out
of them all." This is an assuring thought. Praise Him, we have
an unfailing God. What is your problem? What is your difficulty at this moment? Realize that our God is sufficient. He is

unfailing in His goodness and grace. Take your burden to the Lord in prayer. Cast all your care upon Him. David could say in Psalm 61:2, "When my heart is overwhelmed: lead me to the rock that is higher than I." He knew where to go with his heartaches. Are you able to lean the whole weight of your problem on God with the assurance that He will provide a way of escape?

Some years ago Mr. and Mrs. Clarence Jones, of radio station HCJB in Quito, Educador, were seriously injured in an automobile accident in California. About a month afterwards, I received a letter from them which stated: "Only the Lord knows why the terrific impact of the collision did not put a 'period' to our lives instead of just a 'comma.' Graciously He has intervened in these weeks to recuperate our health to the point where both of us have recently been discharged from the hospital. As outpatients we shall go back for some time to our doctors for checkups and further medical attention. But God is good, and we are so happy to turn over to Him more completely than ever what remains of our lives."

How thrilling to read those words at such a time, "God is good." This is the attitude we should have in every trial of life. He is never anything but good. Even though we may not be able to comprehend His purposes, He is still good. It is for this reason that we can trust Him implicitly, with confidence that He makes no mistakes and that He will provide the needed help, whatever it may be.

Maybe you do not know the Lord. It is possible that you are going through some time of great trial at this moment, and yet you do not know the Burden Bearer. You need Christ. It is He who provides a solid foundation upon which to build. The Bible says, "Other foundation can no man lay than that is laid, which is Jesus Christ" (1 Corinthians 3:11). He is our only hope. If you never have done so, trust Him now, believe Him, receive Him as your Saviour and Lord. You can be sure that He will never fail you, for He is our unfailing God.

JOB 6:1-30; 7:1-21

IN CHAPTERS 6 and 7 Job replies to Eliphaz. It is quite obvious that what Eliphaz said had little effect on him. Job begins by lamenting his sorrowful state. "But Job answered and said, Oh that my grief were throughly weighed, and my calamity laid in the balances together! For now it would be heavier than the sand of the sea: therefore my words are swallowed up." There is the suggestion here that Job feels that his condition is hopeless. God has helped in former times, but now it seems that the grief is too much.

Job is beginning to doubt God. Under normal circumstances true believers do not doubt, but when the pressures of life crowd in upon us, sometimes we are prone to forget that God is all-sufficient for every trial. It is at times like these that we must really pray so that we shall not for a minute doubt the Lord. Someone has said, "When we doubt, we don't trust. When we trust, we don't doubt." Rather than doubt, we should put our cares into the hands of God. When we put our cares in His hands, He puts His peace into our hearts.

Further Job says: "For the arrows of the Almighty are within me, the poison whereof drinketh up my spirit: the terrors of God do set themselves in array against me." Is he intimating that God is trying to kill him? Is his faith wavering? Recall his words which had been spoken only days before, following the death of his loved ones, "The LORD gave, and the LORD hath taken away; blessed be the name of the LORD." His attitude seems to have changed. This should remind us that grief can affect one's spiritual condition if he does not stay close to God.

Because we cannot always understand the Lord's way is no reason to believe that God is forsaking us. Mary and Martha could not understand why Jesus, if He were God, stayed away from their home when their brother was dying. This is suggested in the words of Martha to Jesus, "Lord, if Thou hadst been here, my brother had not died" (John 11:21). Faithful Abraham could not fully understand God's purpose in asking him to offer up his only son. Yet Abraham believed God, and though he could not understand the situation, he walked by faith and not by sight. Moses could not understand the fruitless wandering in the wilderness journey, with a complaining people, rebellious and unconcerned about the principles of God. But he believed. In his heart he knew that even though he could not understand, God would have the answer. Joseph was thrown into confusion because of his circumstances. He could not begin to fathom the mysteries of it all, the treachery on the part of his brothers, his lot with the wicked woman, his imprisonment. How confusing it must have been. But Joseph did not give up. He trusted, and ultimately the reward came.

It may be at this moment you, too, like Job and scores of others of the people of God we read about in the Scriptures, are perplexed about the divine providences at work in your life. May I encourage you not to waver, but, with renewed commitment to the Lord and His purposes, to trust Him for the present moment with confidence that He will not and cannot fail you.

What about it, was God trying to kill Job? Of course not. It was Andrew Murray who said, "Every loss is meant to be filled up by His presence; every sorrow is meant to make His fellowship more to us." God was trying to make His presence real to Job. Have you ever stopped to consider that if one does not have a need in life, God is not really a necessity. It is in the hour of need that most of us find God to be a necessity. We learn how to believe Him and trust Him for all things.

Job continues by confessing his weakness. "Is my strength the strength of stones? or is my flesh of brass?" (6:12) What he is saying here is, "This is more than I can take. I am not made of stone or brass. I am a human. I am a weak, frail, faltering human." I doubt that he had ever realized this before as he realized it at this moment. Sometimes God has to prove to us just how weak we actually are. Even though we profess to be trusting in the Lord, there is always the tendency among us to feel a certain self-sufficiency. Job had come to the end of his rope, so to speak, as far as his self-sufficiency was concerned. At a time like this, one is in a position really to lean on God.

In the hospital I called on a lady who had just undergone serious surgery. She told me of the dread that was in her heart. She said, "I had an operation about a year ago and the worst part of it was when I had to get up and start walking again. I'm so afraid of this now." Several days later I went back to see her and she was sitting up in a chair.

"Well," I said, "I see you are up."

"Yes. Do you recall," she asked, "how fearful I was of getting up? Well, I just committed it all to the Lord and there was nothing to it. I knew I could not do it so I turned it all over to Him."

That is the way God works. When we come to the place where we recognize that there is nothing we can or should do about a situation, that God must do everything, you may be sure He will not fail. The greatest problem is that most of us feel as if we had to help God. He is not dependent upon our help. We must claim His promises and lean upon Him wholly. He says in Isaiah 43:2, "When thou passest through the waters, I will be with thee; and through the rivers, they shall not overflow thee: when thou walkest through the fire, thou shalt not be burned; neither shall the flame kindle upon thee." What is it in your life today that has you bogged down with care and worry? Realize that you are not stone, you are not brass, you are a frail human, utterly helpless before God. Tell Him that, will you? Let Him know that you realize your insufficiency as well as His all-sufficiency.

As Job progresses in his reply it appears that he is drifting away from his former reliance on the Lord. He says, "Therefore I will not refrain my mouth; I will speak in the anguish of my spirit; I will complain in the bitterness of my soul" (7:11). He boldly affirms that he is going to complain.

One of the strangest war incidents I have ever read was about the arrest, trial, and imprisonment of a serviceman who was called "A Discourager." He struck no blow for the enemy. He was not disloyal to his country. He was just a discourager at a very critical time. The fate of the company hung in the balance. He would go along the lines and say discouraging words to the men on duty. The court martial judged it a crime to speak disheartening words at such an hour. And so it was that he was sentenced to a year's imprisonment.

How many Christians there are who might be termed "Discouragers" because of their constant complaining. Rather than praise the Lord for all things, they grumble about most things. What a horrible disease complaining is.

Of course, all complaining is in reality against God. How tragic to see this servant of the Lord complaining against the unfailing God. But let us not be too hard on Job. Have not you and I done the same thing on occasion? We complain so often. But, you say, though I may have complained, I have never complained against God. Yes you have, for all complaining is against God. Romans 8:28 says, "And we know that all things work together for good to them that love God, to them who are the called according to His purpose." If as a Christian you really believe that "all things work together for good," any complaining you do is against God. How much better it would have been for Job to say, "I will trust, I will pray," instead of "I will speak, I will complain."

It takes far less wisdom and effort to trust God than it does to complain, and, to be sure, there is no comparison of the results. One may be sick, but if he complains he will be worse. Small wonder Paul declared, in writing to young Timothy, "Godliness with contentment is great gain" (1 Timothy 6:6). Most of us complain about things that are so insignificant. What a difference it would make if we would trust God for all things.

To trust the Lord may mean to wait for the Lord to act. It is true that God works for him that "waiteth for Him." Most of us will agree that, in the light of the past, God has a time for doing things and it is the best time conceivable. It may not always be to our liking, but it is according to the schedule of the Lord who is never late. Because of our limited wisdom we cannot see why God does not act immediately. As far as we are concerned, one time is as good as another. But never forget it, God has a set time for everything.

We see this in chapter 7 of John, where Christ's brothers said to Him, "Depart hence, and go into Judea, that Thy disciples also may see the works that Thou doest. For there is no man that doeth any thing in secret, and he himself seeketh to be known openly. If Thou do these things, show Thyself to the world" (John 7:3-4). Doubtless you have sensed the strain of sarcasm in these words, because Christ's brothers had not yet truly believed in Him. But notice our Lord's answer to His brothers, "My time is not yet come: but your time is always ready" (John 7:6). How revealing is this statement. As far as we are concerned, one time is as suitable as another. We cannot see why things should not be done immediately. Why should God keep us waiting so? Simply because His "time is not yet come." We are always ready, but He has a specific time for everything.

One of the lessons few of us learn fully is that of waiting on God. We think we have learned this important lesson, when suddenly we are plunged into a serious trial and discover that we know practically nothing about waiting on the Lord. In all of His plans and purposes, God's way is perfect. Ours is imperfect. We stumble and falter all along the way because of our failure to rest in the Lord's perfect plan and wait for His divine moment. One of the most overlooked words, by way of experience at least, in the Old and New Testaments is "wait." In Psalm 27:14 David implores us to "Wait on the Lord." Then he says, "Be of good courage, and He shall strengthen thine heart." And then he makes a further plea, as he says, "Wait, I say, on the Lord." David practiced what he preached. In Psalm 25:5, we read his encouraging words, "On Thee do I wait all the day." If you and I were to wait on the Lord all the day, every day, you may be sure worry and fear would vanish.

Caleb waited for forty-five years to realize God's promise made at Kadesh-barnea. He held on to His promise in spite of peril, changing circumstances, a multitude of funerals, and the passing of a generation. But he discovered that God's promise was as good as the Promiser. He lived to taste the glory of God's provision in the land flowing with milk and honey.

Abraham and Sarah failed to "wait on the Lord" and tried to help God keep His promise of giving them a son. They made a fleshly agreement—and Ishmael was born. Later on God fulfilled His promise and Isaac was born. All his life Ishmael was a "thorn in the flesh" to his parents and to Isaac. In fact, to this day Ishmael's descendants (the modern Arabs) are "a thorn in the flesh" to the modern Jews, and all because Abraham failed to wait on the Lord. Who of us could begin to estimate the mistakes we have made in life because we have overlooked this necessary truth time and time again? We have failed to wait on God.

Oft there comes a gentle whisper o'er me stealing,
  When my trials and my burdens seem too great;
Like the sweet-voiced bells of evening softly pealing,
  It is saying to my spirit— "Only wait."

When I cannot understand my Father's leading,
  And it seems but hard and cruel fate,
Still I hear that gentle whisper ever pleading,
  "God is working, God is faithful—only wait."

When the promise seems to linger, long delaying,
  And I tremble lest, perhaps, it come too late,
Still I hear that sweet-voiced angel ever saying,
  "Though it tarry, it is coming—only wait."

When I see the wicked prosper in their sinning,
  And the righteous pressed by many a cruel strait,
I remember this is only the beginning,
  And I whisper to my spirit— "Only wait."

Oh, how little soon will seem my heart of sorrow,
  And how trifling is our present brief estate;
Could we see it in the light of Heaven's tomorrow,
  Oh, how easy it would be for us to wait!

                                        Author Unknown

Further, Job says, "Let me alone; for my days are vanity" (7:16). Can you imagine a servant of God going so far as to say to the Lord, "Let me alone. Take Your hands off me. Don't persecute me any more"? Then, even worse, he accuses God of departing from him. "How long wilt Thou not depart from me, nor let me alone till I swallow down my spittle?" (7:19) I am sure that most of us can sympathize with Job, because in the hour of trial we too have felt on occasion that God had forsaken us. "If God is God," we have thought, "if He has all power, why doesn't He do something about our need? Why doesn't He answer our prayers?" Well, we may be sure that God is doing something. He always answers prayer. Not always how or when we think He should, but He always answers.

Realize whatever your need today, God is above all; He can do all things. Whatever your need, He is able to provide.

During an earthquake a few years ago, the inhabitants of a small village were much alarmed, but they were at the same time surprised at the calmness and apparent joy of an old lady whom they all knew. At length one of them asked the old woman, "Mother, are you not afraid?"

"No," she said, "I rejoice to know that I have a God who can shake the world." You and I should rejoice too in this assuring truth.

For centuries a sizable lump of rock lay in a brook in North Carolina. Passers-by saw just a lump of rock and passed on. Then one day a man saw in it a heavy stone useful to hold ajar his cabin door. He took it home and put it to that use. Still later a geologist passed by and saw it to be a lump of gold, the biggest nugget ever found east of the Rockies. Thus many looked upon Jesus of Nazareth, saw in Him only a Galilean peasant, and passed on. Others saw in Him a teacher and a prophet and listened. Still others saw in Him the Christ, the Son of God, the Saviour of sinners, and yielded themselves to Him. If you have never seen Him as the eternal Christ, the One who saves to the uttermost, I trust that at this moment you will turn to Him and acknowledge Him as your Saviour and Lord. He is ready to save you, but you must be willing to come. If you are willing, salvation is yours by receiving Christ.

JOB 8:1-22

Now ANOTHER WARRIOR, by the name of Bildad, appears on the scene. He seems to be quite abrupt in his manner of speech, not at all like Eliphaz who, at least at first, was gracious and kind. The sum total of Bildad's argument, as he, too, condemns Job, is that unless God delivers Job soon, it will be quite obvious that he and his family have been guilty of gross sin.

Let us examine a few of Bildad's statements found in chapter 8. He begins with a sharp blast of words, accusing Job of being mere talk, suggesting that Job did not practice what he preached. "How long wilt thou speak these things? and how long shall the words of thy mouth be like a strong wind?" A strong wind envelops an area and rarely does good. Often it destroys property and leaves only debris lying in its path of destruction. It comes and it is gone, but it seems to be of little value. That is what Bildad says about Job.

It does not seem that this was true of Job, but it is true of some people we know. So often when they speak, their words are like a strong wind, producing destruction as far as the lives and characters of others are concerned. Dr. A. B. Simpson was heard to say on one occasion, "I would rather play with forked lightning or take in my hands living wires than speak a reckless word against any servant of Christ, or idly repeat the slanderous darts which thousands of Christians are hurling on others, to the hurt of their own souls and bodies."

Unkind speech is most serious in its consequences. It has separated old friends and brought cruel misunderstandings. It has blasted the reputations of godly men. It has broken the hearts of many of God's dearest saints. It has blocked the power of the Holy Spirit in churches. Well has the tongue been defined as the avenue for Satan's inroads, the index of carnality, the poison that harms one's self and hurts one's best friends. The Christian's manner of speech is an expression of either his spirituality or his lack of spirituality. How we need to pay heed to the exhortation in James 4:11, "Speak not evil one of another, brethren."

Little do any of us realize the influence our words have on others. Guides sometimes warn tourists in the Swiss mountains not to speak as they pass certain points. Even the reverberation of a whisper in the air may stir an avalanche from its place in the crag. We never know when a passing word of ours will decide a soul's destiny. There are times in the history of a soul when life is so delicately balanced that sometimes it depends upon the first word with which a person is greeted whether he sinks into the darkness of despair or lifts up his head in hope. We can say something which will help a soul to Heaven or something which will bring him nearer to hell. We can give a bias to his whole character and influence every part of his life. Thus let us heed the words of Bildad to this extent, that we recognize the seriousness of wrong words, for indeed, they can be like a strong wind, producing devastation and anguish of heart.

Next Bildad assures Job that God will not overlook sin. "Doth God pervert judgment? or doth the Almighty pervert justice?"

God will not side-step evil. This is true; but in his harsh and inconsiderate manner, I wonder if Bildad considered the sin of judging one's neighbor? He appeared to be extremely self-righteous, and when Job needed comfort and help, Bildad seems to beat him down.

This is an evil that has affected many of the followers of Christ. Rather than help lift a brother when he has fallen, by unkind words or actions we beat him down. How contrary this is to the Scriptures. God tells us in Galatians 6:1, "Brethren, if a man be overtaken in a fault, ye which are spiritual, restore such an one in the spirit of meekness; considering thyself, lest thou also be tempted." We are not to be critical or unkind; we are to be loving and thoughtful of the needy brother.

It is very easy to fall into a satanic spirit of continual criticism, constantly picking out flaws in others, failing to see their real value and potential for usefulness. If we have not been able to discover the good in our brother and fellow servant; if our eye has detected only the crooked things; if we have not succeeded in finding the vital spark amid the ashes, the precious gem among the surrounding rubbish; if we have seen only what was of mere nature; then it would be far better if with a loving and delicate hand we drew the curtain of silence around our brother or spoke of him only at the throne of grace.

In Matthew 5 we find grace teaching righteousness; in chapter 6, piety; and in chapter 7, sobriety. How we need these three virtues at work in our lives—grace, piety, and sobriety. Such will rule out every trace of criticism, with the exception of criticizing ourselves. The tendency with most of us is to judge others and not ourselves. It is the easiest possible thing to sit in the judgment seat, to occupy the critic's chair, but it is the most miserable part of any Christian life. Do not permit yourself to get there, child of God. Daily realize that this is a constant danger with all of us. We need to be looking for Christ in one another. An aged Christian said he found it easy for him to esteem others better than himself. It was no doubt because he habitually judged himself. Oh, hear the Word of God as given in Romans 14:13, "Let us not therefore judge one another any more." Do not permit yourself to be engulfed in this evil that had eaten into the heart of Bildad.

Bildad continues by suggesting that if Job were really pure, God would help him. "If thou wert pure and upright; surely now He would awake for thee, and make the habitation of thy righteousness prosperous." This statement contains only a partial truth. The fact that one has been prospered in life does not mean that he has been pure. There are many people who are prospering financially, physically, and other ways, but they are extremely wicked. On the other hand, there are humble saints of God who respect and revere the Lord, who faithfully follow Him day by day, and yet their lives seem to be an unbroken chain of trouble. Bildad is using a very popular argument, that which the world might advance: that prosperity and success are synonymous. This may or may not be true; very often it is not. This is a rather superficial argument which proves to be groundless.

Like the ungodly, the righteous must also suffer. Belief in Christ is no promise that the believer shall escape suffering or trouble. But one marked difference between the ungodly and the godly is evident: when the ungodly suffers, he has nothing beyond to help, to encourage, or to assist him. But when the godly man suffers, he has all the power and provision of Heaven.

My wife and I have for many years been vitally interested in the work of the Missionary Aviation Fellowship. Recently one of their flyers had a most unusual experience. His plane suffered damage as he landed at a seldom-used strip on one of the mission fields. Someone was ill and the plane had been requested. Unable to fly out, the pilot began the long and weary trek back to his base. Along the way he passed through a small town that had only months before been touched with the gospel. The missionary was a bit discouraged and downcast, but in this small town the new believers gathered around and encouraged his heart in the Lord. Think of it, new converts speaking to the missionary of God's precious promises, reminding him that all things work together for good! Then they followed their words of comfort with a gift of two hundred pesos toward repairs.

How marvelous is the provision of our God! He cares for His own. Never does He fail. Trouble may come, but somehow there is always a way with the Lord. Lamentations 3:32 is true: "But though He cause grief, yet will He have compassion according to the multitude of His mercies."

Next Bildad points Job to a backward look. "For inquire, I pray thee, of the former age, and prepare thyself to the search of their fathers: (For we are but of yesterday, and know nothing, because our days upon earth are a shadow:) Shall not they teach thee, and tell thee, and utter words out of their heart?"

"Look back to our fathers," Bildad suggests, "and examine their lives. Those who were successful were blessed of God. Those who were not successful were not blessed of God." This argument was extremely weak and superficial, for it would not always hold good. At times it might, but at other times it might prove to be worthless. It is well for all of us to look back occasionally to see wherein we have failed, to learn by our experiences. But after we look back, then we should do as Paul did, take the upward look. "Forgetting those things which are behind, and reaching forth unto those things which are before, I press toward the mark for the prize of the high calling of God in Christ Jesus" (Philippians 3:13-14). The upward look is far more important than the backward look. Some of us have been looking backward for a long time. Lift up your eyes unto the hills, from whence cometh your help. Forget the past! Look to a greater day which can be found in Christ!

I have met some people who seem to impress me with the fact that, as far as they were concerned, the sun would never shine again: they were called upon to face some tragic experi- ence in their life. Ever since, they have kept their eyes fixed on that experience, unwilling to let God give them the grace to overcome. Oh foolish Christian, if this should be your lot, for- get those things which are behind. But, you say, I have tried to forget. Have you really? Have you asked God to enable you to forget? Remember, our God can do the impossible, but we must be willing to let Him do it.

As far as I am concerned, one of the most intriguing char- acters of the New Testament is the Apostle Peter. Peter had a great asset which is becoming more rare every day. He had a "nevertheless" up the sleeve of his faith. Peter was the kind of man who believed every word of God. Look, for example, at Luke 5:5, "And Simon answering said unto Him, Master, we have toiled all the night, and have taken nothing: nevertheless at Thy word I will let down the net." Doubtless you recall the details surrounding these words. Our Lord had said to Peter and his companions, "Launch out into the deep, and let down your nets for a draught" (Luke 5:4). Such action seemed to be hopeless, for the men had been fishing all night with no success. When Jesus gave the command to launch out into the deep, Peter might have put his hand on his brow and said, "I do not understand this. It is contrary to my reason. I am a beaten man in a beaten boat." But then, placing his other hand on his heart, he shouted out, "Nevertheless." Simple trusting faith overrides any bitter experience. "At Thy word" is God's way and the secret of success in any Christian endeavor. God's Word and Peter's, "I will," linked human effort to sovereign power and brought success.

Don't limit God by your lack of faith. Use what faith God has given you to reach out to the God of all grace, who will most assuredly enable you to forget the past and look forward into the glorious future. But is it not true that we are more will- ing, after examining our circumstances, to look to ourselves and worry than we are really to trust God? While going through the tunnel under the Hudson River in New York, a frightened woman was comforted by her English friend who said reassuringly, "Have cheer, my friend, we're not in a sack; there's a hole at the other end!" For the child of God, there is always a way out. God says in 1 Corinthians 10:13 that He will "make a way to escape." He always does. Not necessarily when we think He should; but in His own choice of time God will "make a way to escape."

Give God time, and even when the knife flashes in the air the ram will be seen caught in the thicket. Give God time, and even when Pharaoh's host is on Israel's heels a path through the waters will suddenly be opened. Give God time, and when the bed of the brook is dry Elijah will hear the guiding voice. Whatever the circumstances, however dark or cloudy it may seem, at the proper time God will be there to provide His way of escape. It is for this reason that we can trust Him unerringly, confidently, with the assurance given by the Holy Spirit that the Lord will not forget our need.

Bildad said to Job, "Prepare thyself to the search of their fathers" (8:8). Can a man by searching find God? Can a man by searching find help? How much better it would have been had Bildad told Job to "trust" instead of "search." Proverbs 3:5-6 says: "Trust in the LORD with all thine heart; and lean not unto thine own understanding. In all thy ways acknowledge Him, and He shall direct thy paths." The way of blessing is discovered by trusting and believing God.

In Song of Solomon 8:5 we read, "Who is this that cometh up from the wilderness, leaning upon her beloved?" How precious are these words, "leaning upon her beloved." The thought of the wilderness flees before us and passes into oblivion. Our Beloved's presence all the way through our wilderness journey makes it bearable. He is our constant strength and faithful stay. Lean hard! Our Beloved is omnipotent. We could not call Him our Beloved were we not beloved of Him. It is because He first loved us that we are now in Him.

If the way seems especially hard and our eyes have been fixed upon the ruggedness of the past, let us look up and see upon whose arm we are leaning—then lean all the harder. Hear His Word as He speaks in Psalm 121:3: "He will not suffer thy foot to be moved: He that keepeth thee will not slumber." Have we become absorbed in our own thoughts as we watched the path? Have we forgotten there is One to lean on? If we are lonely it is because we have not looked to Him for a long while and have even forgotten to lean. The burden that seems to have gotten so heavy is but calculated to teach us to lean on our Beloved. He will bear the load. Look to Him and trust Him.

We are commanded in His Word to "walk in the light, as He is in the light." We are not to stumble along in the darkness. The light is not only on the outside but on the inside, for He who indwells us is the Light. Does the distant howl of the wolf or the roaring of the lion frighten you? Their power is only in the darkness. Look up. Our Beloved is the Light. No fear need depress you if you are in Him. Delight yourself in Him and lean hard on Him.

Bildad reaches the peak of his argument as he accuses Job of being a hypocrite. It is always dangerous to accuse others of this sin, because all of us have so much hypocrisy in our own hearts that we have no right to accuse the other fellow. Nevertheless, that is what Bildad did. Notice this one verse where he says, "The hypocrite's hope shall perish" (8:13). Of course, this is true. The hypocrite's hope will perish.

There are many hypocrites in our day. We find them wherever we go: in business, among our neighbors, in our churches, in the pulpits. This is a great evil. The hypocrite is an actor; he is merely pretending. He is not sincere; he is only pretending to be something or someone. Many pretend to be righteous and holy, while underneath they are abominably wicked. Bildad said that about Job. We should do better to accuse our own selves of hypocrisy rather than the other person. It is so easy to see hypocrisy in those around us, while we completely overlook our own.

A certain soapmaker, having run out of superlatives to define the perfection of his product, hit upon a statement that said in a novel and compelling way the last word that could be said concerning it: "As we couldn't improve our product, we improved the box." We cannot improve the content of the faith once and for all delivered unto the saints, but we can improve the container, ourselves, as we yield to the control and power of the Living Christ. After all, it is "the box" that people see; the box must be made attractive. The hypocrite can never be attractive to others for Christ. All traces of self and hypocrisy must be removed as complete control is given to the indwelling Christ.

In concluding his argument, Bildad gives a slight hope, a faint glimmer of encouragement. "Behold, God will not cast away a perfect man, neither will He help the evil doers: Till He fill thy mouth with laughing, and thy lips with rejoicing" (8:20-21). He is telling Job if there were any righteousness at all in his life, God would not cast him away. There was still a chance. Of course, having the entire Word of God, we know better than this. There are no perfect individuals. Romans 3:23 says, "All have sinned, and come short of the glory of God." But how consoling to know, as we read in 1 John 1:7, "The blood of Jesus Christ His Son cleanseth us from all sin." How comforting is the fact that even though there may be sin in one's life, God will forgive if that person confesses his sin and claims Christ as Saviour and Lord. The moment he does he is saved. Daily, however, we must confess our present sin. The moment we do, God says we are forgiven and we are ready to meet Him should He call.

We must not be too hard on Job. He did not have the Word of God to which he could turn to find the Lord and the Lord's plan. Later in his book he cries out, "Oh, that I knew where I might find Him." You and I do not have to say that today. We can find the Lord immediately, if we desire. Jesus says in John 6:37, "Him that cometh to Me I will in no wise cast out." Let me ask, do you really know the Lord in your heart? Maybe you are going through some great sorrow or facing some perplexing decision. You need more than human ability, more than the advice of your friends. You need the unfailing God. Invite Him into your life by believing on the Lord Jesus Christ. If you will believe, you may be sure He will come into your heart.

JOB 9:1-39; 10:1-22

BILDAD MADE A HEARTLESS ATTACK on God's servant, declaring Job to be a hypocrite. According to Bildad, that was the reason Job was suffering so much affliction and sorrow. In chapter 9 Job replies to Bildad's accusations. He starts out by asking a question. "I know it is so of a truth: but how should man be just with God?" Job knew all about the hypocrisy of his own heart. It was not necessary that he be told about that. He says, "It is not *what* that I want to know, but *how*. I know what I am, I know what my difficulty is. But how can I get out of my suffering?" That is understandable, isn't it?

Most of us are pretty adept at picking out flaws. We find it easy to tell the other person about his errors. There are plenty of faultfinders. But there is a tremendous need for those who will help others in difficulty. God says in Isaiah 40:1, "Comfort ye, comfort ye My people." That is what Christians are supposed to be—comforters, not disturbers or trouble makers.

Job feels that his case is futile because God is so great and Job is so small; what would such a mighty, powerful Monarch

69

have to do with such a frail, insignificant being as Job? Notice these statements of Job regarding God's greatness: "He is wise in heart, and mighty in strength. . . . Behold, He taketh away, who can hinder Him? who will say unto Him, What doest Thou? . . . How much less shall I answer Him, and choose out my words to reason with Him?" In a very definite sense, Job is correct. God is certainly a great God. He is the Creator of the heavens and earth and all that dwells on the earth, but at the same time He is a loving God. We read in 1 John 4:16, "God is love." He is also a forgiving God: "For Thou, LORD, art good, and ready to forgive; and plenteous in mercy unto all them that call upon Thee" (Psalm 86:5). He is merciful and gracious, willing to forgive and to forget.

Oh, how wonderful is the grace of God. When we seek to describe the word "grace," it is difficult to find any words to explain it. It means "everything for nothing to those who do not deserve anything." It is God's love, mercy, and favor bestowed upon helpless, hopeless sinners who receive the Saviour. In Ephesians 2:4-5 we read, "But God, who is rich in mercy, for His great love wherewith He loved us, Even when we were dead in sins, hath quickened us together with Christ." No human merit could earn this blessing. No works of the flesh could purchase this treasure; it is the gift of God's marvelous grace.

How blessed to be able to say, "Once I was blind, but God touched me; Once I was lost, but God found me; Once I was under wrath, but God loved me; Once I was under guilt, but God forgave me; Once I was dead, but God provided new life for me; Once I walked according to the course of this world, but God reversed me; Once I was by nature a child of wrath, but God has begotten me; All of this He did because of His grace."

Another striking thing about the grace of God is that it is inexhaustible. Most of us have had the experience of reading an interesting article only to be brought to disappointment by the words, "To be continued." Yet, applied to other matters, these words bring cheer and satisfaction, for indeed it is a comfort to realize that the Lord's mercy and grace are to be continued. As much as we have experienced in our earthly pilgrimage, we still have not begun to exhaust their abundance. We have a right to our feelings of insignificance before God and His grace, but at no time is it permissible to feel that His grace, mercy, and love are insufficient for our needs.

Job's trouble was the same as the trouble of many present-day believers. He looked at his sin rather than at the grace and mercy of God. If we look to ourselves, we can name a dozen or more reasons why God should not help us; but if we look to Him and realize that He is the God of all grace, who is concerned about His people, who longs to help, then we shall find deliverance. This is the answer to Job's question of "How?" We must look to the Lord by faith and fully trust Him.

Now consider another problem Job had which some of us also have. Job was sure that God was reachable but doubt hindered recourse with God. "If I had called, and He had answered me; yet would I not believe that He had hearkened unto my voice" (9:16). Even though God would hear, Job would not believe it. He would still doubt the fact because God is so great and Job felt that he was so insignificant. This is where faith comes into the picture. God says in Hebrews 11:6, "Without faith it is impossible to please Him." If we sit back and try to reason out God, as Job was trying to do, and alongside of this try to reason out God's dealings, we shall never get any place. We must have faith. How do we get faith? Study the Word of God. In Romans 10:17 we are informed that "Faith cometh by hearing, and hearing by the word of God." If we neglect the Word we shall be weak in faith; only as the believer feeds on the Word can he become strong in faith. As we meditate on the Scriptures, the great facts of the Word will grip our hearts and all doubt will be routed out.

Job continues by emphasizing another important truth: self-justification can never avail. "If I justify myself, mine own mouth shall condemn me: if I say, I am perfect, it shall also prove me perverse. Though I were perfect, yet would I not know my soul: I would despise my life" (9:20-21). Here is a worth-while fact all of us would do well to consider. There is so much self-justification among all of us. Very few people like to think of themselves as being sinners; we much prefer to think of ourselves as being good, upright, and benevolent. Job knew all too well the uselessness of self-justification because he knew that God could see him as he was.

That is what you and I need to realize: God sees us as we are. Some of our friends look at us and say, "Well, now, he is a nice sort of fellow; or, she is a fine young lady." But in 1 Samuel 16:7 we read, "The LORD seeth not as man seeth; for man looketh on the outward appearance, but the LORD looketh on the heart." If a person is dressed up and cleaned up, he looks acceptable to his neighbors, but God sees the blackness of his heart, the deceit, the wicked thoughts, the dishonesty. He sees everything. That is why we need to go to the cross for salvation. We cannot excuse ourselves; before God we are condemned sinners in need of a Saviour. Job did not know everything but he certainly knew this.

Job realized the brevity of life: "Now my days are swifter than a post: they flee away, they see no good. They are passed away as the swift ships: as the eagle that hasteth to the prey" (9:25-26). This made his calamity all the worse. He realized that he was coming to judgment because of his sin; he did not feel that he was ready. Further, he recognized that any works of righteousness which he might do would not avail for God: "If I wash myself with snow water, and make my hands never so clean; Yet shalt Thou plunge me in the ditch, and mine own clothes shall abhor me." Snow water is free from impurities. Would this make Job clean? No, he is certain about that. He was right. Nothing you or I do could ever remove our sins. God says in Titus 3:5, "Not by works of righteousness which we have done, but according to His mercy He saved us, by the washing of regeneration, and renewing of the Holy Ghost."

Job laments the fact that there is no daysman to help: "Neither is there any daysman betwixt us, that might lay his hand upon us both" (9:33). This is an important verse. Job is searching for one who is righteous enough to go into the presence of God and yet human enough to approach needy sinners. A daysman is a go-between. Praise God, the Daysman has come in the person of Jesus Christ, the God-Man who is perfect in His humanity and, at the same time, Deity. He is very God, who came to earth and assumed a body of flesh. He was without sin but He died for sin—your sin and mine. He is our Go-Between; He is our way to God, our only way. We read in 1 Timothy 2:5-6, "For there is one God, and one mediator between God and men, the man Christ Jesus; Who gave Himself a ransom for all, to be testified in due time."

In chapter 10 Job still does not come to the place of real repentance and trust in the Lord. In fact, he seems to be more sorry for the calamity than he is for his own sin. In the opening verse of the chapter he evidences the fact that he would like to end it all: "My soul is weary of my life; I will leave my complaint upon myself; I will speak in the bitterness of my soul." There are many people like Job, without hope, without comfort, and without assurance. Without these things, perhaps Job is right: what is the use of living, anyway? Life is indeed empty without God's constant care and provision. It need not be so, because the Lord wants to help all of us; but we must let Him do it.

The body of a forty-year-old woman was found on the hot sands of the Mojave Desert, fifteen miles northwest of Twentynine Palms, California. She had gone to the desert from Los Angeles, seeking material for a feature story. Search for her began when the owner of a desert cabin found a note written by her, reading, "I am exhausted and must have water.

I do not believe I can last much longer." She had left three dollars to pay for a window she had broken to gain entrance to the cabin. But she found no water there. Apparently she collapsed en route back to her car, which was stuck in the sand two miles away. She died of thirst and exposure just two miles from Surprise Springs, where there was plenty of water.

Prolonged thirst for either literal water or the "Water of Life" is an agonizing experience. Sometimes it is difficult, and even impossible because of circumstances, to secure literal water, but no one need ever thirst for want of the "Water of Life." The Lord Jesus is the Giver of that water, and He is accessible to all, in all places, and at all times. He said to the Samaritan woman at Sycar's Well: "If thou knewest the gift of God, and who it is that saith to thee, Give Me to drink; thou wouldest have asked of Him, and He would have given thee living water" (John 4:10). After one partakes of the Living Water, Christ Jesus, he will find life worth living and will rejoice in tribulation, knowing that the Lord's way is the very best way.

Next Job makes a very foolish statement. He says to God, "Shew me wherefore Thou contendest with me." Here he is again asking "why." He did this earlier, you recall. This is not the important thing: he would have been far better off to stay with his former question, *"How* do I get out of my suffering?" It never does any good to ask God, "Why?" If we knew why we must suffer certain trials in life, it would not help a bit; in fact, it would make matters worse. It is just as well that God does not tell us why.

Job seems to be getting into more trouble all the time. He even goes so far as to condemn God, "Thou knowest that I am not wicked" (10:7). The word "wicked" here means "guilty." "Thou knowest that I am not guilty; and there is none that can deliver out of Thine hand. Thine hands have made me and fashioned me together round about; yet Thou dost destroy me." Surely Job knew that God's standard is perfection. In the light of this we are all guilty. In Ecclesiastes 7:20 we read,

"There is not a just man upon earth, that doeth good, and sinneth not." Of course, what Job meant was that he had not done enough to deserve all the suffering he had to endure. God does not measure sufferings in this light; in fact, we do not know what God's standard is for suffering. In Proverbs 25:2 we read, "It is the glory of God to conceal a thing." No one knows why certain things must come our way. That is why we ought to lean on the Lord all the more; He knows why. Nothing more is necessary.

Job knew better, because he said, "And these things hast Thou hid in Thine heart: I know that this is with Thee." He respected the sovereignty of God. He realized that the Lord in His eternal counsel knows all things and does all things well.

Like Job, all of us forget this fact so easily. Romans 8:28 says, "And we know that all things work together for good to them that love God, to them who are the called according to His purpose." We are not told that all things are good, but God assures us that "all things *work together* for good." Each trial, each testing, each sorrow that comes into the believer's life is a part of God's great plan. I realize that we bring many of our sorrows upon ourselves, but yet God uses even these things to work for good for those who love Him. We may not always understand this completely, but God does, and that is all that matters. He knows what He is doing. He will not forsake us. He has us at heart, at this moment, even though we might think we have been forsaken. If your trust is in Him, you have nothing to fear. His grace is sufficient. He will care for you. He will lead you out of your present calamity as He has done in times past. He will not fail.

We have no promise from the Word that we shall escape calamity altogether, but we do have many promises telling us that the Lord will not fail us in our calamity. Thus it is that we must stay close to Him and rest on His unchangeable promises. He will give the grace and the power to enable us to overcome.

After breakfast, a little boy eagerly skipped out of the house to play, only to discover that his clothing was not warm enough to protect him against the sudden drop in temperature.

"Daddy," he asked later, "why does God make it turn cold?" His mother and father alternated in answering. They tried to explain the value in having different seasons, fall, winter, spring, and summer. As they concluded he said, "I guess I'll just have to dress for the weather."

There are "seasons of the soul" in changing spiritual climates in which we live. As God's children, we are not immune to such drops of temperature as loneliness, misunderstanding, injury, sickness, and sorrow. Cherished friendships may be broken, winds from the North bring clouds, dampness, and chills. Knowing this, we can dress for the weather. We can put on the whole armor of God, that we may be able to stand in the evil day or the good day. Clad with truth and right and the gospel of peace, we can carry the shield of faith and the sword of the Spirit. But keep in mind, in ourselves we are weak. We must depend wholly on the Lord.

If Job had stopped with verse 13 of this chapter, it would have been much better, for he goes on to say, "If I be wicked, woe unto me; and if I be righteous, yet will I not lift up my head. I am full of confusion; therefore see Thou mine affliction" (10:15). It was not necessary that he tell us of his confusion; that is certainly obvious from our reading of the opening chapters. But just a minute: what about you? Are you any better off? It may be necessary for you to confess, with Job, "I am full of confusion." Perhaps you have been having trouble in your home or in your place of employment; you have been trying to understand some people. You are as confused as anyone could be. Your mind is going round and round, just like Job's. You are on a mental merry-go-round and you don't know how to get off. Consider this wonderful verse of Scripture found in Malachi 3:6, "For I am the Lord, I change not." Situations in the home may change; circumstances in business may change; people may change; but God declares, "I change not."

If your heart and life are yielded to the control of Jesus Christ, you have nothing to fear. God will take care of you. He always does. Remember, the devil is under His control. The devil can go only as far as God permits him to go. Oh, he puts on a good front; he tries to deceive us. But God changes not. Tell the Lord you believe Him. Say, as God's servant did, "I will trust and not be afraid." You may be sure the Lord will lead you step by step.

As a young minister in Scotland, Dr. John G. Patton volunteered for the foreign mission field and asked to be sent to some place where no missionary had ever gone. He was assigned to a cannibal island in the New Hebrides. Before sailing he married a charming young woman. In his autobiography he tells of their arrival on the island and how they built a humble cottage and began work. All went well for a year or two, and then a little child was born into the home. The young parents were extremely happy. But within a few weeks death came into the home and took the mother and child within a few hours of each other. He tells how he dug the grave in the garden with his own hands and buried his beloved dead. Then he adds, "If it had not been for Jesus and the fellowship He gave to me, I would have gone mad and died beside that lonely grave." Dr. Patton trusted the Lord implicitly even though he was forced to tread through the darkest valley of his life. But God kept him in the hour of trial, as He will keep all who faithfully trust Him and lean upon Him.

Job seems to be going down and down. "Are not my days few? cease then, and let me alone, that I may take comfort a little" (10:20). "Let me alone!" Isn't that something to tell God? Suppose God took Job at his word and departed from him; what would have happened to Job? I have seen people come to the place where they actually reacted to God in this manner. "Let me alone, I don't want You to bother me." Look where this leads. "Before I go whence I shall not return, even to the land of darkness and the shadow of death; A land of darkness, as darkness itself; and of the shadow of death, without any order, and where the light is as darkness" (10:21-22). Job was depressed and discouraged, he had lost all hope. Even eternity held no light for him. All was as darkness. One can get very disheartened and disconsolate when the Lord is forgotten. But why forget the Lord? Jesus said in John 8:12, "I am the light of the world; he that followeth Me shall not walk in darkness, but shall have the light of life." Are you following the Lord today?

JOB 11:1-20

In this chapter a new character appears on the scene to offer his advice to Job. Like the other two critics, Zophar is convinced that Job is suffering as the result of his sin. Also like Bildad, he accuses Job of being a hypocrite.

Zophar begins his speech by asking, "Should not the multitude of words be answered? and should a man full of talk be justified?" He rebukes Job for speaking in empty words that have not been backed up by a holy life. Further he asks, "Should thy lies make men hold their peace? and when thou mockest, shall no man make thee ashamed?" The word "lies" here is really "vain boasting." This was another way of saying that Job was insincere, he was not real — just so much talk. Zophar felt that this was a mockery of God for which Job would be punished.

The thing that seemed to disturb Zophar most was Job's self-justification. "For thou hast said, My doctrine is pure, and I am clean in thine eyes." This appears to be ridiculous to Zophar. How could a man suffering such judgment at the hand of God be pure and clean? Then Zophar cries out, "Oh that God would speak, and open His lips against thee." He is quite sure that if God would but speak He would tell the truth. Then Job's three comforters would be justified and Job would be condemned. They found it otherwise, however, when God did speak. Look at what is said in the last chapter of the book, verse 7, "And it was so, that after the LORD had spoken these words unto Job, the LORD said to Eliphaz the Temanite, My wrath is kindled against thee, and against thy two friends: for ye have not spoken of Me the thing that is right, as My servant Job hath." God's judgment was the reverse of that which Zophar and his friends thought it should have been. They were judging Job, but God judges them.

It is a dangerous thing to point your finger at someone else. Recall the words of our Lord in Matthew 7:1-5: "Judge not, that ye be not judged. For with what judgment ye judge, ye shall be judged: and with what measure ye mete, it shall be measured to you again. And why beholdest thou the mote that is in thy brother's eye, but considerest not the beam that is in thine own eye? Or how wilt thou say to thy brother, Let me pull out the mote out of thine eye; and, behold, a beam is in thine own eye? Thou hypocrite, first cast out the beam out of thine own eye; and then shalt thou see clearly to cast out the mote out of thy brother's eye." Usually when we criticize our brother for his sin, we have within us other sins that are far worse in the sight of God, so that actually no human is in a position to judge others. Human judgment is extremely faulty.

When D. L. Moody joined a church for the first time, the decision of the examining board was, "He is a very unpromising member." Little did they realize that Moody would be an instrument God would use to shake the world for Christ.

So often our judgment is like this. We are critical and unkind because we do not know all the facts. In Romans 2:2 we read, "But we are sure that the judgment of God is according to truth." God does not see as man sees. He sees everything, He knows all the facts, He is in a position to judge. He is our rightful Judge. But usually when we judge someone, we are sinning. Thus God says in Romans 2:1, "Therefore thou art inexcusable, O man, whosoever thou art that judgest: for wherein thou judgest another, thou condemnest thyself; for thou that judgest doest the same things."

So often the critic is inconsistent. He judges someone else for his sin while he completely ignores his own. It has been said that there would be less faultfinding if all faultfinders had come from the ranks of the faultless. The difficulty is that we are not from the ranks of the faultless; we are from the ranks of the sinful. This thought alone should exclude criticism and judgment.

We need to realize that we are not judged by man's opinion but by God's Word. In everything we must be sure that we are fulfilling the laws and the demands of God as they are prescribed in His Word. We are not responsible to men; we are responsible to God. The true believer in Christ can listen to criticism, accept that which is true and reject that which is untrue. But remember, in all cases, God is the Judge. He setteth up one and putteth down another according to His wisdom and judgment. We cannot fool the Lord. He says in Luke 14:11, "For whosoever exalteth himself shall be abased; and he that humbleth himself shall be exalted." If a man tries to exalt himself by empty and vain speech, God will bring him down. But if, on the other hand, a man humbles himself before the Lord, God will exalt him and make him fruitful.

Zophar continues by informing Job that, if God were to speak, "He would shew thee the secrets of wisdom, that they are double to that which is!" (11:6) This is as though to say that, if God were to speak, He would tell Job that the Lord's ways are greater than man's ways and that Job was a sinner and not righteous as he declared.

Zophar goes on to speak of the grace of God as he says, "Know therefore that God exacteth of thee less than thine iniquity deserveth." Even though Job was a great sinner, Zophar assures him that God does not judge according to one's sin. Of course this statement is true. No sinner has ever been judged by God to the extent of his sin. God always judges with grace.

Zophar then asks two important questions, "Canst thou by searching find out God? canst thou find out the Almighty unto perfection?" The answer to both of these questions is "No." We do not find God by searching; we find God by believing, by believing on His Son, Jesus Christ. Also, we cannot "find out the Almighty unto perfection." That is, we cannot fully understand all His ways. It is not necessary that we do. The thing all of us need to realize is that God loves us and that He gave His Son to die for us. The Bible says, "Whosoever believeth in Him should not perish, but have everlasting life" (John 3:16). What a marvelous promise, that simply by believing on the Lord Jesus Christ one can escape the eternal judgment of God. Oh, the mercy of the Lord, the grace that He has provided!

Zophar elaborates on the subject of God's wisdom by saying, "It is as high as heaven; what canst thou do? deeper than hell; what canst thou know?" (11:8) Who can fully understand the glory of the heavens? Man has gone to the telescope and obtained some knowledge of the perfections of the heavenlies, but he knows only an infinitesimal part of what God knows about the heavens He created. At the same time, what do we know about hell, other than what God has revealed in His Word? God's wisdom is so vast and great. Zophar says, "The measure thereof is longer than the earth, and broader than the sea," suggesting the greatness of God's wisdom. But not only is God great in wisdom, He is sovereign. "If He cut off, and shut up, or gather together, then who can hinder Him?" (11:10) What God decrees to do, He will do.

Zophar applies the truth he is leading up to by saying, "For He knoweth vain men: He seeth wickedness also; will He not then consider it?" He accuses Job of being vain and wicked.

It is true that God "knoweth vain men" and that He "seeth wickedness." He sees your heart and mine. We cannot cover up. We read in 1 Samuel 16:7, "The LORD seeth not as man seeth; for man looketh on the outward appearance, but the LORD looketh on the heart." It may be that your friends have a good opinion of you, and you may have a good opinion of yourself. But on the other hand, there may be sin in your life which God abominates. In Genesis 16:13 God's servant says, "Thou God seest me." Certainly He does! We cannot hide anything from God. If you are a Christian, there may be sin in your life hindering your progress in the Christian experience. You wonder why your witness is ineffective. You wonder why God is not using you in a greater measure. It could be that you have been overlooking some unconfessed sin that has not been dealt with in the light of the mercy of God.

The *National Geographic* magazine tells us about sea lampreys. Using man's canals to get by Niagara Falls, they have invaded the Great Lakes and adapted themselves to fresh water. Clinging with suction-cup mouths to the sides of trout, they hang on like leeches, pierce scales and skin with razorlike teeth, and eventually kill the trout. They are deadly parasites.

The Apostle Peter warns God's people in 1 Peter 2:11, "Dearly beloved, I beseech you as strangers and pilgrims, abstain from fleshly lusts, which war against the soul." In Hebrews 12:1 the writer exhorts us to "Lay aside every weight, and the sin which doth so easily beset us, and let us run with patience the race that is set before us." Secret sin, or open sin, is like the sea lamprey, sucking away your strength, your vitality. The Christian, through the grace of God, can shake off the lampreys of sin that weaken him, for in the cross of Christ God not only provided deliverance from sin, but deliverance from sin's power. In Romans 6:14 we read, "For sin shall not have dominion over you: for ye are not under the law, but under grace." God's people may have victory over any sin, but that victory must be received by faith in the same manner in which we received salvation—through Jesus Christ. The Lord gives the victory but the victory must be appropriated. There is no need for any believer to be overcome by any sin: there is complete deliverance from sin's power through Christ.

Reading on, Zophar says, "For vain man would be wise, though man be born like a wild ass's colt." Man would profess to be perfect. Very often he overlooks his sin, but Zophar says he is "born like a wild ass's colt," he is not tamed or domesticated; that is, he is not controlled by God. Further Zophar tells us what to do. "If thou prepare thine heart, and stretch out thine hands toward Him; If iniquity be in thine hand, put it far away, and let not wickedness dwell in thy tabernacles" (11:13-14). Man in himself is not sufficient to overcome any sin. How then can he prepare his heart? We are told how: "Stretch out thine hands toward God." Turn to Him, confess sin, claim victory over it! God will give the strength to put iniquity far from you. No longer must you be plagued by a besetting sin that seems to be ruining your testimony for Christ.

Zophar also has a message for the unsaved. Here are three essentials for salvation. First of all, "Prepare thine heart." The heart must be prepared, for we are told in Jeremiah 17:9 that it is "deceitful above all things, and desperately wicked." Next, "Stretch out thine hands." Lift your hands and heart in prayer to God. He alone can help you. Only He can save you. Stretch out your empty, helpless hands to Him for mercy which He will shed upon you abundantly. Then thirdly, "If iniquity be in thine hand, put it far away." All iniquity must be put away. "Let the wicked forsake his way, and the unrighteous man his thoughts, and let him return unto the LORD, and He will have mercy upon him; and to our God, for He will abundantly pardon" (Isaiah 55:7).

If you never have done so, turn to the Saviour now. There is no real happiness apart from Christ. Thousands upon thousands of people are wasting precious hours living for self when they could be enjoying all the blessings of God. Will you heed the Word of God today? Prepare your heart, stretch out your hands, turn from your iniquity. Believe on the Lord Jesus Christ, receive Him as Saviour and Lord. Your heart will be prepared immediately to meet God, and you will have the strength to put away all iniquity. God will deliver you from temptation and give you power over sin. But you must obey Him! You must come His way; your way will not suffice, for the Bible says in Proverbs 14:12: "There is a way which seemeth right unto a man, but the end thereof are the ways of death." Christ offers the way of life. He says in John 14:6, "I am the way, the truth, and the life: no man cometh unto the Father, but by Me." Come to Him now, if you never have; receive His abundant salvation and let Him live through your life. Be a witness for Him! Let others see what Christ has done for you, and then get busy for Him. Tell others about Him. Point lost and helpless men to the Saviour who provides eternal life.

Zophar goes on to tell us of the blessed results experienced when one turns from sin to God. Let us consider some of these results. "For then shalt thou lift up thy face without spot" (11:15). God will no longer see us as sinners, for, as He says in 1 John 1:7, "The blood of Jesus Christ His Son cleanseth us from all sin." He sees us as saints in Christ.

Next Zophar says, "Thou shalt be stedfast, and shalt not fear." The word "stedfast" is literally "molten," like metals which become firm and hard by fusion. The sinner wavers: he has no foundation. But when a man completely trusts Christ and permits Him to take away the power of sin, that believer stands upon a solid rock. He no longer wavers. He is right with God. 1 Peter 1:5 says he is "kept by the power of God." He shall not fear regardless of what comes his way. He is no longer like a house built upon sand, for he is built upon the true foundation, Christ Jesus.

In 2 Timothy 1:7 we read, "For God hath not given us the spirit of fear; but of power, and of love, and of a sound mind." The child of God should never be disturbed and distressed. He has a mighty Saviour who promises to undertake for him in every exigency of life. Whatever our trial or testing, God gives us the grace at the needed moment if we trust Him for it. "Let us therefore come boldly unto the throne of grace, that we may obtain mercy, and find grace to help in time of need" (Hebrews 4:16). The phrase "in time of need" is a colloquialism of which "nick of time" is the exact equivalent. Thus we may say that when we come to the throne of grace, trusting God for our trial, we find grace to help "in the nick of time." Grace will be provided whenever and wherever we need it. We are attacked by temptations, but at the moment of assault we look to Christ and the needed grace is there to help "in the nick of time." There need be no postponing of the provision until the evening hour of prayer, but there, out on the street, in the office, in the school, wherever you may be with a flaming temptation in front of you, you may turn to Christ with a cry for help; the grace will be there "in the nick of time."

Further Zophar says, "Because thou shalt forget thy misery, and remember it as waters that pass away" (11:16). It is a wonderful thing to be able to forget the past. The man or woman in sin cannot forget. His sin plagues and haunts him day and night. But after one has been to the cross and laid the burden of his sin on Christ, the Lord enables him to forget the things which are behind, and He gives him the strength to reach forth unto those things which are before, pressing toward the mark of the prize of the high calling of God in Christ. As the waters of the river pass before our eyes and soon are many miles out into the sea, so we are able to forget the old past life lived in iniquity.

In verse 17 we read, "And thine age shall be clearer than the noonday; thou shalt shine forth, thou shalt be as the morning." Do you see those words, "Thou shalt shine forth"? You will not only be illumined after coming to Christ, but you will be a guiding light to direct others to Him. The new light is not of your own kindling, but like the dawning of the day it is the gift of God, the brightest and the best. To each of us God says in Matthew 5:16, "Let your light so shine before men, that they may see your good works, and glorify your Father which is in heaven." Do not hide your light. You have received the glorious light of God through Christ—let it shine.

Notice the security Zophar speaks about, "And thou shalt be secure, because there is hope; yea, thou shalt dig about thee, and thou shalt take thy rest in safety." We have a hope that maketh not ashamed. In Hebrews 6:19 God tells us of this hope. "Which hope we have as an anchor of the soul, both sure and stedfast." There was a day when we had no hope, but the moment we turned to Christ He gave us an everlasting hope. The word "hope" means "confidence." We have the confidence that God will not fail. Men may fail us but God—never!

Zophar says, "Thou shalt take thy rest in safety." Isn't it wonderful that the love of God surrounds us on every side, so that nothing can come into the believer's life except it first pass through the heart of God? In Proverbs 2:8 we are told that He "preserveth the way of His saints." Certainly He does. Step by step as we walk on our earthly pilgrimage, God preserves every step as we trust Him and follow Him.

A mother took her little boy to the front gate to show him the neighbor's house, where he was to go and do an errand for her. It was beginning to get dark and the little fellow was afraid, but as he started out, he said, "I'll not be afraid to go that far, Mother, if you will watch me all the way." Her standing there with her eyes upon him was all that he needed to enable him to make the round trip without a murmur.

That reminds me of Psalm 32:8 where the Word of God says to you and to me, "I will instruct thee and teach thee in the way which thou shalt go: I will guide thee with Mine eye." Thus, how true are these words of Zophar, "Thou shalt take thy rest in safety."

Zophar gives more comfort as he says, "Also thou shalt lie down, and none shall make thee afraid; yea, many shall make suit unto thee" (11:19). The fact that the believer can lie down in the midst of his trouble and sorrow suggests again the almighty providence of God. Sometimes He makes us lie down, as in the case of the shepherd and his sheep spoken of in Psalm 23, "He maketh me to lie down in green pastures." We should realize, however, when God forces us to take rest it is in the green pastures. His love is still there; He is still at work, seeking to help us.

These words, "many shall make suit unto thee," literally are, "many will entreat thy face." This suggests the fellowship that will become the believer's the moment he trusts in Christ. He finds real friends, lasting friends, those of like precious faith, who will work with him and help him. Indeed, true born-again believers can say, "What a fellowship, what a joy divine!" This is a marvelous fellowship, the fellowship of the saints.

Look at Zophar's closing words of the chapter, "But the eyes of the wicked shall fail, and they shall not escape, and their hope shall be as the giving up of the ghost." What a horrible picture. Here is the result of sin. What has been written previously in this chapter is the result of believing on Christ. Here is the wicked man: the man without the Lord still in his sin. Sin has its wages and the Bible says they "are death." But Christ gives life, abundant life.

JOB 12:1-25

JOB HAS PATIENTLY LISTENED to his three friends in their attempt to give advice. Obviously they were of little help. Had they prayed more and argued less they might have helped God's servant in his calamity.

In chapters 12 through 14 Job answered not only Zophar but the other two friends. As he responded to their arguments, he began by giving them the benefit of the doubt saying, "Wisdom shall die with you." He inferred that they were wise. This was a favorable gesture on his part, for in chapter 11 Zophar had implied that Job was stupid.

In speaking of their wisdom, Job reminded them that it would soon vanish. It is for this reason that man needs more than human wisdom. Praise God, we have His Word, the Bible, which contains eternal wisdom. More than that, it is divine wisdom, the wisdom of God. In Proverbs 2:6 we read, "The LORD giveth wisdom: out of His mouth cometh knowledge and understanding." The Bible supersedes all other books, for it is divinely inspired.

Next, Job says, "I have understanding as well as you; I am not inferior to you." In other words, he is saying, "I know all that you have been telling me." In fact, the maxims the three comforters were proffering were well-worn, commonplace.

Further he says, "I am as one mocked of his neighbours." The advice his friends had given was more of mockery than advice. They were laughing at Job in his calamity. "He that is ready to slip with his feet," Job says, "is as a lamp despised in the thought of him that is at ease" (12:5). The word "lamp" is really "torch." When the traveler reached his destination after journeying through the darkness of the night, he threw aside the torch that had guided his steps. Job likens himself to a torch. He had aided his friends when he was in a position to help, but now that he has nothing they throw him aside. They make him the subject of mockery.

People are still doing this. How many times we have known of those who were well-to-do, as far as this world's goods are concerned, but some calamity intervened and they lost their means. Some who had appeared to be their friends, suddenly had nothing more to do with them. There are many people in this life who are interested only in what one has, not what one is. As long as we have things, they are our friends; but when we have little or nothing, we become the object of mockery.

This should never be true of believers in Christ in their relationship to each other. We have a fellowship, a oneness, that binds us together, making us all one in Christ. Each one of us is obligated to help the weaker brother. We should gladly perform deeds of kindness one for another, that Christ might be glorified through us. God says in Galatians 6:10, "As we have opportunity, let us do good unto all men, especially unto them who are of the household of faith." Christians are to be kind to everyone, but especially to other Christians.

A sergeant in the army was asked what had led him to become a Christian. He gave the credit to a private in his company who had been converted.

"We gave that fellow an awful time," the sergeant said. "One night he kneeled to pray. My shoes were heavy with mud and I threw one of them and struck him on the head. The next morning I found those shoes beautifully cleaned and polished. That was his only reply to me. It broke my heart and I came to Christ that day," said the sergeant. This is what the Lord Jesus enables believers to do. Without Christ a man will retaliate and pay back, but if one has really been born again, his attitude will be different.

Job points out the fallacy of Zophar's theory that calamity is always the result of evil. He says, "The tabernacles of robbers prosper, and they that provoke God are secure; into whose hand God bringeth abundantly." Evil men who lie, cheat, and steal are often prosperous. Many gangsters live high; they have plenty of money. Some who refuse to believe in God or obey Him are prosperous. And yet Job says, "into whose hand God bringeth abundantly." God supplies for them. He does not honor them in their prosperity, but were it not for the grace of God He would wipe them off the face of the earth immediately; He would utterly destroy every criminal. But God in His grace permits man to live. In His grace he permits man to steal and to be unkind without immediate judgment.

You may say you cannot fully understand this. Nor can I! The reason is that we are humans. We do not have the grace and love that God has for His creatures. Of course, we must realize that there is a judgment coming when man will be judged for his sins if he is not in Christ. In Hebrews 9:27 God says, "It is appointed unto men once to die, but after this the judgment." God is merciful now, but He will be just in meting out judgment. That is why every unsaved person ought to turn to the Lord during this present age of grace. God says in Isaiah 55:7, "Let the wicked forsake his way, and the unrighteous man his thoughts: and let him return unto the LORD, and He will have mercy upon him; and to our God, for He will abundantly pardon."

There was a poor man about sixty years old who had been a rough sailor, one of the worst men of the village. He was a heavy drinker and delighted in cursing and swearing. One Sunday morning he went to church. The message was about Jesus' weeping over the people of Jerusalem. The minister made the love of Christ so real and practical to his hearers that the poor sailor thought, "What! Did Jesus Christ ever weep over such a wretch as I am?" He thought he was too bad for Christ to care for him. At last he came to the minister and told him of his desire to give himself to the Lord Jesus. The man's life was changed and he became a man of God. Yet he was the last one you would have thought would be reached by the gospel. Does God choose the last men? He not only cares for the diamond, but He picks up the pebble; for He is able, as He says in His Word, out of "stones, to raise up children unto Abraham."

Job has emphasized the fact that sorrow and suffering are not always the result of evil. There are many wicked men who by the grace of God are prospered, in spite of their wickedness. The only explanation we can give to this is that God is merciful. Job continues to elaborate on this point by saying, "But ask now the beasts, and they shall teach thee; and the fowls of the air, and they shall tell thee; Or speak to the earth, and it shall teach thee; and the fishes of the sea shall declare unto thee. Who knoweth not in all these that the hand of the Lord hath wrought this? In whose hand is the soul of every living thing, and the breath of all mankind." Job reminds us that beasts, birds, fish, and plants also reveal the truth he has been presenting, that the violent oftentimes prosper over the weak. The vulture lives more securely than the dove, the lion than the ox, the shark than the dolphin, and the thorn than the rose. In other words, God is sovereign. God is over all. Even though we may not be able to understand many things, God does. One of the most confusing questions of our age is, why do the wicked prosper? Job assures us that it is because of the mercy of God, "In whose hand is the soul of every living thing, and the breath of all mankind."

Job says further in regard to the advice his friends had offered, "Doth not the ear try words? and the mouth taste his meat?" In other words, he was not bound to receive what they had to say. Every man has the right to receive through his ears what he wants to receive. As the mouth is privileged to taste anything it may eat, so we have a right to accept or refuse ad-

vice. Should not this be a reminder to all of us to choose carefully the things we hear and the things we believe? Some people believe anything that comes their way. They are especially
gullible regarding spiritual matters. We must detect truth from
error. How can one detect truth from error? The Word of God
is our standard. It does not matter too much what man says, but
it does matter what God has said.

It is important that every believer be a student of the Word
so he can detect error in the light of the truth. To be able to
recognize truth, we must spend time studying the Bible. God
says in 2 Timothy 2:15, "Study to shew thyself approved
unto God, a workman that needeth not to be ashamed, rightly
dividing the word of truth." Now, to be sure, study means more
than the mere reading of the Bible. One of the weaknesses in
the Christian Church today is that there are too few real students of the Word. We have our pet theories and traditional
doctrines that have been handed down, but too few of God's
people take the time to meditate on the Scriptures to get
God's message for their own hearts.

It might be well to check up on ourselves. How much time
are we actually spending in the Word of God? You say you are
a Christian? You say you love Christ? You say you are one of
His followers? How much time are you taking each day to let
God speak to your heart from His Word? Of course, we know it
is not the amount of time that is of greatest importance, for it is
possible to read much of the Word and get very little out of it
because of an unprepared heart and mind. But we must set
apart enough time to permit God to speak to us. The Bible
teaches in Matthew 4:4, "Man shall not live by bread alone,
but by every word that proceedeth out of the mouth of God."
What you read in the newspapers and in the magazines, and
what you hear and see on television will not feed the soul. You
need to take time to get into God's Word. Do not neglect the
Book, child of God. The Lord wants us to be Berean Christians.
We read of them in Acts 17:11: "These were more noble than

those in Thessalonica, in that they . . . searched the scriptures daily, whether those things were so."

Some Christians get awfully disturbed because they cannot understand everything they read in the Bible. You do not have to understand everything. Just keep on reading! I find that the things that disturb me most are not the things I cannot understand, but the things I do understand. When we eat fish, we do not refrain from eating because of the bones; we lay the bones aside and enjoy the meat. So it is when we come to the hard places in the Bible. We should not be disturbed or distraught because we cannot understand everything. Concentrate on that which you do understand. As you faithfully study the Word, the Holy Spirit will open up many of those things you have not been able to comprehend. As a believer, you have the greatest teacher of all indwelling you in the person of God's Spirit.

The important thing for you and for me is to be diligent students of the Word, not reading into the Bible, not trying to interpret from our background, but humbly beseeching God to speak to us and to guide us in His holy will.

Of course, if you have never taken Christ into your life, the Bible is a closed Book to you. It cannot be understood unless you really know the Author. To know the Author you must be born again, that is, born from above by believing on Christ. You need a spiritual rebirth. This is a miracle of God. You cannot achieve it. You cannot obtain it. You can only receive it by faith by believing on Christ, the Son of the Living God.

From verse 12 through to the end of chapter 12, Job continues to emphasize the wisdom, power, and sovereignty of God in ordering and disposing of all the affairs of the children of men according to His own will. When we come into the full realization of the great fact that God is over all, it gives us a more hopeful view of the catastrophic age in which you and I live. Job says, "With the ancient is wisdom; and in length of days understanding." The word "ancient" here is the word "aged." Elderly folks ought to be wiser than young people because of their years of experience. They have been through many heartaches and pitfalls.

Speaking of God, Job says, "With Him is wisdom and strength, He hath counsel and understanding." God does not find it necessary to acquire wisdom; He is wisdom. He knows all things; He always has and He always will. He knew everything before the world was formed. What is the wisdom of ancient man in comparison to the Ancient of Days? With all we know, there is so much we cannot do. God is unlimited. He can do all things. Job says, "Behold, He breaketh down, and it cannot be built again: He shutteth up a man, and there can be no opening. Behold, He withholdeth the waters, and they dry up: also He sendeth them out, and they overturn the earth." Probably Job is alluding to the flood in these verses.

Job continues by saying, "With Him [that is, with God] is strength and wisdom: the deceived and the deceiver are His." This means that all men are in God's power. No human has ever usurped the authority of God. We have lived in a generation when the world has been distressed by dictators. It is hard to realize sometimes that these men are always under the power and control of God. They are! The Lord is sovereign. He is above all and over all.

Job declares, "The deceived and the deceiver are His." The world has many deceivers. Not a few of them are found in business. But these deceivers are not below the notice of God. They cannot escape His cognizance. Because God is sovereign, He can make fools of the deceivers. He has the wisdom and power to manage everyone and everything in the world. Likewise, He knows how to serve His own purposes by them. We have seen this so frequently in the Bible where deceivers sought to ruin the character of believers. God used the wickedness of these ungodly deceivers to bring about His noble purposes for His own glory. We may be sure that He would not permit sin of any kind if He could not control it and bring out of it praise to Himself. The Lord omnipotent reigns. If He did not, the world would have passed into oblivion centuries ago.

Further in Job 12, God's servant cites instances of wisdom and power of Almighty God in the control of political leaders and authorities. Nations rise and fall under the sovereignty of God. Job reminds us that it is the Lord who "Leadeth counsellors away spoiled, and maketh the judges fools." He is speaking of wicked men, selfish men who cared nothing about God, who were ambitious for worldly glory. They wanted to reach the top. Perhaps they were on the way or maybe they did reach their goal. God humbled them and brought them down because they did not give Him the praise.

In the book of Daniel we read of King Nebuchadnezzar, a vivid illustration of the futility of man to achieve without giving glory to God. Further we read in Jeremiah 9:23-24: "Thus saith the Lord, Let not the wise man glory in his wisdom, neither let the mighty man glory in his might, let not the rich man glory in his riches: But let him that glorieth glory in this, that he understandeth and knoweth Me, that I am the Lord which exercise lovingkindness, judgment, and righteousness, in the earth: for in these things I delight, saith the Lord." There is nothing more important in all of life than knowing and understanding God. How do we come to know Him? Through His Son! This is the only way. The question is, do you know Him? Or have you been trying to reach the top in human strength without realizing that all you are and all you have is through the grace and mercy of God?

Continuing on through to the end of the chapter, Job proclaims again the sovereignty of Almighty God. He says, "He looseth the bond of kings, and girdeth their loins with a girdle." History proves all this. Some kings have been weak and yet God has lifted them to high positions, giving them unusual power. Others have been mighty, with strong supporting armies, and yet God has permitted them to go into captivity. Job says, "He leadeth princes away spoiled, and overthroweth the mighty. He removeth away the speech of the trusty, and taketh away the understanding of the aged."

We have depended upon our fathers for help. We have sought their wisdom from their experience. Suddenly God removed them from us in His providence. "He poureth contempt upon princes, and weakeneth the strength of the mighty. He discovereth deep things out of darkness, and bringeth out to light the shadow of death." In the midst of confusion, God can provide the light to give wisdom, if He cares to. "He increaseth the nations, and destroyeth them: He enlargeth the nations, and straiteneth them again." Truly, God sets up one and puts down another. "He taketh away the heart of the chief of the people of the earth, and causeth them to wander in a wilderness where there is no way." Men look to a great leader, and soon that leader falls. Thus the people "Grope in the dark without light, and He [God] maketh them to stagger like a drunken man."

Job has been emphasizing one of the most important truths of the Bible: God is over all. Though we have been talking about kings, princes, and nations, I believe this subject ought to cause all of us to fall to our knees and praise the Lord that He is interested in you and in me, that every step of our lives, every breath we take, is in the providence of Almighty God who is over all. Today, whatever your need or your problem, God is concerned about it. In 1 Corinthians 10:13 we are told that "There hath no testing taken you but such as is common to man: but God is faithful, who will not suffer you to be tested above that ye are able." God loves you and He can lead you out of your calamity. I am not telling you to grin and bear it; I am telling you to trust in Him. He will not fail. David said in Psalm 18:2, "The LORD is my rock, and my fortress, and my deliverer; my God, my strength, in whom I will trust; my buckler, and the horn of my salvation, and my high tower." Then he goes on to say in the next verse, "I will call upon the LORD, who is worthy to be praised." Whatever your need, whatever your problem, call on the Lord. Trust in Him, He will not fail you. Remember, God is over all. He is still the God of the impossible. He performs miracles. Trust Him!

JOB 13:1-28

JOB CONTINUES HIS REPLY to Zophar by saying, "Lo, mine eye hath seen all this, mine ear hath heard and understood it." He is referring here in particular to God's providence. In chapter 12 he spoke of the many evidences which set forth the sovereignty of God. Thus he says, "Mine eye hath seen all this." He then says, "What ye know, the same do I know also: I am not inferior unto you." His would-be comforters were talking down to him, as though they knew more about God than he did. Yet Job assured them that, if he did not know more, he certainly knew as much about God as they.

Next he informed them that he was not primarily interested in their advice, but that he was going to look beyond them. "Surely I would speak to the Almighty, and I desire to reason with God." More and more Job was convinced the philosophies proffered by his friends were useless. He was wise in going directly to the Lord. I am sure all of us appreciate the help of kind friends during times of trial, but we must go beyond what man can do for us and look to the Lord and trust Him. The

Psalmist said in Psalm 121:1, "I will lift up mine eyes unto the hills, from whence cometh my help." He looked to God, knowing Him to be a miracle-working God. Sometimes our friends would like to help us, but they are limited. There are instances when there is not a thing in the world they can do, other than to pray; but what could be more necessary than prayer?

Recall the incident in Mark 5, where we are told of the woman who had had an issue of blood for twelve years. We read in verse 26 that she "had suffered many things of many physicians, and had spent all that she had, and was nothing bettered, but rather grew worse." I am sure she had friends who tried to help her. She had sought the leading doctors. But no help came. Next we read in verses 27-29 that "She had heard of Jesus, came in the press behind, and touched His garment. For she said, If I may touch but His clothes, I shall be whole. And straightway the fountain of her blood was dried up; and she felt in her body that she was healed of that plague." What man could not do for her, the Lord Jesus did. You may be sure we have the same Christ who cares for us today. The Bible says of Him in Ephesians 3:20 that He "is able to do exceeding abundantly above all that we ask or think." Truly we can sing, "What a Friend we have in Jesus, all our sins and griefs to bear." The question is, do we rest in Him? Do we trust Him as we should? Do we lean on Him for everything?

Once when Martin Luther felt very despondent, he heard a bird singing its evening song. Then he saw it tuck its head under its wing and go to sleep. He remarked, "This little bird has had its supper, and now it is getting ready to go to sleep, quite content, never troubling itself as to what its food will be or where it will lodge on the morrow. Like David, it abides under the shadow of the Almighty. It sits on its little twig content and lets God care for it."

The same God who cares for the birds of the sky cares for His beloved people who have been born of His Spirit. David knew that even though his dearest loved ones were to forsake him, God never would. He said, "When my father and my mother forsake me, then the LORD will take me up" (Psalm 27:10). Your best friend may turn against you but Christ remains the same yesterday, today, and forever. Thus you can trust Him for all things. He will not fail. To you He says, "My grace is sufficient for thee" (2 Corinthians 12:9). Whatever your need, whatever your problem, do not look to men; look to God. "It is better to trust the LORD than to put confidence in men" (Psalm 118:8).

God is a very present help in time of need. The arm of the Lord is not shortened. He can provide a way out of your sorrow and calamity. Oh, how we need to take this third verse of Job 13 to heart, "Surely I would speak to the Almighty, and I desire to reason with God." Perhaps you need to speak to the Almighty today. Your mind has been disturbed by worry and fear. Take your burden to God in prayer! Get on your knees, cast your burden on the Lord! Submit your problem to Him; He has the answers. Do not look to men. Trust the Lord!

Job goes on to say to his friends, "Ye are forgers of lies, ye are all physicians of no value." "Forgers of lies" is literally "artful twisters of vain speeches." Job feels that his three comforters would have done better to keep quiet. "O that ye would altogether hold your peace! and it should be your wisdom." To remain silent would have helped more than the advice that was given. Is it not true that frequently silence is better than words? There are occasions when we should say nothing. Probably there are more times when we should keep quiet than when we should speak. Most definitely, when we have nothing to say, it is better not to speak. "For by thy words thou shalt be justified, and by thy words thou shalt be condemned" (Matthew 12:37). For this reason we need to pray constantly, "Let the words of my mouth, and the meditation of my heart, be acceptable in Thy sight, O LORD, my strength, and my redeemer" (Psalm 19:14).

Job exhorts his friends further to listen to him and consider what he has to say, "Hear now my reasoning, and hearken to the pleadings of my lips." Then he asks, "Will ye speak wickedly for God? and talk deceitfully for Him?" Job is referring to the unreasonableness of their argument that the end justifies the means, that Job was a sinner because he was a sufferer. Such an argument, declares Job, is speaking "wickedly for God."

Next Job reminds his listeners that the day is coming when they, too, will be searched out and tried. "Will ye accept His person? will ye contend for God? Is it good that He should search you out? or as one man mocketh another, do ye so mock Him?" Job is asking what they will have to say, what will they do, in the face of a judgment in their own lives such as Job was facing at the present.

Indeed, man is a poor judge. To each one of us God says in Galatians 6:7-8, "Be not deceived; God is not mocked: for whatsover a man soweth, that shall he also reap. For he that soweth to his flesh shall of the flesh reap corruption; but he that soweth to the Spirit shall of the Spirit reap life everlasting." We are prone to look to our neighbor and say, "Well, I am not as bad as he. I do not do the things he does." My dear friends, God is our judge. The holiness of God is our standard. We are not to look to anyone else. This is the thing Job was trying to point out to his friends. These men had tried to set up vain humanistic standards that would soon crumble.

How do you and I stand in the light of the perfections of Jesus Christ? I will tell you how we stand: we do not stand—we fall. Romans 3:23 declares, "For all have sinned, and come short of the glory of God." That is why all men need the redemption Christ has provided. He died on the cross for your sins and for mine. The moment we trust in Him we are saved, eternally saved. God longs to save you. Do not look to men. Do not look to your good works. Do not look to your morality. Look to Christ, the Lamb that was slain from the foundation of the world.

Having reproved his would-be comforters for their vain philosophies and shallow reasonings, Job goes on to say, "He will surely reprove you, if ye do secretly accept persons." That is, God would judge them if they accepted the philosophies that came from men rather than the eternal truth of God. "Shall not His excellency make you afraid? and His dread fall upon you?" These friends of Job should have been fearful to advance reasonings that were not according to the truth, while they professed to be followers of God.

In verse 12 Job says, "Your remembrances are like unto ashes, your bodies to bodies of clay." The remembrances refer to the proverbial maxims they were offering Job in his calamity. This empty talk was to "become like ashes." What a contrast this is to the Word of God. God says in the Bible, "Heaven and earth shall pass away, but My words shall not pass away" (Matthew 24:35). What man has written will go into oblivion. But the "thus saith the Lord" shall stand for eternity. Those who read and study the Bible readily testify to the difference between God's Word and the philosophies of men. Indeed, there is something different about the Word of God.

This was the experience of Robert Vogeler, the American businessman who was imprisoned for seventeen months by the communists in Hungary. After his release and return to New York, he told of the torment he endured in solitary confinement, and how eventually he was permitted to have a Bible in his cell.

"When my request for a Bible was granted," Vogeler declared, "I treated it as one treats a priceless possession and a thing of great value, a rare treasure." He then told how he read it daily, reading portions from the Psalms and the Old and the New Testaments. Then he added, "It gave me strength and assurance for what to my knowledge at that time were the interminable years ahead."

How many of us could give this same testimony. We have read other books. We have heard many preachers. But there is nothing as satisfying, as inspiring, as comforting, as the Word of the Living God. Thus men's thoughts will some day be but ashes, but the Word of God will still stand. Since this is true, should we not give ourselves to the study of the Book? Should we not memorize it and hide it away in our hearts, that we might enjoy all the blessings God has provided for us there?

Next Job says, "Hold your peace, let me alone, that I may speak, and let come on me what will." He saw little value in their speeches, thus preferring to face anything God would send rather than to continue listening to their empty and shallow advice. He further asks, "Wherefore do I take my flesh in my teeth, and put my life in mine hand?" Here he suggests that he is not afraid to die. He is not simply trying to preserve his life. For notice verse 15, "Though He slay me, yet will I trust in Him." Job states his full confidence and trust in the sovereignty of God at work in his life. Job knew that God was all-wise in everything, thus he was willing to trust Him fully. Next Job says, "I will maintain mine own ways before Him." This he desired to do, not as a hypocrite, but as one with a sincere heart. Then notice his testimony in verse 16, "He also shall be my salvation: for an hypocrite shall not come before Him." However sorely tried, the true believer will not depart from God. Of course, a man who is not really converted may turn against the Lord when he is tried. He may become angry with God for permitting such a trial to come into his life. But not one who has truly met the Lord. Like Job, he will say, "Though He slay me, yet will I trust in Him. He also shall be my salvation." This reminds me of the words of the Apostle Paul in Romans 8:38-39: "For I am persuaded, that neither death, nor life, nor angels, nor principalities, nor powers, nor things present, nor things to come, Nor height, nor depth, nor any other creature, shall be able to separate us from the love of God, which is in Christ Jesus our Lord."

Let me ask you, have you been doubting God? My dear Christian friend, He will not fail you. Possibly you have been looking to your circumstances rather than to your great God. Be assured that "underneath are the everlasting arms" (Deuteronomy 33:27). No matter how far you may go down into the valley of adversity and suffering, these arms are still underneath. That is how Job could say in the midst of his soul-shaking, mind-disturbing sorrow, "Though He slay me, yet will I trust in Him." Is your confidence in the Lord today? Realize the Bible says, "In quietness and in confidence shall be your strength" (Isaiah 30:15). Though sometimes our feet may be in the wilderness, never forget: our names are written on the heart of God and our life is hid with Him. It is quite true that many may not realize the hidden life in its brightness, its peace, and its plentiful provision within the vale. But it is nonetheless a glorious fact. And our dimness of perception or our changeableness of feelings can no more destroy this truth than we can prevent the sun from shining. It is true of every child of God, even the youngest and the feeblest, as of the oldest and most advanced Christian. It does not depend upon age, intelligence, or strength, but upon union with the living Saviour. In Ephesians 5:30,32 we read, "We are members of His body, of His flesh, and of His bones. . . . This is a great mystery: but I speak concerning Christ and the church." This is how we can say, "Though He slay me, yet will I trust in Him." Christ is Lord. He changes not. Think of Him at Nain when He said to the widow, "Weep not." Think of Him on His last journey to Jerusalem, how He took little children into His arms and blessed them. Think of Him as He wept by the grave of a friend He was about to raise to life. He changeth not and He has said, "I will never leave thee, nor forsake thee." What a Saviour! What a promise! Believer, are you trusting Him daily? Have you the new life that He alone can give? Depend not on being remembered in a will, but be in the Father's will.

Do you know Jesus Christ in your heart? I don't mean, do you know about Him? Do you really know Him as your Saviour and Lord? If you do, then you can face the trials of life with the belief and the confidence that somehow God will make a way of escape. God will provide. God will undertake. You will be able to say as confidently as Job said, "Though He slay me, yet will I trust in Him. He also shall be my salvation." Is He your salvation today?

Looking at verse 17 we see that Job speaks out quite strongly to his friends, saying, "Hear diligently my speech, and my declaration with your ears." That is, give attention to what I am about to say. Job proceeds to give his side of the story. He has listened to his friends; now he must answer them. "Behold now, I have ordered my cause; I know that I shall be justified." The word "ordered" here suggests that his own heart is right before God. He has been careful that his own relationship to the Lord is in order. For this reason he says, "I know." There are no doubts in his mind. "I know that I shall be justified." I like the confidence with which Job speaks. To be sure, this confidence is not because of himself, but because of the greatness of his God.

How it disturbs me when I hear people reply to the question, "Are you a Christian?" with "I think so." If there is anything we may *know*, it is the fact that we have been passed from death unto life. Of course, if a person has not had a real conversion experience, I can understand why he may have doubts. The Apostle Paul declared, "I *know* in whom I have believed." He knew because on the Damascus highway he met God. There were no doubts about it. He had an experience. Job had an experience also. For this reason he could declare, "I know that I shall be justified." Job knew that he was saved. Do you know that? Many people think it is presumptuous to say one is saved. On the other hand, we should understand that for one to doubt his salvation is to doubt God's power, for we read in Jonah 2:9, "Salvation is of the Lord." No man can save himself—it is the gift of God. Thus, when one is saved he ought to know that he is saved. How may he know? Simply by receiving the free gift of God—salvation through Jesus Christ. If you have received Christ, you are saved and you should possess the assurance of your salvation.

In a large manufacturing town a man lay on his deathbed. While well and strong, he and his son professed to be infidels, but under the test of his last days, his confidence in his unbelieving principles broke down. There was nothing in them to sustain him. His son, desirous that his father should die as he had lived, went in to fortify him, and said, "Father, be a man and stick to it."

"Ah, but son," he replied, "there's nothing to stick to." How different it is for the child of God. In Hebrews 6:19 we read, "Which hope we have as an anchor of the soul."

> We have an anchor that keeps the soul
> Steadfast and sure while the billows roll,
> Fastened to the Rock which cannot move,
> Grounded firm and deep in the Saviour's love.

Job asks next, "Who is he that will plead with me? for now, if I hold my tongue, I shall give up the ghost." This was to say, if I am wrong and it can be proved that I am wrong, I am willing to keep quiet and die; I will take my medicine. He was willing to stake his life on the sincerity of his own heart.

Job pleads with God to do two things: first, "Withdraw Thine hand far from me," and secondly, "Let not Thy dread make me afraid." Job wanted God to lift His heavy hand of suffering from him, that is, remove his disease. Evidently, what the three friends had said to Job had disturbed him and made him fearful of God. He wanted this fear removed. Also, he wanted to continue in communion with God. He wanted God to speak to him and he wanted to speak to the Lord. "Then call Thou, and I will answer: or let me speak, and answer Thou me."

Job continues by lamenting his sorrowful state: "How many are mine iniquities and sins? make me to know my transgression and my sin. Wherefore hidest Thou Thy face, and holdest me for Thine enemy? Wilt Thou break a leaf driven to and fro? and wilt Thou pursue the dry stubble? For Thou writest bitter things against me, and makest me to possess the iniquities of my youth. Thou puttest my feet also in the stocks, and lookest narrowly unto all my paths; Thou settest a print upon the heels of my feet. And he, as a rotten thing, consumeth, as a garment that is moth eaten." Job is giving a clear-cut confession of his own unworthiness before God, and at the same time giving thanks for God's greatness, His jurisprudence, His holiness, and His complete sovereignty.

In these closing verses of this chapter I see Job once again searching out his own heart before the Lord. In verse 23 he asks the question, "How many are mine iniquities and sins? make me to know my transgression and my sin." This reminds me of David as he prayed in Psalm 139:23-24, "Search me, O God, and know my heart: try me, and know my thoughts: And see if there be any wicked way in me, and lead me in the way everlasting." There is a tendency on the part of man to become proud and self-confident. We need a daily heart-searching before God. It is so easy for us to overlook our own sins and weaknesses. They stand out vividly in the eyes of others, but frequently we overlook them. It would be a great thing for all of us in the Church of Jesus Christ if we were to examine our hearts more frequently, that we might deal with personal sin. We are more prone to deal with our neighbor's sin than with our own. But God says, "Your iniquities have separated between you and your God" (Isaiah 59:2). Many of us are shutting out the blessing of God because of the separation brought about by sin in our lives. It is a serious thing for the unbeliever to ignore his sin, but I believe it is far more serious for the believer to overlook his sin.

I have read that in Colorado there is the ruin of an enormous tree. It was a seedling when Columbus discovered America, and only half-grown when the Pilgrim fathers landed at Plymouth. It was struck by lightning fourteen times. It survived the storms of centuries. Age did not wither it. Lightning did not blast it, nor avalanche move it. But it fell to an army of beetles, so tiny that you or I could crush them between finger and thumb. Some of us are like that tree. Like Samson, we stand up to storms with a certain amount of fortitude, but down we go before a few tiny beetles, a few little sins in our lives which we refuse to deal with in the light of God's power and grace.

Oh, if you are a child of God, let the Lord search you out.

JOB 14:1-22

JOB REPLIES to Eliphaz, Bildad, and Zophar in chapters 12, 13, and 14. In verse 1 of chapter 14 he reminds us of the frailty of human flesh: "Man that is born of woman is of few days, and full of trouble." I think we can understand what Job is saying here. "Man . . . is of few days." Yes, some of us are old and gray-headed. It seems like a matter of only a few years since we were back in youth. The years have swept by so swiftly.

And who of us has not suffered along the way? We have had heartaches, trials, and burdens. Some of us at this very moment are going through extreme and intense suffering. "Few days, and full of trouble," Job says. That is so common to life, and it is all the result of sin. Romans 5:12 says, "Wherefore, as by one man sin entered into the world, and death by sin; and so death passed upon all men, for that all have sinned." Sin brings misery and unhappiness, but, praise God, Christ brings peace and light. When we know Him we can face our troubles, we can weather the storms, we can carry the burdens. The Lord gives us the grace to face every sorrow of life. In 2 Corinthians 9:8 He says, "And God is able to make all grace abound toward you; that ye, always having all sufficiency in all things, may abound to every good work." It is impossible to drain dry the reservoirs of Heaven's grace. No matter what the need or the trial, there is always more grace to sustain us. God's grace can turn the darkness into sunshine and the sorrow into joy because of Calvary. There grace was wrought for you and for me. There the victory was won, so that, whatever the need, God's grace is sufficient.

It is said that one day Ruskin was talking with a friend who picked up a beautiful and costly embroidered handkerchief with a large ink spot in the center of it. The lady was very much vexed and annoyed at the carelessness of the person who had spoiled the handkerchief. She said to Mr. Ruskin that it was a present from a dear friend and would never be of any use to her any more. Mr. Ruskin said nothing, but quietly put the handkerchief in his pocket. Some days afterward he called on his friend and handed her the handkerchief; he had put on it in India ink a beautiful drawing, using the ink blot at the center as the basis of the ornamentation. The effect was exquisite, and the lady expressed her surprise in unmeasured terms.

That is the way God works with the things that touch our lives. As we trust in His grace and leave all things in His hands, He takes the wrong done to us, the injustice or injury, the sorrow or the suffering, as the basis of something good and beautiful. Yes, His grace is sufficient. He knows no limits. The arm of the Lord is not shortened. Whatever your need at this moment, He can help you. He is the mighty God. "Man that is born of woman is of few days, and full of trouble." Certainly there is plenty of trouble but consider the believer's privilege of "Casting all your care upon Him, for He careth for you" (1 Peter 5:7). Let us take our burdens to the Lord. He will not fail.

In speaking of the brevity of life, Job says, "He cometh forth like a flower, and is cut down: he fleeth also as a shadow, and continueth not." Life to him appears to be as a flower and a shadow. Flowers do not last very long. Their beauty soon withers and fades away. Likewise, a shadow is but a fleeting thing. It will soon be lost in the darkness of the night. Indeed this is a true picture of a man without Christ.

In the next verse Job marvels at the thought that God has any interest at all in that which seems to be useless and perishing, such as human flesh. "And dost Thou open Thine eyes upon such a one, and bringest me into judgment with Thee?" Yes, God does have interest in us, so much so that His eye is always on us. In Psalm 32:8 He says, "I will instruct thee and teach thee in the way which thou shalt go: I will guide thee with Mine eye."

Then in verse 4 Job speaks of the utter futility of sinful man to do anything about his condition, apart from the grace of God. "Who can bring a clean thing out of an unclean? not one." As he said in verse 1, we have been born of woman, and the Bible makes it clear that anyone born of woman is born in sin. David said in Psalm 51:5, "Behold, I was shapen in iniquity; and in sin did my mother conceive me." Thus, since man is defiled by sin, how can he be made clean? Job does not give us the answer here, but God does in Romans 3:24: "Being justified freely by His grace through the redemption that is in Christ Jesus." Think of it—the moment one believes in Jesus Christ he is completely forgiven of past, present, and future sin. He is justified, declared to be no longer guilty. How marvelous is the grace of God! Have you experienced this grace? Oh, if not, turn to Christ at this moment. "Who can bring a clean thing out of an unclean? Not one," Job says. In other words, no human can do this. This is impossible without a miracle of God.

You have sin in your life. All of your good works could never blot out your sin. Only the blood of Christ shed at Calvary can do this.

It is needful for you to make your decision for Christ immediately, for Job says of man, "Seeing his days are determined, the number of his months are with Thee, Thou hast appointed his bounds that he cannot pass." Job is not speaking of years but of days and months. The end may be nearer than any of us thinks. In fact, it may be hours or minutes, as far as you are concerned. Your bounds have been appointed, Job says, and beyond these you cannot pass. You need Christ in your heart.

Job pleads for mercy regarding sinful man. He says, "Turn from him, that he may rest till he shall accomplish, as an hireling, his day." The hireling's life was not an easy life. It was filled with hardship and toil. This is another way of saying what Job said in the first verse, "Man is of few days, and full of trouble." Job knew where to turn in his trouble. He went to the One who could give rest. I wonder if you have turned to Him? Have you been too busy for God? Today Jesus says to you in Matthew 11:28, "Come unto Me, all ye that labour and are heavy laden, and I will give you rest." Rest from your cares! Rest from your trials! Rest from your sorrows! Yes, God's grace is sufficient for you. You may have tried other ways but, remember, Christ died for you to provide the one way—God's way of salvation and blessing. Don't look for another way; there is no other.

We have seen what Job had to say about life; now what does he have to say about death? In verse 7 he says, "For there is hope of a tree, if it be cut down, that it will sprout again, and that the tender branch thereof will not cease." Then he goes on to say, "Though the root thereof wax old in the earth, and the stock thereof die in the ground; Yet through the scent of water it will bud, and bring forth boughs like a plant." Thus, if a tree is cut down and the trunk is left in the ground, though it may seem dead suddenly it will sprout forth as the result of the moisture in the earth and the rain from Heaven; the stump is revived and life is evident. But Job reminds us that it is different for man. "Man dieth, and wasteth away; yea, man giveth up the ghost, and where is he? As the waters fail from the sea, and the flood decayeth and drieth up: So man lieth down, and riseth not: till the heavens be no more, they shall not awake, nor be raised out of their sleep." When we go to bed at night, we anticipate rising up in the morning. But when one is placed in the grave, he shall not awake to such a life or such a state as we are now in. We shall not awake, Job says, "till the heavens be no more," actually, until time is swallowed up in eternity.

It should be kept in mind that what Job was thinking about in these verses is the return of man to his present life in his present form. Job was not ignorant of the resurrection hope. He firmly believed in the resurrection of the righteous dead. In Job 19:26 he says, "And though after my skin worms destroy this body, yet in my flesh shall I see God." Of course, from other passages of Scripture we know that what Job is saying here is absolutely true. Though all men will be resurrected, no one will be resurrected to come back to this present life as it exists now, unless God intervenes with a miracle to bring one back from the dead, as in the case of Lazarus. In John 5:28-29 we read, "Marvel not at this: for the hour is coming, in the which all that are in the graves shall hear His voice, And shall come forth; they that have done good, unto the resurrection of life; and they that have done evil, unto the resurrection of damnation." There will be two resurrections, as we see from this verse. They will, however, be separated by a thousand years. The first resurrection will take place when Christ comes for His saints. The righteous will be raised to meet Him in the air. The second resurrection will take place at the end of the thousand-year reign of Christ, when the wicked will be raised to be judged for their sins and then cast into eternal perdition. But as far as coming back into this present life as it is now, Job is absolutely correct. "So man lieth down, and riseth not: till the heavens be no more."

Verse 13 reveals Job's desire to find release from his present suffering in the grave, to await his resurrection. "O that Thou wouldest hide me in the grave, that Thou wouldest keep me secret, until Thy wrath be past, that Thou wouldest appoint me a set time, and remember me!" Job knew that his suffering on this earth was the result of sin, not necessarily his sin but sin in general. All suffering is the result of sin. Thus Job was looking to something better: release from it all through the grave, and then the glory of the resurrection. He speaks of God's appointing "a set time." This is literally "a decreed time." In the decrees of God He has established a day of resurrection for His beloved saints. 1 Thessalonians 4:16 says, "For the Lord Himself shall descend from heaven with a shout, with the voice of the archangel, and with the trump of God: and the dead in Christ shall rise first."

Job further emphasizes this truth saying, "If a man die, shall he live again? All the days of my appointed time will I wait, till my change come." Job answered the question of living again in this present life in verses 10-12: his answer is "No." But for the next life, the glorified life in which there will be no suffering or pain, he answers the question, "Yes." "This is what I am waiting for," he says, "till my change come and till I am delivered from this body of flesh, this dying, sinful, suffering body." Job was to receive a new body, as will every believer at the time of Christ's coming for His own. The words "appointed time" really mean "a set time." Ah yes, the Lord has a set time for the Lord to return. He will not be late, nor will He be early. The time is set. No man knows the hour, but God does, and you may be assured that Christ will come at the appointed time. Hebrews 10:37 says, "For yet a little while, and He that shall come will come, and will not tarry."

Verse 15 seems to come to the climax of this blissful expectation. "Thou shalt call, and I will answer Thee." Paul declares, "For the Lord Himself shall descend from heaven . . . with the voice of the archangel." Job will hear that voice. He will not remain in the cold, lifeless form, but he will arise out of sleep, with all who have believed the truth of God, to see his

Lord face to face. He knew that his body was fearfully and
wonderfully made and that God did not create him to perish
as an animal. He well understood that the best was yet to come,
and that, even though he was to go back to dust, God would
recreate him. He refers to this by saying, "Thou wilt have a
desire to the work of Thine hands." Job was the work of God's
hands at Creation. He would again be the work of God's hands
at the time of the re-creation, the Resurrection.

This is a blessed hope which every believer has. But for the
unbeliever, the picture is not so hopeful. Psalm 9:17 says,
"The wicked shall be turned into hell." The wicked go to hell
not because God sends them there; they go there by choice.
They have either neglected or forgotten God. Jesus says in
John 11:25-26: "I am the resurrection, and the life: he that
believeth in Me, though he were dead, yet shall he live: And
whosoever liveth and believeth in Me shall never die. Believest thou this?" Have you received Christ as your Saviour and
Lord? If so, your future is far brighter than your past.

In verses 16 and 17 Job confesses man's trying to escape the
eye of God. "For now Thou numberest my steps: dost Thou
not watch over my sin? My transgression is sealed up in a bag,
and Thou sewest up mine iniquity." Though we are told in
the first chapter that Job "was perfect and upright, and one
that feared God, and eschewed evil," this does not mean that he
was not a sinner. Job realized his sinfulness as any righteous
man does. In fact, the closer one gets to God, the more obvious
his sins become, for he sees himself in the light of God's perfection. Some there are who think they are escaping the eye of
God. If you are one of them, do not be deceived. In Psalm 44:21
David said of God, "He knoweth the secrets of the heart." God
knows all about your sin, and it may well be that the misery you
are in today is the result of unconfessed sin in your life. If you
were to get right with God and do something about your sin,
you would enjoy His wonderful peace.

In India many of the homes are built on poles and posts in

order to protect the inhabitants from reptiles. As you pass the houses in the morning, you might judge them to be very sturdy. But coming back at night, you may discover that some of those homes which appeared to be durable are complete wrecks. Why? Little white ants, that can scarcely be seen, work themselves into the wood of the posts, literally perforating it. Steadily but surely they go forward with their work until they have eaten away the strength of the supporting posts. Then suddenly a gentle wind will blow the home to the ground.

Sin works in a similar manner. Very often it may be some little thing in the life that seems quite insignificant. It is ignored day in and day out. We say to ourselves, "Well, it isn't much. I can give it up any time I want." Suddenly we find that it has practically destroyed any spiritual concern or interest we may have had. It was just a little thing which we did not think to be very much. God says in Zechariah 4:10, "For who hath despised the day of small things?" God is concerned about small things, and especially small sins. Usually small sins will become big sins. That is why we must deal with all sin. The Christian should confess sin immediately. 1 John 1:9 says, "If we confess our sins, He is faithful and just to forgive us our sins, and to cleanse us from all unrighteousness."

How should the unsaved deal with their sin? Turn to Christ and claim the victory of Calvary. That is the only possible way to deal with sin. Yes, be sure, as Job says, God watches over our sins, He knows all about them, "My transgression is sealed up in a bag." The Bible further states, "The soul that sinneth, it shall die" (Ezekiel 18:20).

Job continues to lament the uselessness of life, that is, the life which we now live, by saying, "Surely the mountain falling cometh to nought, and the rock is removed out of his place. The waters wear the stones: Thou washest away the things which grow out of the dust of the earth; and Thou destroyest the hope of man." The mountains become stones and the stones finally become dust. Everything seems to crumble, even as the body grows older and eventually goes into the grave. It all looks very hopeless as Job presents it here. Then he says, "Thou prevailest for ever against him." That is, God by His superior power and strength prevails against man. Soon man passes into the grave. And though our children be advanced in life, even that will not mean anything to us in the grave. "His sons come to honour, and he knoweth it not; and they are brought low, but he perceiveth it not of them." The concluding verse gives us the agonizing picture of death: "But his flesh upon him shall have pain, and his soul within him shall mourn." He mourns as he leaves his loved ones.

Job has given us in these verses a very dismal picture of life. Yet there are many who live in this manner. These last 5 verses of Job 14 describe perfectly many lives in this world today. They are miserable, unhappy, without the blessing of God, because they don't know Christ. Jesus said in John 10:10, "I am come that they might have life." In describing this life He uses the word "abundant" which means full, enriched with the daily blessing of God. David said in Psalm 37:23, "The steps of a good man are ordered by the LORD: and He delighteth in his way." Further in Psalm 16:11 he says, "Thou wilt shew me the path of life: in Thy presence is fulness of joy; at Thy right hand are pleasures for evermore."

Life need not be as Job describes it. It can be full of blessing and happiness. That does not mean that you will not have trials and testings, but you will have the joy of the Lord in your heart even though you may be surrounded with hardships. This all begins by a new-birth experience. Let me ask you, have you really been born again? I do not mean, are you a church member, or are you doing nice things for others, or are you living a good life? I mean—have you really met God by believing on Christ and by receiving Him into your heart?

Sir James Simpson discovered chloroform in 1864. He was a great doctor in Edinburgh, and made other discoveries in medicine which have helped many a poor sufferer, but chloroform was his greatest medical discovery. Once he was asked, "Do you think anyone has ever made a greater discovery than chloroform?"

"Yes," he said, "I have made a greater discovery myself."

"Really? What was that?" asked the inquirer.

"The discovery that Jesus Christ was my own Saviour." Sir James Simpson was thirty-five when he discovered the use of chloroform; he was fifty before he made the greater discovery, and it was always a regret to him that he had not made it sooner.

It could be that you have not made this discovery as yet in your own life. Christ died for you, and rose again, that you might have everlasting life. Oh, receive Him at this moment. You need Him. You cannot face life alone. Without Him, life is just as Job has described it here—hopeless and meaningless. Take Jesus Christ into your life and you will find that life will take on a whole new meaning. It will be joyous and thrilling with Christ in your heart.

JOB 15:1-35

ELIPHAZ THE TEMANITE is quick to reply to God's servant. You will notice in this chapter that Eliphaz strikes very hard at Job. Because God's suffering servant did not receive the advice of his would-be comforters with praise and adulation, Eliphaz, filled with pride, replied with bitterness in his heart.

First of all, Job is charged with foolishness. He had the reputation of being a wise man, but Eliphaz asks, "Should a wise man utter vain knowledge, and fill his belly with the east wind? Should he reason with unprofitable talk? or with speeches wherewith he can do no good?" Proud Eliphaz, rather than admit his own guilt, becomes more stern with Job, accusing him of offering mere talk without reason. The "east wind" was most destructive in that region. Job's speech was likened unto the east wind, destructive rather than helpful. Eliphaz asks, "Should he reason with unprofitable talk?" "Unprofitable talk" is really "evil talk." It is something all of us must be on guard against continuously. The Lord Jesus said in Matthew 12:36-37, "But I say unto you, That every idle word that men shall speak, they shall give account thereof in the day of judgment. For by thy words thou shalt be justified, and by thy words thou shalt be condemned." How essential that believers speak edifying words, words that honor Christ and bear witness to Him among their friends.

In one of the Virginia campaigns, General U. S. Grant and his staff were gathered around the fire one evening in a country farmhouse. The officers were telling stories. Presently one of them said, "I have a good story to tell," and to indicate what was coming, he added, "I think there are no ladies here."

"No, but there are gentlemen here," General Grant quietly remarked. The story was not told. God says in Ephesians 4:29, "Let no corrupt communication proceed out of your mouth, but that which is good to the use of edifying, that it may minister grace unto the hearers."

Eliphaz accuses Job further of being impious: "Thou castest off fear, and restrainest prayer before God." This was a dangerous attack indeed. How did Eliphaz know that Job did not pray? How did he know that Job did not respect and revere God? We cannot judge others in this light; God is the Judge. Of course, anyone who does not respect and honor God is the loser, and he who does not pray is certainly living a life devoid of much of the blessing of God. In Matthew 7:7 Jesus taught that we must ask Him for all things. If we do, He says, "It shall be given you." If we do not ask, we shall not receive. How much of God's blessing we miss because we do not take the time to pray and wait on Him. I am sure Job must have been a man of prayer, even though his critics refused to give him the benefit of the doubt.

Eliphaz attempts to prove Job's prayerlessness and lack of respect for God by saying, "For thy mouth uttereth thine iniquity, and thou choosest the tongue of the crafty." Eliphaz is correct in his assumption that the tongue is a good index for one's beliefs and attitudes. One who is not a man of prayer will certainly have little control of his tongue. Not only will he offend and disturb others, he will bring much trouble upon himself by the things he says. This is why it is so important that one be saved and know Christ, permitting Christ to live through him so as to control every phase of living, including the tongue. "Thine own mouth condemneth thee, and not I: yea, thine own lips testify against thee," says Eliphaz.

Next we see that Eliphaz becomes very sarcastic. He questions the wisdom of Job, asking, "Art thou the first man that was born?" That is, "Did you live before us? Do you know more than we do?" Then he asks, "Wast thou made before the hills?" In other words, "Are you God, the Creator, that you know so much?" "Hast thou heard the secret of God?" He wonders, "Do you have some inner counsel with the Divine that you can talk to us the way you do?" Like the other friends, Eliphaz claimed that Job was a faulty, erring human, deserving of his suffering. Thus in questioning Job's wisdom he asks, "What knowest thou, that we know not? what understandest thou, which is not in us?"

Eliphaz's presumptuous pride is further seen in his next statement. "With us are both the grayheaded and very aged men, much elder than thy father." He claims to have the voice of experience on his side. He is saying to Job, "We know more than you do," intimating that all the fathers of the faith were of the same opinion as the comforters. This was easily said but not so easily proved. One's age does not always make him an authority. It is regrettable how many older people, living at this moment and standing on the threshold of eternity, have never given definite consideration as to where they will spend eternity. Regarding spiritual matters, they are as little children, without understanding. If such should be your case, before it is too late turn to Christ. Receive the Saviour into your heart. Repent and turn to Him, for the Word of God declares in Ezekiel 18:20, "The soul that sinneth, it shall die." Hear God's Word! He means what He says. Both Job and his comforters may be lacking in wisdom, but the Bible says in James 3:17, "But the wisdom that is from above is first pure, then peaceable, gentle, and easy to be intreated, full of mercy and good fruits, without partiality, and without hypocrisy." The wisdom of the Word of God is truth.

Looking at verses 11-13 of chapter 15 we read, "Are the consolations of God small with thee? is there any secret thing with thee? Why doth thine heart carry thee away? and what do thy eyes wink at, That thou turnest thy spirit against God, and lettest such words go out of thy mouth?" I can understand why Job would not give attention to the words of his comforters, but there is no excuse for any of us to turn from the wisdom of God. Maybe you are a Christian and God is trying to lead you into some path of usefulness. You have been rebelling against His will, or perhaps you are practicing some secret sin. You are turning against God, you are letting His words go out of your mouth. Oh, Christian, get right with God before it is too late.

Eliphaz continues his attack by saying that Job's attempt to justify himself was unreasonable: "What is man, that he should be clean? and he which is born of a woman, that he should be righteous?" What Eliphaz is saying here is true: there are no perfect humans. However, Job did not declare that he was perfect; he admitted his sin and guilt. On the other hand, he had been redeemed by faith; he had trusted in the cleansing power of God, he was a saved sinner. Isaiah 64:6 declares, "But we are all as an unclean thing, and all our righteousnesses are as filthy rags; and we all do fade as a leaf; and our iniquities, like the wind, have taken us away." We are all marked by sin. We are all condemned to eternal hell. But the moment we trust in the living Christ, our sins are blotted out and we are made clean. Only God can do this, because only God can perform miracles.

In verse 15 we see that even the works of creation are contaminated by sin. "The heavens are not clean in His sight." This is what Paul tells us in Romans 8:22: "For we know that the whole creation groaneth and travaileth in pain together until now." All of creation awaits the return of Christ, when everything will be put in order and all will be made right. Notice further in this verse that even the saints of God are not to be trusted, according to Eliphaz. How important that we realize this. Those who have been purchased with the blood of Christ are still living within the bounds of sinful flesh. We cannot trust ourselves. Only as we permit Christ to have first place and to control us, can we expect any degree of blessing and success. Man is not safe with himself; he needs the power of God at work in his life. Notice the utter sinfulness of man as seen in the next verse, "How much more abominable and filthy is man, which drinketh iniquity like water?" As a thirsty man gulps down water to quench his thirst, so man loves sin and the pleasures of sin. Without the restraining force of Christ within he cannot possibly conquer sin.

Having reproved Job sharply for the speech he had just given, Eliphaz presents his old argument once again, that suffering is the result of sin, and because Job is suffering, he must be a wicked hypocrite. He starts out by saying, "I will shew thee, hear me; and that which I have seen I will declare." He is suggesting that he will show him that which is worth hearing and not give so much unprofitable talk. One thing we notice about Eliphaz is that he was always willing to condemn the other fellow but never willing to face up to his own sin. In fact, he doesn't seem to give any intimation that he had any sin. This is a most pathetic position—self-sufficiency, self-righteousness, self-justification—so many are like this.

In verse 20 Eliphaz states his philosophy once again. "The wicked man travaileth with pain all his days, and the number of years is hidden to the oppressor." What he is saying here is absolutely true, but his intimation that Job was suffering because he was a sinner was definitely wrong. Certainly "the wicked man travaileth with pain all his days." Proverbs 13:15 says, "Good understanding giveth favour: but the way of transgressors is hard." Yes, the way of transgressors is a hard way. He who chooses to reject the Lord and live in the way of the flesh is a miserable man. Sin does not bring happiness. It cannot, for sin is the transgression of the law of God. Can a man be happy breaking the law of God? Absolutely not! Someone has said, "Sin puts hell into the soul, and the soul into hell." That is about all we can say for sin. Sin does not pay. Well, yes, it does, in a sense. It pays wages; the Bible says they are the wages of death. But it does not pay the wages of blessing and joy. Praise God, the Bible says, "But where sin abounded, grace did much more abound" (Romans 5:20). There is no reason for anyone to live in sin, for the grace of God is sufficient to forgive all sin if only the sinner will turn to Christ.

There is a peculiar tree of remarkable beauty found in the West Indies. The fruit that it bears is also most attractive. It is beautiful to the eye and has a fragrant smell, but when eaten, it produces certain death. The juice of this fruit is so deadly that the Indians dip their arrows in it to poison their enemies when they wound them. It is remarkable that wherever this tree grows, there is always found, not far from it, a plant, the juice of which counteracts the poison of the tree.

Is this not a picture of the grace of God? Man may be steeped in sin, but the Word gives God's wonderful invitation: "Let the wicked forsake his way, and the unrighteous man his thoughts: and let him return unto the Lord, and He will have mercy upon him; and to our God, for He will abundantly pardon" (Isaiah 55:7). At this very moment you may be living in deep sin. Take Christ into your life and He will forgive you and cleanse you (1 John 1:9).

Now look at some of the alarming statements Eliphaz makes concerning the wicked man, the one who has not turned to God in repentance. "A dreadful sound is in his ears: in prosperity the destroyer shall come upon him." He seems to have no rest. He is harangued by a guilt complex, knowing that the destroyer, death, shall soon come upon him and there will be no hope. The future offers nothing better. "He believeth not that he shall return out of darkness, and he is waited for of the sword. He wandereth abroad for bread, saying, Where is it? he knoweth that the day of darkness is ready at his hand. Trouble and anguish shall make him afraid; they shall prevail against him, as a king ready to the battle."

The deceitful man, the dishonest man, who seems to be enjoying prosperity, lives a life filled with trouble and anguish. One thing after another seems to follow his steps wherever he goes. He drives thousands of miles to take a vacation, but sadly enough, when he reaches his destination he is as miserable as ever. It is all because of sin. He blames it on his nerves, when in reality it is a heart condition, a heart out of tune with God. "He stretcheth out his hand against God," Eliphaz says, "and strengtheneth himself against the Almighty." He resists God. The Lord tries to speak to him but he will not give in. He persists in his sin. "He runneth upon Him, even on his neck, upon the thick bosses of his bucklers." He is striving with his Maker, living in direct opposition to His teachings as they are presented in the Word of God. He tries to hide in his own ingenuity. "Because he covereth his face with his fatness, and maketh collops of fat on his flanks."

Could this be a description of you? Have you been resisting the Lord? God has been speaking to your heart for days, but you have been turning your face from Him. It may be that at this moment He has you flat on your back, that you might think before it is too late. Hear His voice! He is not an angry judge, pursuing you for your evil. He is a God of love and grace. In Jeremiah 31:3 He declares, "I have loved thee with an everlasting love." He has loved you even though you have despised Him. Why not let Him show you what He can do for you? Why not let Him prove to you what real life is? Take Christ into your heart. Believe on Him as the Son of the Eternal God. The days will become brighter, your load of sorrow and care will become lighter. Christ is the answer.

In speaking further of the rebellious nature of the wicked, Eliphaz says, "He dwelleth in desolate cities, and in houses which no man inhabiteth, which are ready to become heaps. He shall not be rich, neither shall his substance continue, neither shall he prolong the perfection thereof upon the earth." Here is a picture of the coming calamity on those who appear to be secure because of their trust in temporal things. This reminds me of the rich fool of Luke 12. He had so much wealth he did not know what to do with it.

"What shall I do," he asks, "because I have no room where to bestow my fruits?" Then he answers himself: "This will I do: I will pull down my barns, and build greater; and there will I bestow all my fruits and my goods. And I will say to my soul, Soul, thou hast much goods laid up for many years; take thine ease, eat, drink, and be merry." But suddenly he heard a voice. It was the voice of God saying, "Thou fool, this night thy soul shall be required of thee: then whose shall those things be, which thou hast provided?"

Eliphaz's words, "He shall not be rich," apply so well to this rich fool. He was rich at the moment, but what about after death? He became a pauper for all eternity, for God says in 1 Timothy 6:7, "For we brought nothing into this world, and it is certain we can carry nothing out." How important it is for a man or a woman to be rich toward God.

In *New Cyclopedia of Prose Illustrations, Adapted to Christian Teaching*, Elon Foster tells that about two hundred years ago the tomb of the great conqueror Charlemagne was opened. The sight the workmen saw was startling. There was his body in a sitting position, clothed in the most elaborate of kingly garments, with a scepter in his bony hand. On his knee there lay a New Testament, with a cold, lifeless finger pointing to Mark 8:36, "For what shall it profit a man, if he shall gain the whole world, and lose his own soul?"

If one could enjoy all this world has to offer, such as vast human wisdom, riches, high position, friends, and honor, even to the place of being a ruler or potentate, what profit would there be if he were not washed in the precious blood of Christ? Riches cannot bring security, but many wicked people think they can and are placing all their confidence and trust in uncertain riches.

Eliphaz continues by saying, "He shall not depart out of darkness." That is, he shall not escape calamity. "The flame shall dry up his branches." This refers to his children; doubtless they will duplicate the ways of their parents. They, too, shall be impoverished because of sin. "And by the breath of His mouth shall he go away." This is God's mouth. The sinner must be judged for his sin. If he was not willing to face Christ as Saviour on this earth, he must some day face Him as Judge in eternity. And then after judgment, what? Matthew 25:41 is clear: "Then shall He say also unto them on the left hand, Depart from Me, ye cursed, into everlasting fire, prepared for the devil and his angels." In verse 46 we read, "And these shall go away into everlasting punishment: but the righteous into life eternal." No man will escape the judgment of God. If he is in Christ, he will be rewarded for his labors. If he has never received Christ, he must be judged with eternal separation from God. There is no other escape.

"Let not him that is deceived trust in vanity: for vanity shall be his recompense," Eliphaz tells us. Vanity refers to that which is unsubstantial. Do not trust in the unsubstantial things. Trust in Him who is eternal. If one does not trust in the Lord, we read that, "It shall be accomplished before his time, and his branch shall not be green" (15:32). "It" refers to the tree to which the wicked is being compared. His life, as suggested in verse 31, will be cut off because of sin. The sinner lives on dangerous ground, for at any time his soul may be snatched from him and his body will become a lifeless corpse. That is why it is so important to be ready to meet Christ, to be prepared, ready to die. God says in Amos 4:12, "Prepare to meet thy God." Of course, the only thing anyone can do to prepare is to receive the Son of God into his heart.

Eliphaz says further, "He shall shake off his unripe grape as the vine, and shall cast off his flower as the olive." Here we see a fruitless life portrayed. Indeed, the sinner's life is fruitless. This is described so well in the first Psalm where we are told of the blessed or the happy man, who is contrasted with the ungodly or the wicked man. Take time to read the first Psalm. Which one of the two men would you like to be? How could anyone reject the upward call, to be the kind of man that "shall be like a tree planted by the rivers of water, that bringeth forth his fruit in his season," with the assurance that "his leaf also shall not wither; and whatsoever he doeth shall prosper" (Psalm 1:3). This is the only kind of life to live. How can it be lived? Only through the power of Jesus Christ at work in our lives.

There are many posing as followers of God. They go to church; they sing in the choir. Some of them teach Sunday school; they are active on church boards. But many of them are hypocrites, underneath the outward garments is abominable wickedness. We read of them in Job 15:34-35: "For the congregation of hypocrites shall be desolate, and fire shall consume the tabernacles of bribery. They conceive mischief, and bring forth vanity, and their belly prepareth deceit." Even though they appear to be righteous, out of their innermost being comes only wicked thoughts and vain imaginations. Though they are religious, they have never had a real heart experience with God. So many are in this category. They are even on the church rolls. You may be one of them.

Now Eliphaz said all this about Job, but he was wrong. He was not wrong in what he had to say in this most complete and detailed description of the wicked man, but he was wrong in applying it to God's servant. He was misjudging a true, sincere child of God. It is better that we look into our own hearts rather than into someone else's.

JOB 16:1-22

GOD'S TESTED SERVANT makes another reply to Eliphaz. He begins by accusing Eliphaz of being repetitious, saying, "I have heard many such things." Eliphaz seems to be saying the same thing over and over again. Of course, repetition is oftentimes worth while in teaching, but Job's friends seem to have one theory which they recite again and again. They fail to offer any solution to the problem, so Job declares, "Miserable comforters are ye all." The word "miserable" here means "burdensome" or "annoying." They were disturbing comforters which, of course, made them no comforters at all. They offered no help to alleviate the affliction, but by their constant reciting of condemnation they made Job's burden heavier.

Next Job asks, "Shall vain words have an end? or what emboldeneth thee that thou answerest?" Indeed, it would be well if vain words never had a beginning. But Job was so wearied by the constant reproving that he hoped their words would end soon. "Why do you keep answering?" Job asks. "You say nothing when you speak."

Further, God's servant says, "I also could speak as ye do: if your soul were in my soul's stead, I could heap up words against you, and shake mine head at you." It is an easy thing to trample on those that are down. Indeed, this is what Job's friends were doing. Job reminded them that, if they were in his predicament, it would take no thought for him to do the same and to give them the treatment they were giving him.

In verse 5 he informs them that, if such were the case, he would be very careful of his speech. "But I would strengthen you with my mouth, and the moving of my lips would asswage your grief." Job is exemplifying a God-honoring attitude. What he said is so needful in our day. It is easy to condemn our brother, to see his faults, and to be critical. Those who know the Lord are to be loving and kind. God says in Romans 14:10, "But why dost thou judge thy brother? or why dost thou set at nought thy brother? for we shall all stand before the judgment seat of Christ." Usually when someone is extremely critical of another, he has flaws in his own life, yet he does not see his own faults as he pours forth judgment upon his Christian brother. Well, the day is coming, God tells us, when we shall all stand before the judgment seat of Christ. And be sure, that will be true judgment. Our judgment is often faulty because we do not have all the facts. But no man can hide from the eye of God; He sees everything. He knows the beginning from the end.

It has been said that a person who kicks continually soon loses his balance. There seem to be many, even among Christians, who are always finding fault. If we knew all the facts, none of us would be so critical of others. We often set ourselves up as self-appointed judges, like Job's three friends, and severely condemn those about us, when our knowledge of all the facts is totally inadequate. If we only knew all the circumstances, we would praise and not condemn.

A man went to the barbershop to get a shoeshine. The boy who polished his shoes was slow with his work. Exasperated, the man spoke to him harshly, whereupon the boy looked up at him with tear-filled eyes.

"Excuse me," said the man, now contrite. "I didn't mean to hurt you."

"It is not that, Sir, which causes these tears. They were there already. You see, my Mother died last night and I am here this morning only because I am trying to earn enough to buy a small bouquet of flowers to go on her grave. My eyes were so filled with tears I could hardly see your shoes. That's the reason I am so slow."

Of course, the man was condemned in his own heart. If he had only known the situation, he would have acted differently. If you and I knew all the facts, we would be less critical and more sympathetic. And be sure, we would also be happier. We need to pray daily that God will give us the understanding nature of Christ. I think of those verses in Hebrews 4:15-16, "For we have not an high priest which cannot be touched with the feeling of our infirmities; but was in all points tempted like as we are, yet without sin. Let us therefore come boldly unto the throne of grace, that we may obtain mercy, and find grace to help in time of need."

Our Lord is always touched with the feeling of our infirmities. He understands what we are going through, He knows all about our heartaches. We need to pray that God will give us an understanding spirit as we deal with those around us. Sometimes we are unkind and harsh to those who love us most. Oh, that we might open our hearts to the love of God, that we may not be critical and censorious. Job said, if the situation were reversed and you were in my shoes, I would "strengthen you with my mouth, and the moving of my lips should assuage your grief." When you speak, do you help others? Do you lift them up? Do you encourage them? Or are your words sharp and disturbing? In Colossians 4:6 God says, "Let your speech be alway with grace, seasoned with salt, that ye may know how ye ought to answer every man." "Alway with grace, seasoned with salt." Is this how you speak? Do your words honor Christ? Do they help your fallen brother? Do they make his burden lighter? We need to ask God to guard our lips that our speech might exalt Christ. I am convinced that Christians sin more with their lips than with any other part of their body. How important it is that we be surrendered to the control of Christ.

Child of God, have you been sinning with your lips? Confess to the Lord. Let Him fill you with Himself. Perhaps you are not a child of God. You thought you were, but because of your manner of speech you are doubtful. Maybe you need a real heart experience with Christ. Why not ask Him to come into your heart now? Get this thing settled. Come to the Lord! Only He can give you victory over an unruly and uncontrolled tongue. God is able, but He works through the power of His Son. Let Him come into your heart. Don't try to do better, don't try to patch up the old life. This will do no good. Even your best is far from being good enough. You need Christ in your heart. He is the only one who can give victory over sin. He is the only one who can enable us to please God.

In verse 6 Job says, "Though I speak, my grief is not assuaged: and though I forbear, what am I eased?" Here Job seems to be about as bitter in his complaint as in any part of the book. He is not quite sure whether he should repress his feelings or express them completely. But in this verse he tells us he has tried both ways and found help from neither. "Though I speak, my grief is not asswaged: and though I forbear, what am I eased?" If Job told his friends how he felt, they criticized him for it. If he refused to give vent to his feelings, then he became depressed and discouraged. Oh, how deep was the sorrow of God's servant.

Consider Job's complaint. "But now He hath made me weary." His children were snatched from him, his riches disappeared, his body was broken, and as the days passed he became more and more weary. All seemed so hopeless and useless. Have you ever felt this way? I am sure you have. But, be sure, we are never alone. The Lord Jesus said in Matthew 28:20, "Lo, I am with you alway, even unto the end of the world." If God be for us, who can be against us? You may be sure, if you are on the Lord's side, God is for you. He has not forsaken you.

Job goes on to say, "Thou hast made desolate all my company." He recalled the days when many friends came to his home, when they sat around his table and had wonderful fellowship. Now he has no friends. Those who seemed to be his friends were provoking him to wrath. More than this, his body was nothing but skin and bones. "And Thou hast filled me with wrinkles, which is a witness against me: and my leanness rising up in me beareth witness to my face." His face was furrowed because of his sickness. He had become so thin and emaciated that his bones were protruding. These, he said, are "witnesses against me." They were witnesses to God's displeasure toward him, and such witnesses as his friends chose to use as a reproach against him.

In addition to all this, Job spoke of his enemy, saying, "He teareth me in his wrath, who hateth me: he gnasheth upon me with his teeth; mine enemy sharpeneth his eyes upon me." Who is this enemy of whom he speaks? It would seem that he is referring to Eliphaz, who had just gnashed upon God's servant once again with thoughtless criticism. But beyond Eliphaz, Job must have had Satan in mind. Primarily his encounter was with Satan. Satan was Job's worst enemy. He hated and despised Job because of Job's love for God. We read of Satan in 1 Peter 5:8, "Your adversary the devil, as a roaring lion, walketh about, seeking whom he may devour." You may be sure he was out to devour Job, but Job was under the protective care of God.

Job continues his speech by complaining of the abusiveness of his friends. "They have gaped upon me with their mouth; they have smitten me upon the cheek reproachfully; they have gathered themselves together against me." I am sure you have already recognized Job, in several verses in this chapter, as a type of Christ. This likeness is portrayed wonderfully in this chapter. Verse 10 seems to be most descriptive of Christ's treatment following the Gethsemane experience: "They have gaped upon me with their mouth; they have smitten me upon the cheek reproachfully; they have gathered themselves together against me."

Job tells us further that, rather than being withdrawn from the ungodly and being protected from them, he was delivered to them: "God hath delivered me to the ungodly, and turned me over into the hands of the wicked." Again, this seems prophetic of the Lord Jesus, who was delivered for our offenses. But remember, His enemies could have had no power at all against Him were it not given to them. Christ was delivered into wicked hands to be crucified and slain by the determinate counsel and foreknowledge of God.

Job reminds us that his trials, though brought about by the enemy, were directed by God. "I was at ease, but He hath broken me asunder: He hath also taken me by my neck, and shaken me to pieces, and set me up for His mark. His archers compass me round about, He cleaveth my reins asunder, and doth not spare; He poureth out my gall upon the ground. He breaketh me with breach upon breach; He runneth upon me like a giant." Job knew that he was being sustained by his mighty God; though the Lord's judgments were severe, Job knew that they were rendered in mercy.

Consider again the Lord Jesus Christ as He is seen in these verses. We can understand why God permitted this to come into Job's life. He was a sinner like the rest of us. Though we deserve these things, yet we complain. But the same judgment, and even worse, was poured out upon God's only Son, who did no sin, who knew no sin, and in whom there was no sin. Christ was chosen to be God's sacrifice for sin. He was to pour out His blood, not for any sin of His, but for yours and mine. Here is a picture of God's great sacrifice, of which we read in 2 Corinthians 5:21, "God . . . hath made Him to be sin for us, who knew no sin; that we might be made the righteousness of God in Him."

It may be that you are one who has never experienced the new birth. What Christ did on the cross, He did for you. Your respectability, your benevolent spirit, your consideration of others, are not enough to save you. Christ died for your sins.

One time I was speaking to a young lady about her soul's salvation. She admitted that she was not a Christian.

"Were you to die," I said, "you would be lost forever."

"Oh, no," she replied, "I feel like God would give me a second chance." I pointed out to her that nowhere in the Bible is such a thing stated.

Do not gamble on what is not written in the Word. While you are living, God gives you thousands of chances to come to Christ. But after you die, there are no more chances. To die without responding to the opportunity to receive Christ is unpardonable: you have sinned against the Holy Spirit, you have rejected God's beloved Son. The Bible tells us for such sin there is no forgiveness.

Next we come to verse 15 where Job says, "I have sewed sackcloth upon my skin, and defiled my horn in the dust." Sackcloth denotes a mourning garment, and the horn was an emblem of power. Job says his horn is in the dust, suggesting his present humiliation in contrast to his former greatness. Eliphaz had condemned Job as being high and haughty, but just the opposite was true, according to Job; the dust was good enough for him.

Further he said, "My face is foul with weeping, and on my eyelids is the shadow of death." Here is another picture of Christ, the Man of sorrows, acquainted with grief. This picture continues in verse 17, where Job reminds us that his suffering was "not for any injustice" of his own hand. Further he assures us that his "prayer is pure." That is, he had met the conditions for effectual prayer. As far as he knew, his conscience did not reveal any serious sin in his life. He would be the first one to admit that he was a sinner, but, comparing himself to other men, he probably was better than most of them. He had a conscience void of offense toward all men, nor had he done any wrong to his fellow men. His suffering was not for any injustice "of his own hands." His conscience was void of offense toward God—his prayer was pure. No one's prayer can be pure as long as there is known sin in the life. Here is a further portrayal of Christ. He died not for any injustice in His own hands. Likewise, there was nothing between the Father and the Son, His prayer was pure.

Job was in earnest. He was desirous that there be nothing in his heart displeasing to God. "O earth, cover not thou my blood, and let my cry have no place." He wanted everything brought out into the light. If there was any trace of sin in his heart, he wanted it revealed. "Cover not thou my blood."

He assures us, on the ground of God's knowledge, that his heart was clean. "Also now, behold, my witness is in heaven, and my record is on high." God, who keeps all the records, is the Judge. Eliphaz was not the judge—God was. Because of this, Job felt a sense of security in the fact that he was well-pleasing in the eyes of the Lord.

Job was certain of his sure refuge in his God. "My friends scorn me: but mine eye poureth out tears unto God." What a blessed privilege we have. Even though we are misunderstood by those who are supposed to be our friends, we have direct access to God. We can pour out all our troubles to Him.

Perhaps at this moment you feel as if your world were crumbling. Oh, look up, pour out your tears to God. He knows all about your heartaches, He knows all about your problems. In fact, He even knows the number of your tears. In Psalm 56:8 we read, "Thou tellest my wanderings: put Thou my tears into Thy bottle: are they not in Thy book?" Yes, God knows every tear that is shed. He loves you. He is able to care for you. Maybe you have been asking God why you must suffer as you do. Would it really console us if all our "Whys" were answered? Why the child had to meet that deadly virus and why he could not fight it off? Why the road was wet just where you skidded and why you were on that curve at the fatal moment? If we had scientific and philosophical explanations for all our bruising questions, would that comfort us?

The child is not comforted by being told why his toy broke or why his finger hurts when it is pinched in the car door. He is really comforted by feeling that his mother loves him and that she can do something about it. In this business of living, we are all children with little minds and not very great wisdom. But God has gone to the great trouble to assure us that He loves us: He has gone the length of Calvary. Today He reminds us again in Jeremiah 31:3, "I have loved thee with an everlasting love: therefore with lovingkindness have I drawn thee."

Weep not, dear child of God. Trust the Lord! He will not fail you. What is your need? Finances?

> Your Father is rich in houses and land,
> He holdeth the wealth of the world in His hand!
> Of rubies and diamonds, of silver and gold,
> His coffers are full; He has riches untold.

Psalm 50:10 tells us, "For every beast of the forest is Mine, and the cattle upon a thousand hills." Further, in verse 12 God says, "If I were hungry, I would not tell thee: for the world is Mine, and the fulness thereof." Surely God can provide for you. He promises in Philippians 4:19 that He will: "But my God shall supply all your need according to His riches in glory by Christ Jesus." Don't weep! Sorrow not. Trust God. Every need will be provided as you wait on Him and believe Him.

Job continues his speech by saying, "O that one might plead for a man with God, as a man pleadeth for his neighbour!" In other words, as a man pleads for his neighbor at the bar of justice in the courtroom, Job is asking for someone to plead his case before God. Praise the Lord, we know who that One is. It is none other than the Lord Jesus Christ, "For there is one God, and one mediator between God and men, the man Christ Jesus" (1 Timothy 2:5). Christ is our go-between. He reaches down to us, but He also approaches the Father and pleads our cause.

In the closing verse of this chapter Job says, "When a few years are come, then I shall go the way whence I shall not return." Job knew well that his broken and suffering body, that pained him so, would soon be placed in the ground to go back to dust. But he knew also that his soul would go to a better country. He possessed the certainty that he would see His Redeemer. What a wonderful hope we have in Christ, that death is not the end! We read in Psalm 116:15, "Precious in the sight of the LORD is the death of His saints." Can death be precious? Yes, when we know Christ, for the Bible tells us that when we die, we go to be with Him immediately. In Philippians 1:23 Paul said, "For I am in a strait betwixt two, having a desire to depart, and to be with Christ; which is far better." Indeed, it is far better, far better than anything you and I have ever experienced.

When death comes to you, where will you go? Not everyone will go to be with Christ—only those who have received Him as Saviour and Lord in this life. In Amos 4:12 we read, "Prepare to meet thy God." The only preparation you can make, and the only preparation God demands, is that Christ become your Saviour and Lord. If you die without Christ, you must go to hell. The Bible declares this. The Bible is God's Word; it is the voice of authority.

Perhaps the Holy Spirit has been speaking to you. You have been going through some time of great trial and tragedy. God is dealing with you. Do not harden your heart against the Lord.

JOB 17:1-16

Job continues his reply to his three so-called comforters. In verse 1 he speaks as a dying man, saying, "My breath is corrupt, my days are extinct, the graves are ready for me." This reminds me of Paul's words in 2 Timothy 4:6-8: "For I am now ready to be offered, and the time of my departure is at hand. I have fought a good fight, I have finished my course, I have kept the faith: Henceforth there is laid up for me a crown of righteousness, which the Lord, the righteous judge, shall give me at that day: and not to me only, but unto all them also that love His appearing." Job was a sick man; Paul was an old man. Both expected death very soon. Usually when one is in either of these two conditions, death seems very near. But we are all dying men and dying women—one need not be sick or old. That is why it is so important to be ready to meet God at any time. We are ready only as we know Christ in the heart. Were we to rely upon our few paltry good works, we would never be ready.

If we have received Christ, then we ought to be busy for

Him, serving Him, realizing that death is not far away for any of us. What Job said applies to each and every one of us, "the graves are ready for me." Thus, if you are a believer, you ought to be living for one purpose only: that of reaching lost men and women with the gospel of Christ. Our Lord Jesus said in John 4:35, "Lift up your eyes, and look on the fields; for they are white already to harvest." Too few of God's people have the kind of vision that will impel them to reach the needy and the lost for the Saviour.

Recently I was reading of Christians in Korea. What a compassion these people have for the lost! A friend tells of a crusade he held among Korean believers, in which they gave three hundred gold rings. Many times he has seen them give the clothes off their back, because they had nothing more to give. Is it any wonder that God has blessed the Church in Korea more than in many other mission fields of the world? Korean Christians have learned the joys of sacrifice. Many of us in America have never learned this privilege. But do not forget it: we are dying men and dying women. Our time may be short. While we are here, we are to redeem the time for God, investing all we have for His glory, that souls perishing without Christ might hear the gospel.

Not only was Job a dying man, he was an abused man. "Are there not mockers with me? and doth not mine eye continue in their provocation?" Here were men pretending to be friends, yet they were insulting Job. Was it not bad enough that he had to endure his calamity without the additional load of words that were mockery?

Job calls on God for help. "Lay down now, put me in a surety with Thee; who is he that will strike hands with me?" This was a plea to the Almighty to attest Job's innocence, since his friends only mocked him. Litigating parties had to lay down a sum of money before the trial, as a surety. Job is calling on God to be his surety. With God as his surety he could say, "Who is he that will strike hands with me?" The surety provided security. Children of God are not left without a surety: "For there is one God, and one mediator between God and men, the man Christ Jesus; Who gave Himself a ransom for all, to be testified in due time" (1 Timothy 2:5-6). Christ is our surety. As we fully trust Him, even the devil and all of his angels cannot claim us. We are forever delivered from the power of sin. We are the Lord's blood-bought children.

Job reminds us further that all wisdom comes from God; the reason his comforters were in ignorance was because God had not revealed His wisdom to them. They had not been willing to open their hearts to receive His wisdom. We read in James 1:5, "If any of you lack wisdom, let him ask of God, that giveth to all men liberally, and upbraideth not; and it shall be given him." In Proverbs 2:6 we are told that "the Lord giveth wisdom: out of His mouth cometh knowledge and understanding." Is it not wonderful to know that whatever our need for wisdom, we can go to God, who will give us of His wisdom liberally, that we might have guidance and direction in making decisions and in taking action? How pathetic for the man or woman who tries to get through the hard places the best way he can. In Psalm 37:23 we read that "The steps of a good man are ordered by the LORD: and He delighteth in his way." Yes, truly it is a delight to walk in the way of the Lord, because that is the best way.

Not only did Job's friends lack wisdom from God, but they were guilty of plotting Job's ruin. Job says, "He that speaketh flattery to his friends, even the eyes of his children shall fail." The flatterer is usually a liar. Job was wise to the tricks of his vain comforters. He knew they were deceivers, hypocrites who would be happy to see him destroyed.

Is it not true that sometimes those we think to be friends prove to be nothing more than vain hypocrites? But be sure, there is one Friend who will always prove Himself true. Who is He? Jesus Christ, the Son of the Living God. The Bible says of Him that He "is a friend that sticketh closer than a brother"

(Proverbs 18:24). Isn't it marvelous to know that even should earthly friends forsake or betray us, Christ remains the same. We can go to Him at any time with the assurance that He will not fail us.

It may be at this moment that you are in need of a true friend. Lift your heart to God through Christ. Trust fully in Him! Believe Him! He will undertake for you. He promises in Philippians 4:19 that He "shall supply all your need." Why not trust Him for it?

Henry Moorhouse, a noble evangelist, was once in very trying circumstances. His little daughter, who was paralyzed, was sitting in her chair. As he entered the house with a package for his wife, he went to his little girl and kissing her asked, "Where is Mother?"

"Mother is upstairs."

"Well, I have a package for her."

"Let me carry the package to Mother."

"Why, Minnie dear, how can you carry the package? You cannot carry yourself."

"Oh, no, Daddy," Minnie said, with a smile on her face, "but you give me the package and I will carry the package, and you will carry me."

You may not be able to carry your burden today; but let Christ carry you with the burden, and you will find that it will all work out the right way. God is faithful, He is the unfailing Friend. Trust Him!

In verse 6 we read, "He hath made me also a byword of the people; and aforetime I was as a tabret." Job claims that he has been made a byword of the people, that is, a laughingstock, the talk of the countryside. Probably the talk that was going around about Job was that he was a great sinner and this was the reason for all his calamity. The word "tabret" here expresses the act of spitting. He says of himself that he was nothing more than one to be spat upon. He was the object of ridicule and disgust, a reproach among men.

Job was also a man of sorrows, as he says, "Mine eye also is dim by reason of sorrow, and all my members are as a shadow." He was nothing but skin and bones, probably the result not only of his disease but of his anxiety. Night and day he was given to weeping because of his suffering and sorrow; he wept so much that he could hardly see. "Mine eye also is dim," he tells us.

Job's sorrow gave him some hope of sympathy: "Upright men shall be astonied at this, and the innocent shall stir up himself against the hypocrite." That is, men who have a hold on God will be moved by the sufferings of the innocent. At the same time, they will not fall in line with the faulty reasoning of the three hypocrites that surround Job and seek to condemn him. Righteous men will accept such sufferings from the hand of God, as the providence of the Lord. They will truly believe Romans 8:28, "All things work together for good to them that love God, to them who are the called according to His purpose." They will not doubt God but believe Him for all things.

Job assures us further that the righteous will not turn from the Lord in seasons of trial. "The righteous also shall hold on his way, and he that hath clean hands shall be stronger and stronger." Job points out a very real truth here. Rather than turn from the Lord in trial, true believers will be drawn closer to Him. The ungodly will curse God for trial, but those who have a hold on the Lord, "upright men" Job calls them, "shall hold on his way," for they realize that the mercy of the Lord is with them that fear Him.

On occasion, I hear people say, "I was so ill I just didn't feel like praying," or, "I was so disturbed I couldn't pray." That is the time when we should be praying. By this I do not mean that we should pray only when we have a need. The true believer should pray without ceasing. But when the burden gets heavy, when the load of care weighs down upon us, then we must go to the Lord. The Scripture is true, "Draw nigh to God, and He will draw nigh unto you." When you need help, go to the Helper. Realize that God's love for us is not a love that keeps us from trial, but it is a love that keeps us in trial. Thus we are told in Hebrews 4:16, "Let us therefore come boldly unto the throne of grace, that we may obtain mercy, and find grace to help in time of need." This verse refers to any kind of need. God does not qualify the need; He simply says "in time of need." Whatever your need, go to the throne of grace, call on the Lord. He will understand and He will undertake.

An English naval officer once told a grateful story of the way he was helped and saved from dishonor in his first experience in battle. The array of enemy ships so terrified him that he almost fainted. The officer over him saw his state, came close beside him, and took his hands, saying, "Courage, my boy, you will recover in a minute or two. I was the same when I went into my first battle." The young man said afterward that it was as if an angel had come to him and put new strength into him.

When we are assailed by sudden temptation and are afraid, Christ comes close beside us and says, "I understand. I met a temptation just like yours. I know the dread you feel. Be brave and strong, and your fear will vanish and you will be victorious." He can say that because He was tempted in every way that we can be, yet without sin. That is why we should go to the throne of grace immediately. Do not turn *from* God in your trial; turn *to* Him. He will help you, He will provide for you. Thus Job says, "The righteous also shall hold on his way, and he that hath clean hands shall be stronger and stronger."

Next Job appeals to Eliphaz, Bildad, and Zophar, suggesting that, if they have anything worth-while to say, they should say it now. "But as for you all, do ye return, and come now: for I cannot find one wise man among you." He implies that he has not heard anything wise from them as yet.

Job reminds me in this chapter of the words of David, found in Psalm 60:11, "Give us help from trouble: for vain is the help of man." Sometimes even when our friends are willing to help, there is really nothing they can do. Thus, it behooves you and me to be sure that our hearts are clean and pure before God, that there is nothing between God and ourselves. If our relationship to Him is right, we can trust Him, whatever the circumstances may be. We read in 2 Samuel 8:6 that "the Lord preserved David whithersoever he went." As He preserved David, He preserves you and me; our God cannot fail. Thus we must trust Him. Maybe at this moment you are going through a time of extreme suffering or trial. Let me ask you a question: is your mind stayed on your trial or on the Lord? Is it not true that we often fix our eyes on the trial rather than on Christ? Ask the Lord to give you the grace to look beyond the trial to Him, who is unfailing in His care and in His love. The future is as bright as the promises of God, and there are no limits to God's promises. Do not worry about tomorrow: God is already there; He has taken care of tomorrow. Thus He says to you and to me, "Sufficient unto the day is the evil thereof." Trust Him for today; He will take care of tomorrow.

In the remaining verses of the chapter, Job sounds a note of discouragement, "My days are past, my purposes are broken off, even the thoughts of my heart." It would seem that all of Job's plans for the future were gone forever. Like any father, he had fond ambitions for his children. But now even his children were gone. I am sure all of us can understand something of Job's plight. But surely you will agree that there is nothing better in life than God's plan. If we have as our utmost desire the fulfillment of God's divine plan, then there need not be any discouragements. Out of the will of God, there can be no such thing as success; in the will of God, there can be no such thing as failure. Recall the words of Abraham's servant, found in Genesis 24:27, "I being in the way, the LORD led me." That is the best place to be, the only place for any of us to be: in the Lord's chosen path. Dr. A. T. Pierson said on one occasion, "To abide in the will of God is to abide in absolute safety." David prayed in Psalm 27:11, "Teach me Thy way, O LORD, and lead me in a plain path." How we need to pray that prayer. The Lord's way may not always be the most glamorous or the most exciting, but it will be the best way to take, for it is according to God's chosen plan. If you are traveling in this direction, you will not be disappointed. But Job, like most of us, had his own plans, and when his plans were frustrated he was disappointed and discouraged.

In speaking of his three comforters again, Job says, "They change the night into day: the light is short because of darkness." By their reasonings they were trying to offer encouragement, endeavoring to "change the night into day"; but any light they might give was only temporary, because the darkness of death was so near.

Job knew that he was near the grave. He said, "If I wait, the grave is mine house: I have made my bed in the darkness." It seemed as though the darkness of death had already surrounded him. "I have said to corruption, Thou art my father: to the worm, Thou art my mother, and my sister." Here he describes the state of the grave as being but corruption and worms. "Where is now my hope? as for my hope, who shall see it?" At this point Job does not answer his question regarding his hope, but he does later in chapter 19, where we read his challenging words, "For I know that my redeemer liveth, and that He shall stand at the latter day upon the earth: And though after my skin worms destroy this body, yet in my flesh shall I see God" (19:25-26). He had an enduring hope, the resurrection hope, the same hope you and I have in Christ.

Next he tells us that even this hope will go down into the grave with him, "They shall go down to the bars of the pit, when our rest together is in the dust." But in chapter 19 he assures us that both he and his hope will rise again. The grave is not the end; the body will be joined to the soul in the presence of the Lord. That is, it will if we have known the Lord. Job had hope, the hope of someday seeing his Saviour and Lord.

Any man in business, who owns valuable buildings which he finds, for some reason, have not been adequately insured against fire, will let everything else wait until he has the evidence of proper insurance on those buildings, a policy or "binder" carefully tucked away in his vault. But there only a few paltry dollars are involved; here eternal life is at stake. Oh, do not play around with God. You may play fast and loose with your friends, your business associates; but do not play with God. Listen to Psalm 89:48, "What man is he that liveth, and shall not see death? shall he deliver his soul from the hand of the grave?" Be sure, as Job has told us in chapter 17, the grave is near. We need to be ready to meet God at any time. You are not ready to meet God·unless you have been born from above.

JOB 18:1-21

ONCE AGAIN Bildad expresses his feelings about Job. He seems to be more exasperated than ever at the reasoning of God's suffering servant. Bildad appears to be irritated not only because of Job, but because of the other two comforters. Verse 2 is probably addressed to all three—Eliphaz, Zophar, and Job. "How long will it be ere ye make an end of words? mark, and afterwards we will speak." Bildad accuses them of endless talk, words without real meaning.

Bildad was very bitter in his accusations of Job. "Wherefore are we counted as beasts," he asks, "and reputed vile in your sight?" Job had called his friends "mockers" but he did not call them "beasts." Doubtless Bildad was very proud. A proud man often misinterprets what is said. Thus we see Bildad trying to put evil words into Job's mouth. When one is proud, he is easily offended. It is quite obvious that this was the case with Bildad.

Verse 4 is addressed in particular to Job, blaming him for his own suffering, as before. But now Bildad says that much of

Job's difficulty is the result of his anger, "He teareth himself in his anger." This argument is mere self-justification, for, if Job had been angry, I am sure he was no more so than Bildad. But let us pause to reflect the truth in what Bildad said. A man really does harm himself by his anger. Though he may offend others and cause much distress in the lives and hearts of others, the worse damage is done to himself. In Ecclesiastes 7:9 God says, "Anger resteth in the bosom of fools." A man given to anger is a foolish man. Someone has said, "Getting mad will never get you anything else." How true that is.

I am reminded of a pious but cranky old lady who was greatly annoyed because her neighbors forgot to ask her to go on their picnic. On the morning of the event they suddenly realized their affront and sent their little boy to ask her to come along.

"It's too late now," she snapped, "I've already prayed for rain."

Out of anger comes the sin of retaliation. This can bring only misery into one's life. How we need to heed the words of James 1:19-20: "Wherefore, my beloved brethren, let every man be swift to hear, slow to speak, slow to wrath: For the wrath of man worketh not the righteousness of God." Did you get that? "The wrath of man worketh not the righteousness of God." Wrath and righteousness are direct opposites. Are you given to outbursts of anger? Oh, let God give you victory in your heart. He can, for as the Scriptures teach, there is no sin He cannot overcome. We must be willing, however, to let Him have complete control.

Next Bildad asks Job two questions. "Shall the earth be forsaken for thee? and shall the rock be removed out of his place?" In other words, as we have seen before in these studies, Bildad accused Job of being a sinner and having to suffer as the result of his sin. Job had been begging God for deliverance from his anxiety, but Bildad reasoned that God has certain laws that cannot be overcome: if a man is sinful, he must suffer. Since

Job was a sinful hypocrite, as Bildad has already claimed, then he must expect to suffer. Can God change the laws of this earth because of one man? Will God remove mountains out of our paths for our convenience? There are set and fixed laws of life. Thus Bildad argues that Job cannot expect help from God.

How pharisaical this legalist was! He accused Job of knowing nothing of the grace of God. But, someone replies, how could he be expected to know anything about the grace of God? Bildad knew only the Old Testament dispensation. Surely you will agree with me that, whether it be Old Testament or New Testament, the grace of Almighty God is manifested on every page of the Bible. There has never been a time when the grace of God has not been exercised. The very fact that God permitted Bildad and his two friends to thrust their disturbing arguments at Job, without immediately judging them for it, was an act of God's marvelous grace. How wonderful is the grace of Almighty God! We read in 2 Corinthians 9:8, "And God is able to make all grace abound toward you; that ye, always having all sufficiency in all things, may abound to every good work." Think of it, an endless outpouring of God's grace for you and for me! In every situation His grace abounds and far exceeds our worthiness.

A man driving through West Virginia stopped in Salem and left his car by a parking meter. He overstayed his allotted time and fully expected upon returning to his car to find a ticket for a violation. Instead of a ticket, however, he discovered a red tag with this astonishing message: "The Chief of Police of Salem, West Virginia, has deposited five cents in the meter rather than tag you. You want him to have his money back, so hand this card with the amount he has paid to him or leave it at any place of business and it will be returned to the Chief. Thank you, and come back."

Obviously this generous gesture on the part of the chief was an act of grace. But far more wonderful is the grace of God; He does not even charge us a nickel. We read in Romans 3:24, "Being justified *freely* by His grace." At no cost to us, those who believe on Christ are justified freely by His grace.

A very important lesson Bildad needed to learn was the lesson of grace. Have you learned this lesson? If you are not a Christian, have you ever stopped to realize that God loved you enough to send His Son to the cross to die for you? This is grace. You do not deserve it. None of us deserves it. But it is by the grace of God that we are saved.

It may be you have backslidden. You have not fallen *from grace* but you have fallen *in grace*. You are stumbling in the paths of sin today, even though at one time you walked with the Lord. Realize, will you, how greatly God loves you and how concerned He is about you. He wants you to come back to Him. Why not get right with Him? You know you are not happy as you are. Come back today! The Bible says in Isaiah 55:7: "Let the wicked forsake his way, and the unrighteous man his thoughts: and let him return unto the LORD, and He will have mercy upon him; and to our God, for He will abundantly pardon."

Beginning with verse 5, Bildad gives a remarkable description of the horrible calamities that are to come upon the wicked when judgment falls upon the lawless and disobedient. I do not think there is any other portion of the Bible more powerful and descriptive than this one. But the sad feature is that Bildad is applying it to a man of God rather than to those who have no regard for the Lord. Let us examine a few of these enlightening verses, for certainly they are most worth while.

In verse 5 we read, "Yea, the light of the wicked shall be put out, and the spark of his fire shall not shine." You have met people, I am sure, who say, "Well, I am not perfect. I know I have sin in my life, but I am not all bad. I do some good things." On the basis of these "good things" they feel that they will merit Heaven. Not only verse 5 teaches the unreasonableness of such an argument; there are many other verses in the Bible which say the same thing."The light of the wicked shall be put out, and the spark of his fire shall not shine."

Further we read, "The light shall be dark in his tabernacle, and his candle shall be put out with him." God says in Matthew 8:12 that the wicked "shall be cast out into outer darkness: there shall be weeping and gnashing of teeth." Think of those words, "cast out into outer darkness." All the darkness of hell will be the lot of the ungodly, who will be forever separated from God in eternal torment. Who could begin to fathom the awfulness of such a state? Would to God that every man outside of Christ would consider these words today. Unless you repent and turn to the Lord, "outer darkness" will be your place of abode throughout all of eternity. In spite of the flames of hell, it will be darkness because of the emptiness of the soul and the absence of God and His power.

Bildad informs us next that "The steps of his strength shall be straitened." He is speaking of the strong man who will be brought low because of his own rebellion against the way of the Lord. "Straitened" here means that he is no longer able to move about in his own strength as he has done in the past. Here is a healthy, virile man brought low by his own wickedness. "His own counsel shall cast him down." He has his own ideas; he thinks he is right. But he will soon find that his ideas are as nothing because they have opposed the Word of God.

Further we are told that "He is cast into a net by his own feet, and he walketh upon a snare." In other words, the wicked man's own plans will be the cause of his downfall. The phrase, "he walketh upon a snare," means that he lets himself be caught in a net. He takes no precaution. He is careless and indifferent to warnings.

Is this not descriptive of the ungodly in our day? The Bible is filled with hundreds of warnings. God says, "Seek ye the LORD while He may be found; call ye upon Him while He is near" (Isaiah 55:6). But what does man do? He lives on in his quest for money and more money. He disregards the laws of

God. He treats the Lord's Day as any other day in the week. He takes no time for worship. He does not read the Bible. Thus "he walketh upon a snare." He permits himself to fall into difficulty after difficulty.

The wicked are not really happy. "The gin shall take him by the heel, and the robber shall prevail against him. The snare is laid for him in the ground, and a trap for him in the way" (verses 9-10). His sins are constantly bringing him into misery. He thinks he can escape divine judgment, but how mistaken he is. God declares in John 5:28-29, "Marvel not at this: for the hour is coming, in the which all that are in the graves shall hear His voice, And shall come forth; they that have done good, unto the resurrection of life; and they that have done evil, unto the resurrection of damnation." As we are told here, "All that are in the graves shall hear His voice, and shall come forth." There will be no exceptions. Every one who has failed to come to Christ in this life must stand before God in judgment, and then the result—eternal hell. You can believe anything you want about this. You can laugh at it, deny it, ridicule it; but that does not change it in the least. That is why people ought to be ready to meet God. That is why you ought to be saved if you are not. Try as you may, you cannot escape judgment.

Then look at these words: "Terrors shall make him afraid on every side, and shall drive him to his feet. His strength shall be hunger-bitten, and destruction shall be ready at his side. It shall devour the strength of his skin: even the firstborn of death shall devour his strength. His confidence shall be rooted out of his tabernacle, and it shall bring him to the king of terrors" (verses 11-14). Practically every phrase in these verses suggests fear and unrest of the heart and soul. There are so many people like this today. They know nothing of the peace of God, all because of their unconfessed sin. They have not come to Christ and permitted Him to be their Sin-Bearer.

I wish there were some way by which God would enable us to help everyone to see what they are missing by their refusal to receive Christ. Oh, if only they could understand about His marvelous peace. Jesus said in John 16:33, "These things I have spoken unto you, that in Me ye might have peace. In the world ye shall have tribulation: but be of good cheer; I have overcome the world." Tribulation? Yes, we all have tribulation. But in Christ we have peace. Do you know this blessed peace? Have you received it from Him, the Son of God? He wants to flood your heart with His peace.

During a recent year, fifty million prescriptions were written for tranquilizers, according to Dr. Theodore R. VanDullen, health columnist. "Aspirin," he said, "alleviates the pain but does not cure the cause. . . . Sedatives induce sleep but do not correct the cause of insomnia. Tranquilizers are even less specific in their action, and yet some people consider them to be the answer to all their problems. As yet, there is no ideal tranquilizer."

As far as medicine is concerned, this learned and experienced doctor is right. "There is no ideal tranquilizer." But, thank God, there is One who can give perfect peace and quietness of soul. He quiets the storms in the soul with the same infinite perfection that He brought peace to the raging sea. He gives lasting and unshakeable peace to the disturbed and the guilty. If only man would come to Him and rest on His promises. Jesus Christ takes away frustration and gives fruitage. He supplants unrest in the heart with His own assuring peace. He delivers from sin and gives rest.

In verse 15 we read, "It shall dwell in his tabernacle, because it is none of his: brimstone shall be scattered upon his habitation." "It" refers to the terror reigning in the hearts of the wicked, described in the previous verse. Terror is a characteristic mark of the wicked. What a horrible situation! Wherever he goes, even though he may travel hundreds of miles to get away from it all, he finds unrest as soon as he arrives. He cannot escape the terror which reigns in his soul. In Isaiah 57:20-21 we are told of this unhappy state: "But the wicked are like the troubled sea, when it cannot rest, whose waters cast up mire and dirt. There is no peace, saith my God, to the wicked." No matter in what direction he may turn, regardless of what he might do, "there is no peace, saith my God, to the wicked." Godlessness cannot, under any circumstances, produce peace. The Lord alone can produce peace, and only as one comes God's way can he find peace.

Further, Bildad says, "Brimstone shall be scattered upon his habitation." This suggests the continual judgment that rests upon the sinful man. He can never produce good works, pleasing to God, because he is vile. Notice the description of the wicked given in the third chapter of Romans, beginning with verse 12: "They are all gone out of the way, they are together become unprofitable; there is none that doeth good, no, not one. Their throat is an open sepulchre; with their tongues they have used deceit; the poison of asps is under their lips: Whose mouth is full of cursing and bitterness: Their feet are swift to shed blood: Destruction and misery are in their ways: And the way of peace have they not known." Worst of all, "There is no fear of God before their eyes." They know not the way of peace because "there is no fear of God before their eyes."

Notice verse 16, "His roots shall be dried up beneath, and above shall his branch be cut off." This is just the opposite from the saved man of Psalm 1. In writing of the believer, David said, "He shall be like a tree planted by the rivers of water, that bringeth forth his fruit in his season; his leaf also shall not wither; and whatsoever he doeth shall prosper" (Psalm 1:3). The wicked man finds himself drying up because he has not received of the Water of Life that sustains the soul.

The thought, "above shall his branch be cut off," suggests his posterity. Very often if a parent does not follow in the way of the Lord, neither will his children. Thus the children, likewise, will suffer the judgment of God because they will continue in the wickedness of their parents. For this reason, parents must set a godly example in the home. It is needful that they know Christ and have a family altar, reading God's Word, and praying each day for and with their children. We read in Ezekiel 16:44, "As is the mother, so is her daughter." This is so true. We could also say, "As is the father, so is his son." Children fashion their lives after their parents. That is why it is so needful, mother and father, that you know Christ and follow Him closely.

Verse 17 says, "His remembrance shall perish from the earth, and he shall have no name in the street." Even worse, the unsaved man will have no name in the Lamb's Book of Life. He will be unknown in Heaven. At the same time, he will soon be forgotten on earth. A wicked man will not long be remembered. "He shall be driven from light into darkness, and chased out of the world." This is suggestive of Psalm 9:17, "The wicked shall be turned into hell." Then Bildad says, "He shall neither have son nor nephew among his people, nor any remaining in his dwellings." Here we see God's continuing judgment on the posterity of the wicked because of sin. "They that come after him shall be astonied at his day, as they that went before were affrighted." This embodies all wicked men of every age and generation. Those before and those after will meet the same end. How terrible is the judgment of God.

Notice the summary of it all, the key to the whole chapter, verse 21: "Surely such are the dwellings of the wicked, and this is the place of him that knoweth not God." The word "place" could be translated "condition": "This is the *condition* of him that knoweth not God." Thinking of what we have just read in this chapter, what is the condition of him that knoweth not God? It is one of willful ignorance; he does not desire to know. He has no interest in seeking after God. Thus he lives on, carelessly neglecting his many opportunities to believe on the Lord. But God assures us that the end of it all is eternal judgment.

JOB 19:1-29

GREATLY PERTURBED, Job replied to Bildad without hesitation. He began by asking, "How long will ye vex my soul, and break me in pieces with words?" Doubtless the criticism coming from the lips of Job's three friends was about as painful as the physical suffering he was enduring. He appeared to be greatly disturbed, wondering how much longer they planned to keep up their agitating, which vexed and grieved him. Surely it was bad enough to suffer physically without all of this added discomfort. There are some people who glory in browbeating somebody else. They are never happier than when they are criticizing or adding to someone else's misery. These three comforters seemed to have this special gift.

Job continues by saying, "These ten times have ye reproached me: ye are not ashamed that ye make yourselves strange to me." There had been a time when Job possessed wealth and position, and at that time these three men were very friendly toward him. Now they acted as strangers, and rather than looking up to him they looked down upon him.

Is it not interesting the way people change when our circumstances change? A man is never wealthier than when he has a real friend or two who remain the same regardless of the circumstances. Of course, the wonderful thing about our Lord is that He never changes. We read in Hebrews 13:8, "Jesus Christ the same yesterday, and to day, and for ever." Isn't that wonderful? He never changes. He is always friendly, ready to help with His love and care. How different were Job's friends. "These ten times have ye reproached me," Job said. "Ten" as used here means many times. Over and over again, repeatedly, they had reproached him and become strangers to him.

Further Job says, "And be it indeed that I have erred, mine error remaineth with myself." "Erred" here in the Hebrew means "unconsciously erred." Job did not claim perfection. He readily admitted that he had sinned, but it was not willful sin. He knew of no unconfessed sin in his heart.

Job's friends not only became strangers to him, but they became very proud and ridiculed him with scorn. Thus Job says, "If indeed ye will magnify yourselves against me, and plead against me my reproach; Know now that God hath overthrown me, and hath compassed me with His net." It was bad enough for the three friends to turn against Job, but Job suggests that even God had turned from him. Further he says, "Behold, I cry out of wrong, but I am not heard: I cry aloud, but there is no judgment." It seemed that God had turned a deaf ear toward Job. It only seemed that way, for it was not so. The only time God turns a deaf ear to His people is when there is unconfessed sin in their hearts. David said in Psalm 66:18, "If I regard iniquity in my heart, the Lord will not hear me." If there is any trace of unconfessed sin or known sin in the heart, until one goes to God and confesses it, claiming forgiveness through the cleansing blood of Christ, there can be no effectiveness whatsoever in prayer. The channel must be open. Sin blocks communication with God. In Isaiah 59:1-2 we read, Behold, the LORD's hand is not shortened, that it cannot save;

neither His ear heavy, that it cannot hear: But . . . your sins have hid His face from you, that He will not hear." Known sin in the believer's life is one of the greatest hindrances to prayer power.

There may be times when we feel that even though we have confessed all sin, still God does not hear, such as in Job's case. I am sure every believer has experienced this uncertainty on some occasion. We pray, but our prayers seem to go nowhere. In fact, sometimes the situation even worsens and our needs become greater. Do not let the wicked one deceive you, child of God. If you really know the Lord and all is right between you and Him, your prayers are being heard and God is at work. He does not always act the moment we think He should; the book of Job is a commentary on this fact. You may be sure, however, God will undertake in His divinely appointed time. So keep praying! Do not give up. Be faithful in prayer even though you are not seeing the slightest trace of an answer. God is at work. There are some who stop praying as soon as they fail to see any visible results from prayer. This is a sorrowful mistake. Every time you pray, you are actually saying, "Lord, I need You." When you neglect prayer you are saying, "Lord, I don't need You." The believer is on dangerous ground when he neglects to pray.

I have heard some say, "Well, God is sovereign; He can do all things; He knows what I need. I don't have to pray. He will undertake." The Bible does not say that. The Bible says, "Ask and it shall be given you; seek, and ye shall find; knock, and it shall be opened unto you" (Matthew 7:7). What does this mean? If you do not ask, it will not be given; if you do not seek, you will not find; if you do not knock, it will not be opened. God expects His people to come to Him with childlike faith, asking Him to work, and expecting Him to work.

Centuries ago the throne of Russia was occupied by two boy princes. They sat side by side and gave their decisions on the gravest questions. Their judgments were so wise and just that men marveled that princes so young and inexperienced could know so much of statecraft and speak with such discretion on questions so difficult. The secret was that close behind the throne where they sat, hidden by a thin wall, was Princess Sophia. She heard the cases that were brought to them and she gave the decisions which they delivered. They let her decide in every question and waited until she had whispered to them the wise answer which they gave out.

In a similar manner, believers are to refer every matter to God and wait for His answer. Never make a move until you have His answer. You may feel as Job, that God has not heard you; but He has. If you know the Lord Jesus in your heart and if you are right with Him, He has heard. This is the promise we find in His truth. Of course, if you are not a Christian, He does not hear, unless it is a prayer of repentance while calling on Christ for salvation. But to enjoy the privilege of daily prayer fellowship with God, you must be born again. Prayer is useless without the Mediator, Christ.

Job began to complain bitterly because of God's treatment. It is obvious that he was extremely discouraged, feeling neglected and forsaken, for he said, "He hath fenced up my way that I cannot pass." In other words, Job felt helpless and forlorn. He could do nothing he wanted to do. Not only that, the next statement suggests that there was misery in every step he took. "He hath set darkness in my paths." Further he says, "He hath stripped me of my glory, and taken the crown from my head." Job had been brought low through his sufferings, so that even his dearest friends turned against him. Penniless, he no longer had any standing in society. Seemingly he had lost everything.

Job's situation appeared to be hopeless. "He hath destroyed me on every side, and I am gone: and mine hope hath He removed like a tree." Everything he sought to do failed. Thus, depressed and discouraged, he was without hope. Then in verse 11 he says, "He hath also kindled His wrath against me, and He counteth me unto Him as one of His enemies." We can sympathize with Job in his suffering. It is difficult for us to realize, while enduring the long hours of severe trial, that God has not turned from us. But this cannot be, for God says in Hebrews 12:6, "For whom the Lord loveth He chasteneth, and scourgeth every son whom He receiveth." Job thought his suffering was the result of God's wrath, when actually it was the effects of God's love. This is difficult to understand, but nevertheless, it is true. Consider God's Word in Isaiah 55:8-9: "For My thoughts are not your thoughts, neither are your ways My ways, saith the LORD. For as the heavens are higher than the earth, so are My ways higher than your ways, and My thoughts than your thoughts." Who of us can understand the mind of God? For this reason we should not question His providence. No, it was not the wrath of God being poured upon Job. Behind all of his anxiety and suffering was God's marvelous love.

Further Job says, "His troops come together, and raise up their way against me, and encamp round about my tabernacle." As soldiers besieged a strong city, cutting off all the roads of entry and shutting out provision, Job felt that the tabernacle of his body was being treated in like manner by God. But was that so? Never! Psalm 34:7 tells us differently: "The angel of the Lord encampeth round about them that fear Him, and delivereth them." God is never at war with those who are on His side.

Next Job blames God for the loss of his earthly friendships. "He hath put my brethren far from me, and mine acquaintance are verily estranged from me." In the next few verses he elaborates upon this. Not only were his three friends against him, but as he says, "My kinsfolk have failed, and my familiar friends have forgotten me. They that dwell in mine house, and my maids, count me for a stranger: I am an alien in their sight. I called my servant, and he gave me no answer; I entreated him with my mouth." Even his wife turned against him. "My breath is strange to my wife, though I entreated for the children's sake of mine own body." Little children on the streets ridiculed Job, he was a laughingstock among them: "Yea, young children despised me; I arose, and they spake against me."

He sums it all up by saying, in verse 19, "All my inward friends abhorred me: and they whom I loved are turned against me." There is no question about it, Job's suffering was real. It was not imaginary. Yet on the other hand, is not all suffering real? Your suffering is real and so is mine. But we have a great God, an unfailing God. He has not left us alone; He has given us a Book filled with His marvelous promises. Whatever our need may be, we may be sure that He will not fail His promises. God's servant said in 1 Kings 8:56, "There hath not failed one word of all His good promise, which He promised by the hand of Moses His servant." You and I can say the same thing. God will not fail His promises. Then why don't we trust Him? Why don't we believe Him? Do you have any doubts in your mind at this moment? Doubting is sin. Whatever your need, whatever your affliction, trust the Lord! He will not fail.

Grace E. Troy has written these lovely words entitled, "Rest."

I would not ask Thee why
My path should be
Through strange and stony ways—
Thou leadest me!

I would not ask Thee how
Loss worketh gain,
Knowing that some day soon—
All shall be plain.

My heart would never doubt
Thy love and care
However heavy seems
The cross I bear.

Nor would I, Father, ask
My lot to choose,
Lest seeking selfish ease
Thy best I lose.

Giver of every gift
Thy choice is best.
All-wise Eternal Love,
In Thee I rest.

Yielding to Thy wise hand
Safe in Thy will—
Not asking why or how,
Let me be still.

Looking on things unseen
By faith I see
Glory exceeding great
Worketh for me.

Yes, and this glory is working for you. Do not doubt the Lord. Even though earthly friends may have forsaken you, even though dearest loved ones may have turned against you, God is still the same. He loves you. In fact, He says in Jeremiah 31:3 "I have loved thee with an everlasting love: therefore with lovingkindness have I drawn thee." Maybe your way does seem hard and discouraging; God has not forgotten you. Trial is no sign that the Lord has turned His face from you. He loves you and He will help you, but you must believe Him. You must not fail to trust.

Lamenting his sorrowful state, Job continued by saying in verse 20, "My bone cleaveth to my skin and to my flesh, and I am escaped with the skin of my teeth." He must have been in a pitiful condition. The phrase, "my bone cleaveth to my skin," suggests that he was extremely thin, nothing but skin and bones, and the proverbial statement, "the skin of my teeth," suggests that he was just holding onto life by a thread. He pleads with his friends to have some consideration rather than add sorrow to sorrow by their complaints and criticisms. He says, "Have pity upon me, have pity upon me, O ye my friends; for the hand of God hath touched me." In the next verse he asked, "Why do ye persecute me as God, and are not satisfied with my flesh?"

Now Job turns to a new theme. Of all the words spoken to his three friends, nothing was as important and valuable as that which we are about to consider. In one of the most distressing chapters of the book we see Job ascending to his highest pinnacle of faith. Hear him as he cries aloud, "Oh that my words were now written! oh that they were printed in a book! That they were graven with an iron pen and lead in the rock for ever!" What Job asked for here was fulfilled. In this same chapter he had declared that God would not hear him, but how wrong he was. Every generation since has read these words. I cannot help but feel that when God's servant reached his lowest ebb, the Spirit of God came upon him and buoyed him up to heights before unknown. Philippians 4:19 applies so well to this experience, "My God shall supply all your need according to His riches in glory by Christ Jesus."

Consider Job's confession of faith in verses 25 through 27, "For I know that my redeemer liveth, and that He shall stand at the latter day upon the earth: And though after my skin worms destroy this body, yet in my flesh shall I see God: Whom I shall see for myself, and mine eyes shall behold, and not another; though my reins be consumed within me." Praise God, though Job descended to the lowest depths, he did not stay there. He knew that the hour would come when his Redeemer would return to claim the bodies of every believer from the grave. At death, Job's sickly, weak, emaciated body would go back to dust, but it would be raised a glorious body. God's servant knew he would see his Lord, for he declared, "Whom I shall see for myself, and mine eyes shall behold." I believe he was speaking by divine revelation of the great event of which we read in 1 Thessalonians 4:16-18: "For the Lord

Himself shall descend from heaven with a shout, with the voice of the archangel, and with the trump of God: and the dead in Christ shall rise first: Then we which are alive and remain shall be caught up together with them in the clouds, to meet the Lord in the air: and so shall we ever be with the Lord. Wherefore comfort one another with these words."

When our wonderful Lord returns for His Church, "the dead in Christ shall rise first." All who have believed on the Lord will be raised to meet Him in the air. No wonder Paul calls this the "Blessed Hope." It is "blessed," indeed. On that most welcome day we shall join Job, singing with praise in our hearts, "I know that my Redeemer liveth." We know Christ lives at this moment, but we shall know it then as we never knew it before, for we shall see Him as He is. We shall recognize Him by His nail-scarred hands and feet. With joy in our hearts we shall shout, "My Lord, and my God!"

I never think of Job's confession of faith without thinking of the words of the Lord Jesus Himself as they are found in John 11:25-26: "I am the resurrection, and the life: he that believeth in Me, though he were dead, yet shall he live: And whosoever liveth and believeth in Me shall never die. Believest thou this?" Our Lord said further in John 14:19, "Because I live, ye shall live also." As Christ came forth from the grave, even so will every true believer arise. Death could not hold Him, and it will not hold us. When the trumpet shall sound, the dead shall be raised first. The grave of every Christian will be opened. Our bodies will be recreated and quickened and we shall gather in the presence of Christ to meet Him in the air, as prophesied in the Word of God.

Many people are afraid to die, but Christians should never fear death. The grave is but the waiting place for the body until it is called to life again at the coming of our Lord. Of course, the soul does not lie in the grave. Immediately at death, the soul of the believer goes to be with Christ. But the day is coming when the body will be joined to the soul. What a wonderful hope we have to sustain us when dearest loved ones are called away by death. It is not the end. We shall meet them again, and then we shall spend eternity with them in the presence of our Lord. These few brief years of waiting are not long. We shall be together soon.

> We shall sleep but not forever,
>   There will be a glorious dawn,
> We shall meet to part—no, never—
>   On the resurrection morn.
>
> For death is but a covered way,
>   That opens unto light,
> Wherein no blinded child can stray
>   Beyond the Father's sight.
>
> Beyond this vale of tears
>   There is a life above,
> Unmeasured by the flight of years,
>   And all that life is love.

Job was discouraged but he was not defeated. He knew where he was going; he was ready to go.

In the closing words of the chapter the Lord's servant offered a warning to his unkind friends. "But ye should say, Why persecute we him, seeing the root of the matter is found in me? Be ye afraid of the sword: for wrath bringeth the punishments of the sword, that ye may know there is a judgment." These are worth-while thoughts to follow Job's marvelous confession of faith. Not everyone will be raised to meet the Lord face to face. Many will remain in the grave until the second resurrection. This will be the resurrection of God's wrath, "bringing the punishments of the sword, that ye may know there is a judgment." This will take place at the end of the thousand-year reign of Christ. The wicked, those who have never believed on the Lord, will be raised to face their Creator in judgment. What a horrible day that will be! It will be too late for repentance or change; judgment must be faced. Thus Job informs his friends that they would do well to stop pouring out their wrath upon him, for only God is the author of wrath. They would do better to get right with the Lord.

JOB 20:1-29

FOLLOWING JOB'S LAST SPEECH, Zophar is quick with another response. From verse 2 we notice that he was greatly disturbed by what Job had just said. For this reason he could not keep still; he had to speak. "Therefore do my thoughts cause me to answer, and for this I make haste." It would seem that Zophar had overlooked completely anything worth-while Job recounted in his speech and picked up only that which disturbed him. In verse 3 he says, "I have heard the check of my reproach, and the spirit of my understanding causeth me to answer." Zophar took what Job had to say as a personal affront. Like most humans, Zophar found it difficult to accept criticism, thus he was quick to retaliate with sharp words. With his usual bitterness, he accused Job of wickedness and hypocrisy.

Next Zophar emphasized the brevity of life for the wicked, "Knowest thou not this of old, since man was placed upon earth, That the triumphing of the wicked is short, and the joy of the hypocrite but for a moment?" Surely you will agree that what Zophar said is absolutely true. He argued that this philosophy has been known in every age. And, indeed, it has;

in fact, it still prevails. God tells us that "the wages of sin is death" (Romans 6:23). Whether the wicked rebel blatantly against the grace of God or practice their evil under cover, posing as pious religionists, they soon perish, for sin produces death. God says in Psalm 119:128, "I hate every false way." Because He hates every false way, He will judge every false way, as He has declared throughout His Word. As Zophar says, wicked men may prosper for a time but their prosperity is brief. Judgment must come.

Zophar elaborates on the prosperity of the wicked saying, "Though his excellency mount up to the heavens, and his head reach unto the clouds; Yet he shall perish for ever like his own dung: they which have seen him shall say, Where is he? He shall fly away as a dream, and shall not be found: yea, he shall be chased away as a vision of the night." In the eyes of the world the wicked go to the top, so to speak. But the problem is, the higher the sinner goes, the greater is the fall when he comes down. In the Berkeley version, the word "pride" is used in place of "excellency" in verse 6. "Though his pride may mount up to the heavens . . . yet he perishes forever." A man need not reach the pinnacle of success in actual experience; he needs only to reach it in his pride. Whichever may be the case, he is guilty. The inevitable fall must come. Oh, how delusive is the sin of pride! Many have stumbled and fallen because of this evil. "A man's pride shall bring him low," we are told in Proverbs 29:23. God hates a proud heart. This evil is no respecter of persons. It strikes saved and unsaved alike. Many of the problems common to our churches in our present day are the result of pride.

It is related that when a famous but highly temperamental soprano soloist was rehearsing to sing, Toscanini, the conductor, painstakingly gave her instructions just as he gave them to members of his orchestra. This proved too much for the vanity of the famed lady and she broke out with, "I am the star of this performance." To this Toscanini quietly answered,

"Madam, in this performance there are no stars." Toscanini knew that unless the soloist, members of the chorus, and the orchestra were ready and willing to work together in perfect harmony, there could be no performance worth hearing.

Unity of thought and movement in any effort are highly essential to success. Nowhere is this more true than in Christian work. We need good leadership, but there can be no real advance if everyone desires the solo parts. We are all one in Christ Jesus. In the sight of God each member of His body is as important as the other. There is no room for pride. Pride brings sorrow, misery, and unhappiness. For the wicked, God says that it brings death: "He shall perish for ever."

A proud man is usually despised by those who know him. Zophar says, "He shall be chased away as a vision of the night." A proud man is rarely acceptable among those with whom he lives and works. He is a constant source of irritation and disturbance.

Further we read, "The eye also which saw him shall see him no more; neither shall his place any more behold him." What a tragic picture this is of a man engrossed in himself, who has never learned to think of others but has been so busy exalting himself that he has missed the best in life. The Apostle John said of Diotrephes that he "loveth to have the preeminence among them" (3 John 9). Have you ever met a Diotrephes? Maybe you are one yourself, you love to have the preeminence, you find it difficult to play second fiddle. Anyone who cannot play second fiddle well will never be able to play first fiddle. God says in Galatians 6:3, "For if a man think himself to be something, when he is nothing, he deceiveth himself." Have you been deceiving yourself by your pride?

One time a seminary student began preaching his class sermon in a conceited manner, but he soon forgot it and retired in confusion. A professor kindly remarked, "If you had gone into the pulpit as you came out, you might have come out as you went in."

How much more effectual our service for Christ would be if we were really to die to ourselves and become alive unto Him; if we could say with Paul, and really mean it, "I am crucified with Christ" (Galatians 2:20). God cannot use a proud man. Only as we are completely possessed and controlled by the Holy Spirit can we overcome pride, because at heart we are all proud. Do you want a full measure of God's grace in your life? If so, remember first of all you must be empty, emptied of your pride. For consider what we read in James 4:6, "He giveth more grace. Wherefore he saith, God resisteth the proud, but giveth more grace unto the humble." And then in verse 10 God says, "Humble yourselves in the sight of the Lord, and He shall lift you up." Are you willing to go down at this moment, that you may be lifted up in the power of Christ? Then tell the Lord so. Such a confession on your part would be a delight to the heart of God. Let Him fill you with Himself.

Zophar further describes a hypocrite, saying, "His children shall seek to please the poor, and his hands shall restore their goods." What a sad lot falls upon the children of the wicked man. They must suffer the humiliation of making right the wrongs of the evil deeds of their father. "To please the poor" as used here means that they will restore the property which their father stole. Their wicked father oppressed the poor and used them as instruments to make himself rich. The children try to save their name by making things right.

Let me say to you fathers, I hope when you die your children will not have to do that for you. I trust that they will not find it necessary to salvage your name out of the dump heaps of sin. Are you a real testimony to your children right now, or are you a hindrance to their spiritual development? Many fathers are a stumbling block to their children when it comes to eternal things. They take little or no time for God. How can they expect their children to be interested in the things of God?

Wicked practices of later life are frequently the result of

uncontrolled lust in the years of youth. Zophar says, "His bones are full of the sin of his youth, which shall lie down with him in the dust." Here is a true picture of one living primarily for the gratification of the flesh. No life could be more miserable or encompassed by greater sorrow. Verses 12 and 13 suggest that the wicked man loves his sin so much that he refuses to give it up: "Though wickedness be sweet in his mouth, though he hide it under his tongue; Though he spare it, and forsake it not, but keep it still within his mouth." To "keep it still within his mouth" evidences his obstinacy. He persists in living in sin, even though humble saints may have appealed to him to forsake his wicked ways. Boldly he chooses the broad road that leads to destruction. In John 3:19 we read of men who "loved darkness rather than light, because their deeds were evil." In business they cheat and steal just to make another dollar. They know it is wrong. Time and time again they have been warned by others, but to them, what is the difference? Ah, there will be a difference someday, for sooner or later the catastrophe must come. More than that, the Bible makes it clear that even now there can be no happiness. We read in Proverbs 4:19, "The way of the wicked is as darkness; they know not at what they stumble." Life for them is an unbroken chain of suffering and sorrow. But even though God is dealing with them all along the way, they refuse to recognize the hand of the Lord at work in their lives. Oh, that they might repent and turn from sin to the living God.

Look now at what Zophar has to say about the present misery of the unrepentant sinner. "Yet his meat in his bowels is turned, it is the gall of asps within him." His ill-gotten gains produce no joy, only misery and unhappiness. "He hath swallowed down riches, and he shall vomit them up again: God shall cast them out of his belly." This is not a pleasant picture, is it? The wicked man loses his money as fast as he makes it. At the same time, the more he makes the more he loses. As he feverishly toils night and day, his ill-gotten gains seem to produce no satisfaction. "He shall suck the poison of asps: the viper's tongue shall slay him." This speaks of trouble, never-ending trouble. It is a picture of the wicked man rebelling against God. We are told in Proverbs 28:13, "He that covereth his sins shall not prosper." No matter what he does or how he does it, his sin cannot produce inner peace and satisfaction. "He shall not see the rivers, the floods, the brooks of honey and butter." He is ever clamoring for that which satisfies, but he never finds it. Then, note, very often his sin will catch up with him. "That which he laboured for shall he restore, and shall not swallow it down: according to his substance shall the restitution be, and he shall not rejoice therein. Because he hath oppressed and hath forsaken the poor; because he hath violently taken away an house which he builded not." Zophar is speaking about the oppressor who deceives and robs the innocent to fill his own pockets. To the wicked this looks like an easy way, but he finds that it is a most difficult way.

Next Zophar says, "Surely he shall not feel quietness in his belly, he shall not save of that which he desired. There shall none of his meat be left; therefore shall no man look for his goods. In the fulness of his sufficiency he shall be in straits: every hand of the wicked shall come upon him." No matter which way he turns, the wicked man seems to fall into trouble. He cannot win, no matter how hard he tries, "In the fulness of his sufficiency he shall be in straits." Full — yet empty! How true this is of the man who refuses to yield to the control of the Lord.

Park Tucker in his book, *Prison Is My Parish,* tells of asking an inmate in the federal penitentiary at Atlanta to give a theological analysis for the redemption of man. The inmate took his Bible and said, "I am a Christian because I have *accepted*— 'Behold, now is the *accepted* time.'" He turned to another portion and said, "I am a Christian because I *believe*—'Believe on the Lord Jesus Christ and thou shalt be saved.'" He turned to another portion and showed Mr. Tucker the monumental

Scripture, "If we confess our sins, He is faithful and just to
forgive us our sins, and to cleanse us from all unrighteousness."
He added, "Chaplain, it's just plain ABC—accept, believe,
confess." That is it, it could be no simpler: accept, believe, confess!

Having stressed the fact that the wicked man is never at rest,
that even his so-called prosperity brings only misery, Zophar
proceeds to show us now that the miserable life of the wicked
will be climaxed by utter ruin. "When he is about to fill his
belly, God shall cast the fury of His wrath upon him, and
shall rain it upon him while he is eating." In verse 22 we saw
that the hand of the wicked shall come upon him, but the consequences are even worse in verse 23, where we are told that
the fury of God's wrath will be upon him. It is bad enough to
be at odds with men, but to be on the losing side with God is
far worse.

But even this is not enough to humble some. "He shall flee
from the iron weapon, and the bow of steel shall strike him
through. It is drawn, and cometh out of the body; yea, the
glittering sword cometh out of his gall: terrors are upon him."
There are some so steeped in unbelief that they still try to
resist, but without success. They are able to elude the trap set
by their enemies, but they cannot escape the judgment of God.
"It is appointed unto men once to die, but after this the judgment" (Hebrews 9:27). It will be too late to make any amends
then. Opportunities will be past, there will be no second
chance. God says in Hebrews 10:26-27, "For if we sin wilfully
after that we have received the knowledge of the truth, there
remaineth no more sacrifice for sins, But a certain fearful looking for of judgment and fiery indignation, which shall devour
the adversaries." The wicked man will seek to hide his sins and
in many instances he will rejoice, feeling that he has out-
smarted his neighbor. But God's Word assures us that "All
darkness shall be hid in His secret places: a fire not blown
shall consume him; it shall go ill with him that is left in his

tabernacle. The heaven shall reveal his iniquity; and the earth shall rise up against him." What we do in the dark is clearly seen in the secret places of God. The Bible is clear: the day is coming when "heaven shall reveal his iniquity." We may fool our friends and neighbors and even dearest loved ones, but we cannot fool God. He sees our sin and keeps an eternal record of all the evil we have committed. Some day it will all be brought out into the light.

The story is told of Ruth Wheeler who one morning left her home in a great city to seek work, and never came back. Some days afterward, a burnt torso was found in a box. Officers secured all the possible evidence. They saved bits of the dress and jewelry and other evidences. A man by the name of Albert Wolter was finally arrested. The day of the trial came. The accused man was there, and the sister of Ruth Wheeler was placed in the witness chair. The attorney had the little bits of evidence in a small box, and his plan was to identify the torso as being the mangled body of Ruth Wheeler. He held up bits of the dress and said to the sister, "Did you ever see cloth like this?"

"Yes."

"Where did you see it?"

"Ruth wore a dress like that the morning she disappeared."

He did the same with rings and bracelets.

"Gentlemen," he said, addressing the jury, "I have shown you beyond a doubt that this burnt torso is Ruth Wheeler's body. This torso contained a hand that held in it six human hairs. Under the microscope it is clear that they are not hers. They are different in color and texture. But comparing them with the hair of another, they are the same as the hair of this man, Albert Wolter. Here, gentlemen of the jury, is the brutal murderer of Ruth Wheeler." So suddenly did this attorney prove his case that Albert Wolter confessed the whole brutal crime.

Proving the guilt of a murderer is not always as successful as it was in this case. There are many murderers and criminals

who have escaped the hand of the law. But be sure, no murderer, criminal, or sinner will escape the hand of God's judgment. When the books are opened at the Great White Throne,
everything will be revealed. Every sin, regardless of its nature,
large or small, will be uncovered. Who will be able to stand at
the judgment of God? I will tell you who—only those who
have been redeemed by the blood of the Lamb, only those who
have come to Jesus Christ for eternal salvation. When Christ
died on the cross, He paid the price for all sin, providing eternal deliverance for anyone who will trust in His redeeming
grace. Apart from Him, judgment must be faced. Then after
judgment, eternal hell, eternal separation from God, endless
torment.

Zophar says further that after the wicked man is gone, "The
increase of his house shall depart, and his goods shall flow away
in the day of his wrath" (20:28). One commentator says, "Ill
got—ill gone." That which he got easily but wickedly is taken
from the members of his family as quickly as the wicked man
got it. Ill-gotten gains seldom bring permanence.

Zophar summarizes the chapter by saying, "This is the portion of a wicked man from God, and the heritage appointed
unto him by God." Many there are who would readily excuse
themselves from all of this because they declare that they are
not wicked. I find it necessary to disagree with them, for the
Bible teaches that all men are wicked in God's sight, because
all men are sinful. God says in Isaiah 64:6, "But we are all as
an unclean thing, and all our righteousnesses are as filthy rags;
and we all do fade as a leaf; and our iniquities, like the wind,
have taken us away." Let no one boast of his goodness before
God, because in the light of the Lord's perfection, all men are
abominably wicked. If this is the case, is there any hope? Ah,
yes, Christ is our hope! We read in Hebrews 6:19, "Which
hope we have as an anchor of the soul, both sure and stedfast." In Him we are safe and secure; outside of Him we are
lost forever. Have you made your decision? If not, decide now.
"How long halt ye between two opinions?" (1 Kings 18:21)

JOB 21:1-34

DETERMINED TO BE HEARD, Job pleads with his friends to give considerate attention to what he has to say. "Hear diligently my speech, and let this be your consolations." All he asks for is a fair hearing, and then, after they listen carefully, if his friends desire to continue to mock him, they may do so. "Suffer me that I may speak; and after that I have spoken, mock on."

In verse 4 Job reminds his friends that they are not his judges. "As for me, is my complaint to man? and if it were so, why should not my spirit be troubled?" If Job's three friends were his judges, there would be little need of complaining, for they were quite unsympathetic. But Job reminds them that God is his Judge and it is to Him he is appealing. God would judge between Job and his friends. If Job's appeal were only to his friends, there would be good reason for his spirit to be troubled. But since his appeal is to God, he is assured of being heard.

Would it not be sad if God dealt with us as some people do? Often humans are inconsiderate, but there is no end to the mercy of the Lord. In Micah 7:18 we read, "Who is a God like unto Thee, that pardoneth iniquity, and passeth by the transgression of the remnant of His heritage? He retaineth not His anger for ever, because He delighteth in mercy." Though we may be misunderstood by men, we are always understood perfectly by God. That is why we can go to Him at any time with all our problems and needs. We are assured of this in 1 John 5:14-15: "And this is the confidence that we have in Him, that, if we ask any thing according to His will, He heareth us: And if we know that He hear us, whatsoever we ask, we know that we have the petitions that we desired of Him." Job was resting in this blessed certainty: even though his friends would not listen, he knew God would.

A young businessman, who had been severely tested and whose heart was again and again tempted to rebellion during the process of trial, came to a Christian worker for help. His motherless babies, two and five years old, clung one to each hand. Though still in his early thirties, his hair was snow-white from the hours of anguish through which he had passed. An income of $20,000 a year was gone, his capital was swept away, his home was gone, his car was up for sale. Stripped of everything but the two lovely children, the big, broad-shouldered father, towering over six feet, looked steadily at the Christian worker and said, "In looking back upon my sufferings, I find that God makes no mistakes."

What a thrilling confidence this man had in his heart. What he said is absolutely true—God makes no mistakes. If you truly believe in Jesus Christ you can say the same thing. Even though you may be going through a time of severe trial at this very moment, God makes no mistakes. Job could say this even though he was tempted and tested by his three so-called comforters. He could look above their criticisms, realizing God's unfailing care.

Again Job suggests that his comforters say no more, for their words seemed to be of little avail. "Mark me, and be astonished, and lay your hand upon your mouth." What they had to say resulted only in fear and distress as far as Job was concerned. "Even when I remember I am afraid, and trembling taketh hold on my flesh." Recalling what they had said thus far, it only disturbed Job, rather than providing him needed comfort.

Next Job turns his attention to the repeated argument used by each of his three friends in their latest discourses, that of the unsatisfactory conditions of the wicked in this world. Job concedes that the wicked do suffer much in this world, but even so, it is not what they rightfully deserve. "Wherefore do the wicked live, become old, yea, are mighty in power?" Wicked people often live to a ripe old age, Job informs us. They are prosperous, rising to places of leadership. Even their children may be prosperous. "Their seed is established in their sight with them, and their offspring before their eyes." They have lovely homes in which to live and they appear happy, seemingly escaping sorrow and suffering. "Their houses are safe from fear, neither is the rod of God upon them." Is it true that the rod of God is not upon them? Yes; that is, not yet. Presently it is the age of grace, but the wicked will not escape retribution. If they persist in wickedness and refuse to receive Christ, then they must suffer the consequences in eternal hell. But right now God is merciful toward the wicked. The reason is given in 2 Peter 3:9, "The Lord is not slack concerning His promise, as some men count slackness; but is longsuffering to us-ward, not willing that any should perish, but that all should come to repentance." God longs that they turn from their wickedness to Christ. Those who choose sin, rather than turn to God and His way, are blind because of their sins. Understanding their condition, God is merciful to them and gives them every opportunity possible that they might turn to Him.

It may be that you have given little time to God. You have lived for yourself and this world. Much of your prosperity is ill-gotten gain. You have thought nothing of lying and scheming. You boast of the fact that, though you have neighbors who are honest and go to church, you are far better off than they are and you go to no church. If you mean by "far better off" that you have more money, this may be true. But let me ask, do you have real joy and happiness in your heart and soul? Are you blessed with family happiness? Do you possess the peace of God in your life? Without Christ none of these are possible.

Further Job says, "Their bull gendereth, and faileth not; their cow calveth, and casteth not her calf." This verse informs us that the mercy of God extends even to dumb animals. In spite of the wickedness of their owners, the cattle are cared for by God. Then notice verses 11 and 12, where Job informs us that the wicked usually provide for sensual pleasures for their children though there is no provision for worship. "They send forth their little ones like a flock, and their children dance. They take the timbrel and harp, and rejoice at the sound of the organ." How many parents are like this! Early in life they teach their children how to dance, so that they will be well-adjusted socially, but these same parents rarely read the Bible to their children or teach them how to pray. What a tragedy that many children are being fed mere husks, spiritually speaking, having never tasted of the corn that provides life for the soul. One of the worst problems of our day is not so much delinquent children but delinquent parents. The pronounced wayward-ness of modern children can be traced almost entirely to way-ward and negligent parents.

Recently a daily newspaper carried two pictures. One was of a five-year-old boy, who was found trying to get out of a locked theater at one-thirty in the morning. After forcing the door, a police officer discovered that this very frightened little boy had fallen asleep and had been locked in when the theater closed. Let me ask, would you rest if your five-year-old failed to arrive home by nine o'clock, to say nothing of one-thirty in the morning? The other picture showed a disheveled but good-looking boy of seventeen, who had been charged with drunkenness. Reporters discovered that he had started drinking at the age of fifteen.

The awful consequences of gross neglect in the moral training of the nation's children is a national disgrace. The appalling lack of concern for their children's spiritual welfare on the part of many parents is a tragedy from which many of them will never recover. Oh, that parents would get right with the Lord and then lead their children in His way. God in His grace has entrusted us with children. Out of appreciation and respect for His goodness we should guide these little ones into His chosen paths.

In speaking further of the wicked Job says, "They spend their days in wealth, and in a moment go down to the grave." The word "wealth" as used here means prosperity. The latter phrase means that they die without the pain and agony of a lingering illness. In other words, what Job is saying is that the wicked seem to die a much easier death than he anticipated. Job tried to do what was right in God's sight but suffered untold agony. Thus it is not necessarily because a man is wicked that he suffers, for many wicked people often escape suffering in this life.

Job continues by reminding us of the attitude of the wicked in spite of God's grace. "Therefore they say unto God, Depart from us; for we desire not the knowledge of Thy ways. What is the Almighty, that we should serve Him? and what profit should we have, if we pray unto Him?" The wicked may not say this in so many words, but by their attitude and conduct they express it. Their hearts are hardened toward God. With a smug complacency they are satisfied in their prosperity. Since they have everything, so to speak, they do not think they need God. Carelessly they disregard any thoughts regarding their soul's salvation. They give little or no regard to the certainty of hell. Thus, though God has been gracious and merciful in pro-

viding them with their prosperity and health, they completely
ignore Him.

Job is quick to remind the wicked that "their good is not in
their hand." It was not through their own wisdom or ingenuity that they achieved; it was through God's grace. Thus says
Job, "the counsel of the wicked is far from me." Even though
they prosper in their wickedness, Job wanted nothing of it. He
preferred to suffer with the assurance that he was right with
God rather than to be away from the Lord and in prosperity.

The fact must not be overlooked that the wicked do not always escape misery. "How *oft* is the candle of the wicked put
out! and how *oft* cometh their destruction upon them! God
distributeth sorrows in His anger. They are as stubble before
the wind, and as chaff that the storm carrieth away." Even
though they are prosperous, the wicked are of little help to
others. They are as "stubble" and "chaff" when it comes to
being an aid to society. They live for themselves and their own
interests. Because their evil habits and sinful ways are usually
duplicated by their offspring, judgment likewise falls upon the
children. "God layeth up His iniquity for his children: He
rewardeth him, and he shall know it. His eyes shall see his destruction, and he shall drink of the wrath of the Almighty."
The wicked and his prosperity will end ultimately, for the
wages of sin is death. It is very possible that you may be revel-
ing in your prosperity. You are proud of your possessions. Realize that you have what you have and you are what you are because of the grace of God. He has been good to you. Yet you
have been satisfied to be on the receiving end, taking but never
giving! God gave His Son to die on the cross for you, that you
might have eternal life. Soon your life of sin will be over. Then
what? The facts are clear—judgment and hell. Oh, turn to
Christ before it is too late. Jesus said in Luke 13:5, "Except ye
repent, ye shall all likewise perish." Turn from sin to our living
Lord and He will save you for eternity.

In verse 21 Job asks, "For what pleasure hath he in his house after him, when the number of his months is cut off in the midst?" Job is continuing his discourse here relative to the wicked. Many years later the Lord Jesus told us of the rich man in hell. Certainly he had no pleasure "in his house after him." His cry was, "I am tormented in this flame." Sin can produce only sorrow, if not on this earth, certainly in eternity to come. Now Job asks, "Shall any teach God knowledge? seeing He judgeth those that are high." We cannot question why the wicked are prospered. God is sovereign. It is not for us to say who should be punished and who should be spared. If God ordains that the wicked be prospered and the righteous suffer, this is within His power and jurisdiction.

Job further reminds us that death is no respecter of persons. "One dieth in his full strength, being wholly at ease and quiet. His breasts are full of milk, and his bones are moistened with marrow." Here is a healthy, vigorous man who, to everyone's amazement, is suddenly overtaken by death. On the other hand, "Another dieth in the bitterness of his soul, and never eateth with pleasure." Here is one sick in body, or possibly in mind, lingering day in and day out. This does not appear altogether reasonable but it is certainly descriptive of life as we know it. "They shall lie down alike in the dust, and the worms shall cover them." No one, whether healthy or sick, shall escape death. Then what? For those who have trusted in Christ, they shall ever be with Him. For those who have neglected or rejected Christ, there remains endless suffering in hell.

Speaking directly to his three friends Job says, "Behold, I know your thoughts, and the devices which ye wrongfully imagine against me." They had condemned Job as a wicked man, but he has pointed out to them that many wicked men do not suffer as he. In fact, on the other hand, they are prosperous. Thus his suffering does not prove that he has been wicked. "For ye say, Where is the house of the prince? and where are the dwelling places of the wicked?" The comforters had accused

Job of being wicked because he had lost his property. As was often the case, wicked men did suffer loss of property, but this was not necessarily a proof that Job was wicked. So he appeals to his friends to seek the advice of fellow travelers that might be passing by. "Have ye not asked them that go by the way? and do ye not know their tokens, That the wicked is reserved to the day of destruction? they shall be brought forth to the day of wrath." "Ask those that pass by," Job is saying, "they will tell you the same thing I have told you: that sinners will be punished after death, that they do not necessarily receive their just dues in this life. Thus it is not to be thought strange if they prosper now." Judgment is most certainly coming.

Now Job asks two important questions. "Who shall declare his way to his face? and who shall repay him what he hath done?" Few there are who will confront the wicked man regarding his sins. Even many preachers say little about sin so as not to offend any in their congregations. But some day, when man stands before God, you may be sure God will confront the wicked with his sins, for every sinner must give an account of his wickedness before Him who judgeth righteously. After death, oftentimes the wicked is brought to the grave in great pomp and ceremony, as Job tells us in verse 32: "Yet shall he be brought to the grave, and shall remain in the tomb." The phrase, "remain in the tomb," refers to a monument of some kind being placed on the tomb. In other words, his wicked companions will make much ado about his death.

Further Job says, "The clods of the valley shall be sweet unto him, and every man shall draw after him, as there are innumerable before him." They shall make the grave as attractive as possible. The casket will be shrouded and surrounded with beautiful flowers, with the hope that this might change the sad situation. But all this human effort is meaningless in the eye of God, for this man died with a wicked heart, having never been redeemed. Is it not true that many in our day pass into eternity in this very same manner.

Job concludes the chapter by saying, "How then comfort ye me in vain, seeing in your answers there remaineth falsehood?" He tells his friends that their boasted consolations are contradicted by the facts. They were wrong. It is not only the wicked who suffer; the righteous suffer as well. Job was not a wicked man, in spite of what others said.

I am sure you have realized that this chapter is a clear and solemn warning to those who live for this world and forget God. They have been too busy for the Lord! They have neglected to put first things first. It may be you are one of them and you reply quickly, "Well, I am all right. I have done nothing wrong. I am not a wicked man as those described in this chapter. It is true that I don't go to church, but I believe I am going to be saved because of the good things I have done." If Christ is kept on the outside of your heart, something must be wrong inside. Christ represents all that is holy and good; if you do not want Him in your life, there must certainly be something wrong. As far as the Bible is concerned, there is something wrong with all of us. In Romans 3:23 we are told that "all have sinned, and come short of the glory of God." All men are sinners; none is excluded. Christ is the Saviour. He shed His blood that you and I might be saved. If you never have, put your faith and trust in Him. You cannot save yourself. You will ultimately go to your grave and spend eternity with the wicked in hell. Christ is your only escape.

JOB 22:1-30

ELIPHAZ is about to give his third speech. As we have seen formerly, what he had to say in the main is good. But the mistake is that he applies it all to Job.

Eliphaz begins by asking, "Can a man be profitable unto God, as he that is wise may be profitable unto himself?" This is a worth-while question because so many people think that, by their so-called goodness and by the deeds they perform, they are helping God. We do not help God. He is sovereign; He needs no help from us. Any righteous acts we perform are valuable to ourselves, but they in no way provide benefits for God. He is not dependent in any measure upon humans. He is the Creator; we are His subjects. Thus, Eliphaz was correct in saying that by practicing righteousness one may be "profitable unto himself." In verse 3 several additional questions are asked relative to this same thought. "Is it any pleasure to the Almighty, that thou art righteous? or is it gain to Him, that thou makest thy ways perfect?" Of course the answer to these questions is the same as the first found in verse 2. Surely God is pleased with righteousness in His people, but we should never take the attitude that we are profiting God. What we do is really of no gain to Him. It is profitable to us, but He is sufficient unto Himself.

Eliphaz asks further, "Will He reprove thee for fear of thee? will He enter with thee into judgment?" Does God chasten us because He is afraid of us? Of course not. He chastens us because He loves us and longs to help us. He permits trials that we might give attention to His voice and perform His will. In the temptation of Adam and Eve, Satan insinuated that God did not want them to eat of the tree of knowledge for fear that they would become as gods and be on an equal basis with the Almighty. This, of course, was a lie. Satan sought to deceive the first humans into thinking that God was fearful of losing His position. Nothing could be more ridiculous. Pharaoh oppressed Israel because he feared them. Herod slew the children of Bethlehem because he feared the loss of his popularity. But God has no such fear. He will not enter into judgment with any man, for He is the sovereign Lord of all.

Up until this point Bildad, Eliphaz, and Zophar generalized in their arguments against God's servant. Now Eliphaz becomes quite pointed. He accuses Job of specific crimes and misdemeanors. "Is not thy wickedness great? and thine iniquities infinite?" As far as the three friends are concerned, the answer to both of these questions is "yes." According to them, Job would not be in the condition he was in if his wickedness were not great and his iniquities infinite. The word "infinite" used here is the word for endless. But Eliphaz is saying that, regardless of any attempts Job might make to better his condition, it would be useless because his iniquities would result in continuous suffering.

Notice the first charge. "For thou hast taken a pledge from thy brother for nought, and stripped the naked of their clothing." He charges Job with oppression and injustice. What he is saying is that Job not only failed to do good with his money, he did a great deal of harm. Further he accuses him of being thoughtless of the poor and needy. "Thou hast not given water to the weary to drink, and thou hast withholden bread from the hungry." In verse 8 Eliphaz says that Job catered to the wealthy and mighty. "But as for the mighty man, he had the earth; and the honourable man dwelt in it." While bowing down to those in high positions, according to Eliphaz, Job sent the helpless away in their need and poverty. "Thou hast sent widows away empty, and the arms of the fatherless have been broken." Eliphaz assures Job that such action can only produce trouble. "Therefore snares are round about thee, and sudden fear troubleth thee; Or darkness, that thou canst not see; and abundance of waters cover thee." According to Eliphaz, those guilty of treating their fellow men in such a cruel and harsh manner must suffer the punishment Job was enduring.

Eliphaz's arguments sound quite plausible, but anyone familiar with the teachings of the Bible and the experiences of life knows that many times the unrighteous, who are often unkind and thoughtless toward others, are prospered in life. They are not always judged immediately for their wicked deeds. But rest assured, their day of judgment will come and there will be no escape. Those who have deceived their fellow men and have been unkind and spiteful toward them, often get away with it now. But as surely as we have read these profound words from the book of Job, the day is coming when these men must stand before their Creator and Judge.

This being the case, what hope will there be for any of us? There is none, without Christ. But for all who have believed on Him as Saviour and Lord, there is abundant forgiveness. For it is He who went to the cross for our sins. He knew that we could never fulfill the righteous demands of His law. This He did when He died on the cross. Once and for all He satisfied perfectly every demand of God's law.

The moment we put our faith and trust in the Lord Jesus,

we are declared to be no longer guilty. Notice these verses found in Romans 3:24-26: "Being justified freely by His grace through the redemption that is in Christ Jesus: Whom God hath set forth to be a propitiation through faith in His blood, to declare His righteousness for the remission of sins that are past, through the forbearance of God; To declare, I say, at this time His righteousness: that He might be just, and the justifier of him which believeth in Jesus." Did you get that? Christ is just; He is perfect. He is also "the justifier of him which believeth in Jesus." Because of His death on the cross, because of the price He paid with His blood, He can justify all who believe. He declares them righteous and holy before God on the grounds of His sacrifice. But He must be received as Saviour and Lord if one is to claim the promises of these verses.

Now notice what Eliphaz says in verse 12, "Is not God in the height of heaven? and behold the height of the stars, how high they are!" Yes, God is in the height of Heaven. No matter how high one may go, God is there. Recall the words of the Psalmist in Psalm 139:7-10: "Whither shall I go from Thy spirit? or whither shall I flee from Thy presence? If I ascend up into heaven, Thou art there: if I make my bed in hell, behold, Thou art there. If I take the wings of the morning, and dwell in the uttermost parts of the sea; Even there shall Thy hand lead me, and Thy right hand shall hold me."

Eliphaz accuses Job of attaching the wrong application to this scriptural teaching. In verses 13 and 14 he says, "And thou sayest, How doth God know? can He judge through the dark cloud? Thick clouds are a covering to Him, that He seeth not; and He walketh in the circuit of heaven." According to Eliphaz, Job believed that God dwelt in the highest Heaven, but since His dwelling place was so far from the earth, God was not aware of what was transpiring on the earth. There does not seem to be a single instance in the book of Job where such a philosophy is advanced on Job's part. But thoughtless and wicked men do not always stop at what others say; often they speak their own words for them, as Eliphaz did here.

Let no one think for a minute that, because God is in the high heavens, He is too far away to see what is going on. Some would attempt to mislead us into thinking that, because of the condition of the world today, God is so far away from us that He is insensible to present reality. The Bible teaches that, not only does God see and know everything, He is aware of every thought in the mind of every human. This seems almost incredible as we try to reason it out from the human standpoint, but the fact must not be overlooked that our God is the God of all. He knows no limits nor bounds.

Considering this great fact, it is comforting to know that whatever our need or problem, God sees and understands. Sometimes it seems in the hours of suffering that God is far away from us. We might be tempted even to say, as did Eliphaz, "How doth God know? can He judge through the dark cloud? Thick clouds are a covering to Him, that He seeth not; and He walketh in the circuit of heaven." But consider 2 Chronicles 16:9: "For the eyes of the Lord run to and fro throughout the whole earth, to shew Himself strong in the behalf of them whose heart is perfect toward Him." God's eyes are on you today. You may think you have been forsaken, but you have not. Keep trusting the Lord! In Psalm 27:14 He says, "Wait on the Lord: be of good courage, and He shall strengthen thine heart: wait, I say, on the Lord." God has not failed you in the past; He will not fail you now. Somehow, in His own miraculous power and in His own chosen time, He will open the door that will lead you out of your present affliction. But you must believe that He is able and you must trust Him to undertake.

One time a small boy, on returning from church, was asked about the services. Among other things, he said that the congregation had sung a hymn called, "Trust and O.K." Of course he misunderstood the title of the well-known hymn, "Trust and Obey." That young boy has given us an important truth. If we trust the Lord fully and lean on His Name, to be sure, everything will be O.K. God will always undertake.

During an earthquake that occurred a few years ago, the inhabitants of a small village were greatly alarmed. They were at the same time surprised at the calmness and apparent joy of an old lady whom they all knew. At length, one of them asked her, "Mother, are you not afraid?"

"No," she said, "I rejoice to know that I have a God who can shake the world."

It may seem that God is far away from you. But cheer up: He is not; He is close by your side. Do not be deceived by the tempter. Walk by faith and trust God completely.

Next we find Eliphaz telling Job that God always judges sin. Doubtless Eliphaz had in mind Job's argument that God often blesses and prospers the sinner in mercy. "Hast thou marked the old way which wicked men have trodden? Which were cut down out of time, whose foundation was overflown with a flood" (22:15-16). Judgment came to these evil men, according to Eliphaz, because of their wickedness. They had "said unto God, Depart from us: and what can the Almighty do for them?" These men were cut down before their time. They were wiped off the face of the earth bcause of their sin. Doubtless Eliphaz had in mind those who lived in Noah's day. God's judgment was severe because of their sin. The Lord had appealed to these people through His servant Noah, but they cried out, "Depart from us." They would have nothing to do with God's message of grace.

With sarcasm, Eliphaz continues by reiterating Job's philosophy. "Yet He filled their houses with good things: but the counsel of the wicked is far from me." Job had contended that because of His great mercy, God blesses the unjust as well as the just. Eliphaz was quick in his attempt to repudiate Job's claim of God's grace. Further he said, "The righteous see it, and are glad: and the innocent laugh them to scorn." In other words, Eliphaz would have us think that the righteous rejoiced in the judgment of the wicked. With satisfaction in their hearts, they were glad when the wicked were taken away. Such action is legitimate, Eliphaz would have us to believe; it is to be expected. As he says in verse 20, "Whereas our substance is not cut down, but the remnant of them the fire consumeth." That is, God will preserve the righteous but He will destroy the wicked.

On the basis of his argument, Eliphaz appeals to Job to get right with God. Notice the presumption of verse 21: "Acquaint now thyself with Him, and be at peace: thereby good shall come unto thee." He is actually declaring here that Job does not know God. "Get acquainted with God," is Eliphaz's appeal. What pride, what arrogancy, to question another's relationship with the Lord! As one gets right with God, "good shall come," Eliphaz says. How utterly ridiculous this argument is. I have known of godly people who loved the Lord with the entire heart, who for years had sought the will of God for their lives, yet they suffered endlessly, day in and day out. To be right with the Lord is no promise of an easy road, free of sorrow and suffering.

Of course, let us not overlook the importance of being right with the Lord. The best life of all is to know God and to walk with Him. Do you know Him? If you do, then come what may, you can trust Him for all things, with the assurance that "all things work together for good to them that love God, to them who are the called according to His purpose."

Eliphaz says, "Receive, I pray thee, the law from His mouth, and lay up His words in thine heart." This, likewise, is worthwhile and timely advice for millions of unhappy, restless souls today. Of course, no one can benefit from the Word of God until he comes to know the Lord. Without this relationship, the Word is a closed Book. Certainly Eliphaz has given us the rightful order.

After the Apostle Paul came to the Lord, his first question

was, "What wilt Thou have me to do?" (Acts 9:6) He was
ready to let the Word of God have free course in his life. It is
doubtful that there was any of the Word in written form in
Job's day, but there was the will of God to be done. In our day,
God frequently speaks through His Word to reveal His will.
For this reason believers ought to be storing up His Word in
their hearts, with a willingness to obey. There are too many
hearers of the Word. God declares that we are to be more than
hearers, we are to be doers.

Someone has wisely said, "Apply thyself wholly to the Scriptures, and the Scriptures wholly to thyself." If all believers
would do this, they would certainly keep in touch with God.
Someone has written these thoughtful words:

My Bible and I

We've traveled together through life's rugged way,
O'er land and o'er water, by night and by day;
To travel without it I never would try;
We keep close together, my Bible and I.

In sorrow I've proved it my comfort and joy,
When weak my strong tower which nought can destroy;
When death comes so near me 'tis thought I would die,
We still are together, my Bible and I.

Does God's Word have the place it should have in your daily
routine? There are many weak, emaciated Christians simply
because they do not take the time they should to feed on the
Word of God. Eliphaz is to be commended on his sound advice, "Lay up His words in thine heart."

Next he says, "If thou return to the Almighty, thou shalt be
built up, thou shalt put away iniquity far from thy tabernacles." This is so true. Those who are right with the Lord will be
conscious of any sin in their lives. Only when one is following
the Lord afar off will he persist in practicing secret sins. Could

it be that you have some pet sin in your life, robbing you of spiritual vitality? Oh, do not rob your soul of God's best. Get right with Him! Let Him possess your soul fully. "Then shalt thou lay up gold as dust, and the gold of Ophir as the stones of the brooks. Yea, the Almighty shall be thy defence, and thou shalt have plenty of silver."

Here is God's promise of blessing for those who are right with Him. This does not necessarily mean that you will be wealthy in material things, for much greater than that is to be wealthy in spiritual things. The child of God who is in fellowship with the Lord is indeed a wealthy person, for he enjoys all of the spiritual blessings God has intended for him. Thus Eliphaz says in verse 26, "For then shalt thou have thy delight in the Almighty, and shalt lift up thy face unto God." I do not know of anything better, in the whole wide world, than to be in fellowship with the Lord, for as Eliphaz says in verse 27, "Thou shalt make thy prayer unto Him, and He shall hear thee, and thou shalt pay thy vows." Many people pray, but their prayers do not get beyond the ceiling of their room simply because they are not right with God. There is no use praying unless we are in fellowship with Him. Sin hinders prayer. We read in Isaiah 59:1-2: "Behold, the Lord's hand is not shortened, that it cannot save; neither His ear heavy, that it cannot hear: But your iniquities have separated between you and your God, and your sins have hid His face from you, that He will not hear." Sin is the separating force between God and man. Thus, if one is to have prayer power, he must have a clean heart.

Notice the blessedness of walking with God. "Thou shalt also decree a thing, and it shall be established unto thee: and the light shall shine upon thy ways." Does this mean that whatever you decree will come to pass? Not necessarily. When one is yielded to God, he will want only one thing—the Lord's holy will. He will be so in tune with the Lord and His purposes that whatever comes will be what the yielded believer decrees; even though it may be affliction or sorrow, God gives the assurance that "the light shall shine upon thy ways." God will not fail.

Consider these next two wonderful verses. "When men are cast down, then thou shalt say, There is lifting up; and He shall save the humble person." No one can ever descend too low for God's mercy. There is always forgiveness. God will lift the sinner up and He will save all who are willing to humble themselves as little children in His sight. Further, "He shall deliver the island of the innocent: and it is delivered by the pureness of thine hands." "The innocent" are those who are no longer guilty before God. They have had their sins forgiven. They have been delivered from the bondage of a wicked life, as well as from the wrath of God. Have you had this marvelous experience? If not, God longs to transform your life. He desires to live through you to show you what real living is. Why not surrender your heart and life to Him at this moment?

JOB 23:1-17

JOB REFUSES TO GIVE UP in spite of the fact that his thought-less friends rebuked him severely. Thus, ready with another speech, he says, "Even to day is my complaint bitter: my stroke is heavier than my groaning." Irrespective of all that his three friends had said, Job felt that his complaining was justifiable on the ground of his pain and suffering. But though he complained in his misery, he did not think that his complaining and groaning were equal to the weight of his burden. If one does more complaining than needful, he is certainly in a sorrowful state. If Job were to have said, "My groaning is heavier than my stroke," we should hold little hope for him.

There appears to be a ray of hope for Job. Though he had undergone excruciating pain and mental anguish, he recognized that behind it all was the Master Architect, who had a perfect plan. Fed up with the shallow arguments of his would-be comforters, Job longs to go before God's bar of justice, that he might be heard and understood. Hear his cry in his deep anguish of soul, "Oh that I knew where I might find Him! that

I might come even to His seat!" Job had suffered so much misery that he felt entirely forsaken by the Lord. To him it seemed as though God had departed unto the unknown. Looking to his circumstances and listening to the vain reasonings of the three friends, he failed to realize that God was by his side. Those who truly believe, need never search for God, for He is ever near. He promises in Isaiah 41:10, "Fear thou not; for I am with thee: be not dismayed; for I am thy God: I will strengthen thee; yea, I will help thee: yea, I will uphold thee with the right hand of My righteousness." We need not see Him to be assured that He is with us; His Word is enough. Our need is to believe Him.

A fine young athlete was considering the foreign mission field for his life work. He was asked to open a new work in a far distant land. He hesitated and said, "I just can't bring myself to go out there alone."

"Would you go there," he was asked, "with a man like David Livingstone?"

"Yes," he replied.

"Would you go there with a man like Dan Crawford?"

"Yes, I would be glad to go."

"Then why not go with Jesus Christ?"

The Lord Jesus does not call us to a life of loneliness but to a life of companionship with Him in His work. What He actually says is, "Come, and We shall do it together." One of the most precious of all our Master's names is "Emmanuel," which means "God with us." Maybe you have felt on occasion that you needed to search for God. If you know Him and have trusted in His beloved Son, Jesus Christ, He is with you. In fact, He is in you. Thus, with reliant confidence, you must lean upon Him for all things.

Next Job says, "I would order my cause before Him, and fill my mouth with arguments." He would unload the burdens of his heart before the Lord and tell Him all about his grief and suffering. Of course, this is our marvelous privilege in prayer at any time or place. God assures us in Isaiah 65:24 that "it shall come to pass, that before they call, I will answer; and while they are yet speaking, I will hear." What a blessed prerogative is ours in Christ, to unload the entire weight of our care upon Him.

Well did Job realize that he would not receive the same treatment from God that he had received from the hands of his friends. He says in verses 5 and 6, "I would know the words which He would answer me, and understand what He would say unto me. Will He plead against me with His great power? No; but He would put strength in me." God would be gracious and considerate regarding Job's problem. Job rejoiced in the confidence that the Lord God Almighty would not condemn him but strengthen and encourage him. This is the way the Lord always works with His people.

Recall the incident when the scribes and Pharisees approached Jesus in the Temple, dragging before Him a woman taken in adultery. They cried out, "Master, this woman was taken in adultery, in the very act. Now Moses in the law commanded us, that such should be stoned: but what sayest Thou?" (John 8:4-5) Jesus simply knelt and wrote something on the ground with His finger. They continued to cry out, "Moses in the law commanded us, that such should be stoned: but what sayest Thou?" Our Lord stood and said, "He that is without sin among you, let him first cast a stone at her." They were convicted of their own sins, and every one of them turned and left. Then with heartfelt sympathy, manifesting the grace and love of God, our Lord concluded His words with the woman by saying, "Neither do I condemn thee: go, and sin no more."

God understands. He always does. Friends, and sometimes even dearest loved ones, may misunderstand us, but not God. As we go to Him in prayer, unloading our burdens upon Him, we find comfort and deliverance from care. John the Apostle writes, "And whatsoever we ask, we receive of Him, because we keep His commandments and do those things that are pleasing in His sight" (1 John 3:22). What a marvelous privilege is ours to take all of our burdens to the Lord Jesus, with the assurance that He will understand; even more than that, He will undertake.

Job reminds us that not only does God understand us, but He puts strength in us. He helps us. Few of us utilize the power of prayer that is our possession in Christ. Oh, if we would only take the time we should to meet God at the throne of grace!

One time a clergyman was walking along a road. He observed a poor man breaking stones and kneeling on the ground to do it more effectually. As he passed he said to the man, "Friend, I wish I could break the stony hearts of my hearers as easily as you are breaking those stones."

"Perhaps, Pastor," the man replied, "you do not work on your knees—that's the secret."

Prayer brings down the power that can break the hardest heart. It may be you are disturbed because of the attitude of a dear loved one toward Christ. Have you thought of agonizing in prayer for his salvation? Get hold of Job's message. God will understand what you have to say to Him and He will answer prayer. Take time to wait on Him.

Job longed for an escape from his three persecutors, that he might stand before God and find justice. He says in verse 7, "There the righteous might dispute with Him; so should I be delivered for ever from my judge." Again he reminds us that God's judgment is righteous judgment. The Lord was not like the three friends, who gave no consideration whatsoever to Job's arguments. But he knew the Lord would listen.

Job's real problem seemed to be that he thought he had lost touch with God. It seemed that he could not reach the Lord. "Behold, I go forward, but He is not there; and backward, but I cannot perceive Him: On the left hand, where He doth work, but I cannot behold Him: He hideth Himself on the right hand, that I cannot see Him." Of course, God had not lost sight of Job, but because of his affliction and extreme suffering, Job thought God had forsaken him.

It is well that Job did not end his speech with verse 9, for a glimmer of light appears in verse 10: "But He knoweth the way that I take: when He hath tried me, I shall come forth as gold." The Lord always knows the way that we take. That is, He knows the purposes behind our trials. We do not always know the way, but He does. It is not necessary that we know, as long as God is all-wise and understanding. In Psalm 37:23 we read, "The steps of a good man are ordered by the LORD." Job was discouraged and downcast, feeling that his future was hopeless. But each step that he took was ordered by the Lord. There were no flaws or mistakes in God's plan for Job. Thus it is delightful to hear God's trusting servant cry out, "He knoweth the way that I take."

Even more, look at what Job says next. "When He hath tried me, I shall come forth as gold." Job had not yet lost sight of the purpose of his suffering. Sometimes the going gets awfully difficult, but we must keep our eyes fixed on the goal. You may find it difficult to satisfy your own curiosity as to why you must endure your present sufferings, but cheer up, child of God, there is a better day coming. The Word of God tells us so; in Psalm 30:5 God says, "Weeping may endure for a night, but joy cometh in the morning." Further, in Psalm 31:24 we read, "Be of good courage, and He shall strengthen your heart, all ye that hope in the LORD." Do not be downcast! Do not pity yourself! God has not turned His face from you. Consider the words of our Lord as they are found in Matthew 28:18, "All power is given unto Me in heaven and in earth." The word "power" is really our English word for "authority." Think of that—all authority is committed unto Christ in Heaven and on earth. Very often we are fearful because we think that the authority is in our burden, that for some reason the Lord is not great enough and strong enough to overcome the burden. The authority is in Christ. Whatever it is disturbing your heart at this moment, realize it, the authority is not in your trial. Your trial is subject to the authority of Christ. Claim this promise if you know the Lord; it is your possession in Him. You may be in the furnace of affliction, but God is not through. You will "come forth as gold."

It may be that God is trying to say something to you in your trial. You will notice here that as Job speaks about his afflictions and the future, he thinks of his present and says, "My foot hath held His steps, His way have I kept, and not declined." This is the correct approach to all of the Lord's chastenings. We should practice the inward look. Job examined himself to be sure that there was nothing within that was offensive to God. After a thorough heart examination, he made this declaration, "My foot hath held His steps, His way have I kept, and not declined." Oftentimes in our afflictions we become aware of some practice of disobedience. In the normal experience of life, we might continue to overlook some particular sin, but as God chastens us, we are made aware of our need.

It may be that this is your problem at the moment. You have spent so much time looking at your affliction and your sorrow that you have overlooked examining your own heart. Look away from your burden to Christ, and as you look to Him, remember the inward look in the light of His holiness and perfection. Is there anything there hindering your Christian advance? Is God trying to say something to you at this moment? Do not miss the purpose of your trial. Hear His voice and obey Him.

Every affliction should be a call to an examination of one's heart before the Lord. God says in Psalm 4:4, "Stand in awe, and sin not." This is for you and for me. God hates sin, and we should, too. So often, living in a sinful world as we do, it is easy to become tainted with evil. Thus it is necessary for God to chasten us that we might realize the need of our heart. Just one little sin, which may seem very insignificant to you, may be a detriment to your testimony for Christ.

W. Y. Fullerton used to tell the impressive story of a lighthouse off the coast of Florida, which many years ago failed to act its accustomed part and became the instrument of death and destruction rather than of preservation and safety. A window in the lamp room had broken. There was no time to repair it and a piece of tin was substituted. That night, during a furious storm, because of the darkened window a vessel beating off the coast was sent astray with results fatal to the crew.

What a warning this is to those of us who are Christians. We must see that the light of a Christ-controlled heart shines from every phase of the life. Take a self-examination at this moment! Let God cleanse you with the blood of Christ.

After declaring, "My foot hath held His steps, His way have I kept, and not declined," Job said, "Neither have I gone back from the commandment of His lips; I have esteemed the words of His mouth more than my necessary food." Job's life was governed by the Word of God. He was obedient to God's commandments and sought to follow in the chosen paths of the Lord. To him the Word of God was more important than daily food. Job had discovered that he could get by without physical food, but under no circumstances could he exist without the spiritual.

What a difference it would make if all the Lord's people were to react in a similar manner toward God's Holy Word. The Psalmist had something of this deep appreciation for the truth, for he said in Psalm 119:72, "The law of Thy mouth is better unto me than thousands of gold and silver." What a striking comparison, when millions in the world, even professed followers of God, seem to be clamoring after gold and silver. Here we have it: one realizes that God's Word is more essential than food for the body; the other that the Word is more valuable than wealth, to provide comforts for the body. What does the

Word of God mean to you? Doubtless most of us spend far more time in feeding our bodies than we do in feeding our souls from the Word. What a difference it would make spiritually and physically if we were to reverse the procedure, giving greater place to the Word than to physical food.

One time Dan Crawford, the missionary, was home on furlough. In Cleveland, Ohio, he was asked to give a talk at one of the local clubs. They informed him that they did not want a sermon but a lecture on the geography and peoples of Africa. Mr. Crawford vowed to do his best. He had spoken only a few minutes, telling of his travels in Africa, when almost unconsciously he lifted his New Testament from his coat pocket and looking at it said, "Where would I be without you, Blessed Book? How you have helped me as I traveled here and there." Suddenly he realized what he was saying, apologized, and slipped the Bible back into his pocket and continued to speak about the geography of Africa. In a few minutes, in speaking of another area of Africa and recalling how God used the Word to speak to hearts in that vicinity, out came the Bible again.

"Oh, Blessed Book, how much you meant to me in that city. Excuse me," he said, "I was to talk about geography." This happened five or six times during the first part of his message, and then holding up his New Testament he apologized again saying, "I am so sorry, friends, but this Book means so much to me. It is difficult for me to speak without saying something about it." His was a similar experience to Job's. It was certainly obvious that the Word of God meant more to Dan Crawford than "necessary food." He was in love with God's Word because he was in love with the Lord Jesus Christ.

In the closing verses of the chapter, Job descends to a more depressing note, saying, "But He is in one mind, and who can turn Him? and what His soul desireth, even that He doeth. For He performeth the thing that is appointed for me: and

many such things are with Him." Job is certain that God has
an unalterable plan, that even man's strongest arguments cannot possibly change the mind of God. What Job is saying is indeed true. Prayer has been used to change God's providence,
but never does it change His will or purposes. God has an in-
contestable sovereignty, in addition to uncontrollable power.
Because He is perfect, holy, and all-righteous, we can rejoice in
the fact that His will is always the very best. It is for this reason
that we need not fear the fact that His plan cannot be altered.
We can rejoice because we know that whatever the result, it
is for God's glory and our good.

In the light of all this, Job says, "Therefore am I troubled at
His presence: when I consider, I am afraid of Him." There
is such a thing as holy awe and reverence of God. This was
not what Job had in mind. He was needlessly disturbed and
frightened as he considered God's dealings. Further he says in
verse 16, "For God maketh my heart soft, and the Almighty
troubleth me." It is well for us to have tender hearts in the light
of the Lord's providence, but never should we fear His divine
plan.

The chapter concludes with a pathetic note: "Because I was
not cut off before the darkness, neither hath He covered the
darkness from my face." Job is sorrowful because God did not
take his life from him before all of his trials, nor did God
prevent sorrow from coming to him. Job, like most of us, had
the problem of little faith. He was up, and then down, depending upon the circumstances. He lacked spiritual stability. Oh,
if we could wholly lean on the promises of God! If we could
say as David said in Psalm 16:8, and really believe it, "I have
set the LORD always before me: because He is at my right hand,
I shall not be moved." David did not say, "I have set the LORD
sometimes before me." Most of us act as though that is what
we have done. David "set the LORD *always* before him." And
the blessed result was stability, assurance, peace, and blessing.

Have you set the Lord always before you, or have you set your trial always before you? Can you see only the trial, not the Lord? Look beyond your heartache to Him who can heal the broken-hearted, even Christ our wonderful Saviour.

JOB 24:1-25

JOB CONTINUES HIS SPEECH which began with the previous chapter by asking, "Why, seeing times are not hidden from the Almighty, do they that know Him not see His days?" This question suggests that Job must have been thinking on another question that has disturbed so many of the Lord's people of every generation: "Why must the righteous suffer?" Of course, no believer in Christ should ever ask God, "Why?" But oftentimes, though we do not ask this question verbally, we express it in our attitude. Job realized that God was sovereign in all things, yet he seemed to feel that there was a trace of unfairness in God's dealings with His own people in comparison with His dealings with the wicked.

Notice now what he has to say about the wicked: "Some remove the landmarks; they violently take away flocks, and feed thereof." That is, by shrewd and clever manipulation they get control of the property of others. Somehow they remove or destroy the "landmarks" so that the rightful owner loses control of that which should be his possession. This kind of dishonesty is being practiced every day. The ungodly have no regard to propriety or fairness. As Job says, they even rob orphans and widows of their bare pittance to satisfy their selfish and covetous hearts: "They drive away the ass of the fatherless, they take the widow's ox for a pledge."

Further, they have no regard for the poor, completely ignoring their needs. Often the wicked take advantage of the poor and use them for selfish gain. Job says, "They turn the needy out of the way: the poor of the earth hide themselves together." Knowing the unreasonableness of the wicked, the poor hide from them in an effort to escape their unjust dealings.

In verse 5 Job describes the wicked as "wild asses in the desert." This suggests the unconverted man who has not yet been humbled by the grace of God. It is well to consider that the word "humility" really means "to be domesticated." As a wild animal is domesticated or tamed, so a humble person is one who has been brought under the control of God. In James 4:9 we read, "Humble yourselves in the sight of the Lord, and He shall lift you up." In other words, if we are brought under the control of the Lord, we enter immediately into His blessing. The wicked are not so; they are as "wild asses in the desert." Job says further of the wicked, because of this they go "forth to their work; rising betimes for a prey: the wilderness yieldeth food for them and for their children." Seeking every evil way, they ignore the claims of God on the soul.

Notice, too, that one wicked man steals from another. "They reap every one his corn in the field: and they gather the vintage of the wicked." Job tells us the wicked have no regard for human rights. "They cause the naked to lodge without clothing, that they have no covering in the cold. They are wet with the showers of the mountains, and embrace the rock for want of a shelter." Regardless of how much one may be in need, the hearts of the wicked are untouched; they are cruel and wicked. Next Job says, "They pluck the fatherless from the breast, and take a pledge of the poor. They cause him to go naked without clothing, and they take away the sheaf from the hungry; Which make oil within their walls, and tread their winepresses, and suffer thirst." It is obvious that the wicked have a seared conscience. They have no feeling other than for themselves. They have no regard for anything except their own interests. What a sorrowful way to live. Yet millions of people live like this. Without question, selfishness is the basic sin of present-day civilization. It has always been the underlying evil of every form of wickedness. How different when one comes to Christ and permits Christ to live through him. The true believer can say with Paul, "I am crucified with Christ: nevertheless I live; yet not I, but Christ liveth in me: and the life which I now live in the flesh I live by the faith of the Son of God, who loved me, and gave Himself for me" (Galatians 2:20). Here we see self defeated and Christ victorious.

A man was complaining of his neighbors.

"I never saw such a wretched group of people," he said, "as those who live in this town. They are mean, greedy of gain, selfish, and careless of the needs of others. Worst of all, they are forever speaking evil of one another."

"Is it really so?" asked an angel who happened to be walking with him.

"Yes, it is," said the man. "Why look at this fellow coming toward us. I know his face, though I cannot just remember his name. See his little sharp, white, cruel eyes darting here and there like a ferret? And the lines of covetousness about his mouth? The very droop of his shoulders is mean and cringing, and he slinks along instead of walking."

"It is very clever of you to see all this," said the angel, "but there is one thing which you did not perceive."

"What is that?" asked the man.

"We are approaching a mirror!"

Because of our selfishness, we see the faults of others, but we have not realized the evils of our own heart. It may be that you need victory in Christ today. On the other hand, possibly you have never been converted. You are still controlled by the self-life; you know nothing of the Christ-Life. In humble repentance, bow before Him claiming Him as your Saviour and Lord, and know the victory only He can give. He can give you a love for others, He can enable you to deny self. Respond to His message, and as He becomes the possessor of your soul, you will receive victory over the destructive sin of selfishness.

Job declares in verse 12, "Men groan from out of the city, and the soul of the wounded crieth out: yet God layeth not folly to them." The statement, "God layeth not folly to them," does not mean that the wicked will escape judgment. It means that God does not judge them immediately. Because they are permitted to persist in evil, it would seem that God is overlooking their crime. But anyone who knows the Scriptures understands well that God never overlooks any crime. The Bible teaches that all sin must be judged, though not always immediately.

Job further describes the wicked by saying, "They are of those that rebel against the light; they know not the ways thereof, nor abide in the paths thereof." This reminds me of John 3:19 where we read, "And this is the condemnation, that light is come into the world, and men loved darkness rather than light, because their deeds were evil." The wicked love darkness and hate the light. That is, they love sin and hate Christ. We read in John 1:9 that Christ is "the true Light, which lighteth every man that cometh into the world." There are many who prefer to cling to their sin rather than come to Christ. They rebel against the light.

In their rebellion, often the wicked feel that they are unseen by the eye of God. Job cites the case of the murderer who, "rising with the light killeth the poor and needy, and in the night is as a thief." In the daytime he destroys human life, at night he robs and plunders. He feels that he does this in darkness, that he is unseen.

Further, Job tells of the adulterer who thinks that he, too, has covered up his evil. "The eye also of the adulterer waiteth for the twilight, saying, No eye shall see me: and disguiseth his face." The adulterer thinks he commits his deeds unseen and unnoticed. In the next verse we read of the thief who thinks the darkness can hide his crime. "In the dark they dig through houses, which they had marked for themselves in the daytime: they know not the light." Thus Job tells us of the murderer, the adulterer, and the thief rebelling against the light, thinking their deeds of evil are committed in seclusion.

Much of what Job has said here has to do with physical darkness, but how much worse is the spiritual darkness in which these ungodly men live. How ridiculous that foolish humans would even think that they could possibly hide in the darkness of sin from the eye of the all-seeing God. We read in Hebrews 4:13, "Neither is there any creature that is not manifest in His sight: but all things are naked and opened unto the eyes of Him with whom we have to do." No man can hide from God. Because of this, sin must be judged. God says in Isaiah 13:11, "I will punish the world for their evil, and the wicked for their iniquity; and I will cause the arrogancy of the proud to cease, and will lay low the haughtiness of the terrible." No, let us not think that anyone can hide his sin from God.

It may be that you have been walking in the darkness of a sinful life. Oh, give attention to the Word of God! Come to the light! Come to Him who declared, "I am the light of the world: he that followeth Me shall not walk in darkness, but shall have the light of life." Christ longs to fill your heart with joy and blessing. He wants to deliver you from the darkness of sin and lead you into the light of His glory. But you must come to Him—Christ, the Son of God, who died on the cross for your sins. God says in Proverbs 28:13, "He that covereth his sins shall not prosper: but whoso confesseth and forsaketh them shall have mercy." If you were to turn to God and repent of your sins, calling upon Christ, God would hear you and forgive you of all your sin. Not only that, He would enable you to claim a complete victory over the particular temptation that has been ruining your life. Few of us realize the powerful grip just one little sin can get on a person.

Never shall I forget hearing of Henry White, who was awakened in the dead of night to go to see a dying man. Arriving at the house, which was nothing more than a tumble-down shack, he found a man of about forty years of age, already within the touch of the hand of death. He bent over the bed as he talked to him and offered to pray for him. As he spoke he noted a sudden gleam in the man's eye. Still he went on talking of things past and things to come. Then, as the woman who had led the preacher to the house stood sobbing her heart out, the man of God knelt and prayed. When he arose from his knees, the man was dead, his fast-stiffening fingers clasping the chain of the preacher's watch. For many years this man had been a thief, in and out of jail time and time again. And even as he lay dying, the sight of a gold watch and chain was too much for him. As the pastor prayed, the dying thief tried to pick his pocket.

In speaking further of the wicked Job says, "The morning is to them even as the shadow of death: if one know them, they are in the terrors of the shadow of death" (24:17). Those who live in the throes of evil are plagued constantly by the horrors of a guilty conscience. Those who lie, cheat, and steal live under the continual burden of being caught. They are "in the terrors of the shadow of death." But is it not tragic, though they fear the eye of men, they have no concern as to the eye of God. Far worse than man's judgment is the judgment of God on sin. Oh, that evil men might realize that God sees their wickedness. They cannot hide from Him. But it is of even greater importance that they realize that God longs to forgive them if only they will trust in His beloved Son.

Job adds, concerning the wicked, "He is swift as the waters; their portion is cursed in the earth: he beholdeth not the way of the vineyards." This describes the man who chooses to live in crime. He appears to be adept at stealing. He is clever and fast. Not willing to work for an honest living like other men, he prefers the easy way, at least that which seems to be the easy way. "He beholdeth not the way of the vineyards." He has no interest in earning an honest day's wage. He is forever grabbing for easy money. But look at his future: "Drought and heat consume the snow waters: so doth the grave those which have sinned." Though the wicked may be prospered for a while, ultimately and all too soon they come to their premature end. As the seasons come and go, so do the wicked.

Few mourn the death of the wicked. One who has been a hindrance to society will soon be forgotten. Job declares, "The womb shall forget him; the worm shall feed sweetly on him; he shall be no more remembered; and wickedness shall be broken as a tree." He will be forgotten because he had little interest or concern for others. "He evil entreateth the barren that beareth not: and doeth not good to the widow."

It seems conclusive from verse 22 that the wicked are energized by diabolical power. "He draweth also the mighty with his power: he riseth up, and no man is sure of life." Certainly no human could perform the exploits many of the wicked do without superhuman wisdom and strength. As Satan entered into the heart of Judas and directed him to betray Christ, so the wicked are possessed by the evil one and diabolically prompted to perform their destructive deeds.

But notice the grace of God as it is revealed in the next verse: "Though it be given him to be in safety, whereon he resteth; yet His eyes are upon their ways." God is merciful to all men. So often we hear the question, "Why are the ungodly permitted to prosper?" It is because of the mercy of God. The Lord gives wicked men hundreds of opportunities to repent and turn to Him. But if they habitually continue in their wickedness, refusing to appropriate the mercy of God, the end must come, as Job says: "They are exalted for a little while, but are gone and brought low; they are taken out of the way as all other, and cut off as the tops of the ears of corn." It is said that crime does not pay. We might qualify that to this extent: crime may seem to pay, at least for a little while. Some do reap a temporary success in crime. Ultimately it does not pay, other than the sorrowful wages of eternal death.

In the closing verse of the chapter Job defies his friends to challenge what he has just said. "And if it be not so now, who will make me a liar, and make my speech nothing worth?" It would be impossible for the three friends to challenge Job, for all that he had spoken was the truth.

One time F. B. Meyer was boarding a train when a man, recognizing the great preacher, approached him and asked the question, "How may I be saved?" Not having time to stay and discuss the matter, as the train was pulling out, Mr. Meyer replied, "Turn to Isaiah 53:6. Go in at the first 'all' and come out at the last 'all.'" The man went to his home, turned to the verse, and through reading it was converted. Isaiah 53:6 says, "*All* we like sheep have gone astray." That is the first "all." Every one of us is by nature a sinner; we need to be saved. But God goes on to say, "The LORD hath laid on Him the iniquity of us *all*." There is the second "all." God the Father laid on Christ, His beloved Son, the iniquity of us *all*. Your sin, my sin, everybody's sin was laid on Christ at the cross. To be saved you must go in at the first "all," realizing that you are a sinner, then come out at the second "all," trusting Christ as your Saviour and Lord. Have you had this wonderful experience? If not, claim Christ as your very own. Call on Him. Tell Him you want to be saved, and tell Him that you now receive Him as your Saviour and Lord.

JOB 25:1-6

BILDAD is the speaker once again. In the opening verses he tells us how great and wonderful God is. Then he goes on to show what man is, in contrast to God's greatness.

God is the Sovereign Lord. Bildad says, "Dominion and fear are with Him." We may not always understand the Lord's ways, but this gives no liberty to question His divine counsel. He declares in Isaiah 55:8-9, "For My thoughts are not your thoughts, neither are your ways My ways, saith the LORD. For as the heavens are higher than the earth, so are My ways higher than your ways, and My thoughts than your thoughts." No, we must never doubt the providence of God. We are to trust in the fact that our Sovereign Lord makes no mistakes.

One time a Christian man was walking with John Wesley. Rehearsing his many troubles, he said he did not know what to do. They approached a stone fence, over which a cow was looking.

"Why is that cow looking over the wall?" Wesley asked.

"I don't know," replied the man.

"I'll tell you," said Wesley, "because he can't look through it. That is what you must do with your troubles—look over them."

In Christ we can look over our troubles. We cannot see through many of the things we are called upon to bear in life; but trusting the Lord, we can look over them, for our God is all-powerful, the great God who is not limited in any way.

"He maketh peace in His high places," Bildad tells us. This means that in Heaven there is perfect peace. God never becomes disturbed or upset. Everything He does is orderly, resulting in peace. Well, you ask, why do we not have peace on earth? Why must we have so much trouble and bloodshed? Simply because men and women refuse to take Christ into their lives. We could have this same heavenly peace on earth were the unsaved to respond to the claims of Christ. Jesus said in John 14:27, "Peace I leave with you, My peace I give unto you: not as the world giveth, give I unto you. Let not your heart be troubled, neither let it be afraid." This is heavenly peace, intended for you and for me; but it must be received by faith through Christ. Oh, that rebellious, hardened hearts might yield to the control of Christ and know this wonderful peace on earth even as it is known in Heaven.

From verse 3 we are reminded of God's unconquerable power. The greatness of earthly monarchs was known by the size of their armies. Bildad asks, "Is there any number of His armies?" Literally this reads, "Who can count His armies?" God has legions of angels under His control. He can motivate humans to respond to His will. Could man ever hope to war against God? Some have tried, and even the devil will make one final attempt before he is cast into the lake of fire, but how ridiculous, for God has numberless armies at His disposal.

Consider further God's vast dominion. "And upon whom doth not His light arise?" Whoever it may be—the Eskimo in Alaska, the Indian in South America, the Japanese in the Far East—God's providence and care are showered upon them. David says in Psalm 138:8, "Thy mercy, O LORD, endureth for ever." Indeed, it does! The mercy of God is shining upon you today. You may not realize it, but God in His great love has been trying to speak to your heart. You have been too busy to listen. Oh, hear His voice! You who have never taken Christ into your heart, turn to Him before it is too late. God's mercy is sufficient.

There are many who are trying to save themselves, but look at the next two questions Bildad asks. "How then can man be justified with God? or how can he be clean that is born of a woman?" Everyone born into this world is born with a sinful nature. No man by his good works can do anything to change his sinful nature. He needs the work of God's grace in his heart. Man is naturally mean and vile. He lies and steals, he has impure thoughts, he is proud and selfish. His so-called righteousness at its best falls far short of God's standard. Listen to Galatians 3:22, "But the scripture hath concluded all under sin, that the promise by faith of Jesus Christ might be given to them that believe." The Scriptures are clear, all men are under sin. One can be saved only by believing on the Lord Jesus Christ. He is the Perfect One who was sent by God the Father to die for your sin and for mine. There is no other way. Christ is man's only way to God.

In verse 5 Bildad informs us that even the moon and the stars are not perfect. "Behold even to the moon, and it shineth not; yea, the stars are not pure in His sight." All of creation was affected by the fall of Adam. Nature, as well as humans, awaits complete redemption at the return of Christ. We read in Romans 8:22-23: "For we know that the whole creation groaneth and travaileth in pain together until now. And not only they, but ourselves also, which have the firstfruits of the Spirit, even we ourselves groan within ourselves, waiting for the adoption, to wit, the redemption of our body." Soon all of nature, which was cursed as the result of the Fall, will be perfected by the power of Christ.

Notice the concluding verse of the chapter, "How much less

man, that is a worm? and the son of man, which is a worm?" This is but a further portrayal of man in his state of utter sinfulness and helplessness. The Hebrew word used here for "worm" suggests man's corruption and weakness. But look what we read in one of the Messianic Psalms. "But I am a worm, and no man; a reproach of men, and despised of the people" (Psalm 22:6). Here is a prophecy of Christ, who became sin for us. As our Sin-bearer, He put Himself on our level, not only that He should understand us but that He should be our sin offering, dying for you and for me. Have you believed on the Lord Jesus Christ as your Saviour? Do you know Him as the Lord of your life? Be assured that you cannot save yourself.

JOB 26:1-14

BILDAD has just given his very brief speech. As usual, he was profound, but it is obvious that he did not help Job very much. Job says, "How hast thou helped him that is without power? how savest thou the arm that hath no strength? How hast thou counselled him that hath no wisdom? and how hast thou plentifully declared the thing as it is?" I marvel at the patience of Job. Though he suffered excruciating pain, and though extremely handicapped, he could still answer his critics.

What Bildad had to say seemed to be worth while, but as far as Job was concerned, it was useless talk. "To whom hast thou uttered words? and whose spirit came from thee?" This was as if to say, "What you are saying, Bildad, does not apply to me. Your scholarly thoughts are well and good; but it is help I need, not speeches."

It would seem that there are several important lessons here for all of us. It is so easy to criticize our neighbor, but how infrequently we help him in his hour of need. Further, Job accuses Bildad of speaking merely in the flesh, without being led of the Spirit. How often we are guilty. When one speaks in the Spirit, he does not stop at talking, but he does his best to lift his weak or fallen brother. Are not most of us guilty of a spiritual pride that prompts us to look down upon the weak and erring one, rather than lift him up? Do we not find ourselves gossiping about the fallen brother, rather than going to his aid? God asks, "But why dost thou judge thy brother? or why dost thou set at nought thy brother? for we shall all stand before the judgment seat of Christ" (Romans 14:10). In Galatians 6:1-2 Paul declares, "Brethren, if a man be overtaken in a fault, ye which are spiritual, restore such an one in the spirit of meekness; considering thyself, lest thou also be tempted. Bear ye one another's burdens, and so fulfil the law of Christ." Do you see what God tells us here? We are to be kind, and by the grace of God we are to be helpful to our neighbor.

I. R. Miller in one of his books tells of Sir Bartle Frere, who was always helping someone and serving God in some way. He had been absent for quite a while on one of his African explorations and was to return by train. Lady Frere sent a servant to meet him at the station. The servant was new and never had seen Sir Bartle. He asked his mistress how he would know him.

"Oh," she said, "look for a tall man helping somebody." The servant went to the station, and when the train arrived, he eagerly watched for his new master, trying to identify him by the given description. Soon he saw a tall man helping an old lady out of the train, and he knew at once that it must be the person he sought. He went to the man and inquired, and indeed it was Sir Bartle Frere.

It was this kindness that Job expected from his friends, not the critical spirit they were exercising. God would have those of us who profess to be His followers show forth His kindness to all those around us who are in need.

In the rest of the chapter, Job turns his attention again to the infinite glory and power of God. In these verses God's servant uses a variety of pictures to portray God's wisdom and power in His creation and preservation of the world. In verses 5 and 6 Job portrays God's greatness as it is manifested in hell; in verse 7, on the earth; in verses 8 to 11, in the sky; in verse 12, in the sea; and in verse 13, in the heavens.

In chapter 25, verse 2, Bildad stated that God's power existed in the high places. Job is quick to reply that God cannot be limited to the high places only. His realm pervades the region of the dead, so that He controls all the departed spirits. "Dead things are formed from under the waters, and the inhabitants thereof. Hell is naked before Him, and destruction hath no covering."

Our God is the God of all. He is at every point of space at every moment of time. David said in Psalm 139:7-10: "Whither shall I go from Thy spirit? or whither shall I flee from Thy presence? If I ascend up into heaven, Thou art there: if I make my bed in hell, behold, Thou art there. If I take the wings of the morning, and dwell in the uttermost parts of the sea; Even there shall Thy hand lead me, and Thy right hand shall hold me." Here is a marvelous promise for the distressed child of God. Sometimes we feel alone, but it is never so, for God assures us that "Even there shall Thy hand lead me, and Thy right hand shall hold me." It may be that you feel that you have been forsaken of God. But you have not. If you have received Jesus Christ into your life, God is with you at this moment. Turn your eyes on Him and trust fully in Him. Friends and even dearest loved ones may have failed you, but Jesus never fails.

The other day I read this statement: "God's part we cannot do. Our part He will do." Sometimes we want to rush God to answer our prayers. We cannot do His part, but praise Him, He can and will do our part. So cheer up, child of God, He will find a way of escape for you. Wait on Him!

In verse 7 Job says, "He stretcheth out the north over the empty place, and hangeth the earth upon nothing." In His creation God stretched the heavens out like a vast veil to cover the earth. They continue to remain stretched out by His sustaining grace. Notice, He "hangeth the earth upon nothing." The earth upon which you and I walk rests upon no pillars, no foundation of stones, but only upon God's almighty power.

Next we read, "He bindeth up the waters in His thick clouds; and the cloud is not rent under them." Here is another marvelous act of God's providence. He keeps the waters of the clouds from pouring down upon the earth, as they did in the time of the flood. Job says, "the cloud is not rent under them." That is, they do not burst forth with their tons of weight and pour water on the earth as through a spout. Rather, through the mercy of God the water falls to the earth drop by drop, in small rain or great rain, as God so desires.

Next we are told that "He holdeth back the face of His throne, and spreadeth His cloud upon it." God would have all of us walk by faith and not by sight. Neither He nor His ways are visible to any of us. God and all of His doings are shielded from us as by a cloud. Does this mean that God is inaccessible? Not at all. We are told in John 1:18, "No man hath seen God at any time; the only begotten Son, which is in the bosom of the Father, He hath declared Him." God is known through Christ, His beloved Son. There is no other approach to Him except by believing on the Lord Jesus Christ.

Note further God's providential care as seen in verse 10: "He hath compassed the waters with bounds, until the day and night come to an end." More literally, "He hath drawn a circular bound around the waters." Indication is given here of the global form of the earth. Also we see that God in His providence prevents the waters of the sea from flooding the earth. Were it not for the sustaining care of God in preserving His creation, the earth might be totally submerged by floods. In Jeremiah 5:22 the Lord has promised that such will not be the case: "Fear ye not Me? saith the Lord: will ye not tremble at My presence, which have placed the sand for the bound of the sea by a perpetual decree, that it cannot pass it: and though the waves thereof toss themselves, yet can they not prevail; though they roar, yet can they not pass over it?" Here God reminds us of His all-sufficient providence, but, in addition, of our human inadequacy.

Job continues, "The pillars of heaven tremble and are astonished at His reproof." The "pillars of heaven" as used here is a poetical expression referring to the mountains that appear to reach into the heavens. Our mighty God shakes the mountains and removes them at will. In addition to this, "He divideth the sea with His power, and by His understanding He smiteth through the proud." As He chooses, He may stir up the sea or He may cause a perfect calm. Possibly this verse refers also to the division of the Red Sea at the time of the crossing of the Israelites. There was a mighty miracle wrought by our great God.

Job continued by saying, "By His Spirit He hath garnished the heavens; His hand hath formed the crooked serpent." That is, by His Holy Spirit, that moved upon the face of the waters at creation, God garnished the heavens. Not only has He made them exquisitely beautiful, but He has studded them with the stars, the sun, and the moon, that likewise are kept in their places by His power. "The crooked serpent" as used here would seem to mean the darkness which was dispelled by the light. Thus we could read this verse, "By His Spirit He garnished the heavens; and His hand dispelled the fleeting darkness."

Coming to the concluding verse of the chapter we read, "Lo, these are parts of His ways; but how little a portion is heard of Him? but the thunder of His power who can understand?" Job says these are only parts of His ways. We could not begin to describe all that God does, "How little a portion is heard of Him?" In spite of all the discoveries God has made known to us, we still know only an infinitely small part of His divine wisdom. Paul's words found in Romans 11:33-34 are so true, "O the depth of the riches both of the wisdom and knowledge of God! how unsearchable are His judgments, and His ways past finding out! For who hath known the mind of the Lord? or who hath been His counsellor?"

No, we cannot begin to fathom the ways of God, but we who are in Him can certainly trust Him and believe Him for all things. If you are a child of God by faith in Christ, surely you are glad that you have such a God as Job has described—One who not only created the universe but sustains it in every detail. How foolish we are to worry when we have a God who can do all things. Read these verses again from Job 26. Consider them in the light of your present problems and realize that what God has said in Ephesians 3:20 is absolutely true: He "is able to do exceeding abundantly above all that we ask or think, according to the power that worketh in us." The power that works in us is the same power that brought the world into existence and has sustained it until this day; the power that will continue to sustain it until the heavens and the earth pass away under the judgment of God.

JOB 27:1-23

UP TO THIS POINT it would seem that Job has won the battle of words. Rightfully, according to the structure of the book, it was Zophar's turn to speak. But as he and the other two were silent, probably silenced by Job's arguments, Job speaks again.

You will notice that the opening verse reads, "Moreover Job continued his parable." The word "parable" here means that what he had to say was highly instructive, the essence of his speech being grave and weighty. It suggests, too, that he spoke with authority. I am convinced that it was the authority of God.

He begins by saying, "As God liveth, who hath taken away my judgment." He speaks well of God by calling Him the "God who liveth," or, the "ever-living God." But he speaks poorly of Him as he declares that God "hath taken away my judgment." That is, he accuses God of not intervening and taking his part before the three friends. Job expected God to come immediately and defend him against the accusations of the three hypocrites.

Most of us are like Job in this regard. We expect God to act at our beck and call, overlooking the fact that He says, "Wait on the LORD: be of good courage, and He shall strengthen thine heart: wait, I say, on the LORD" (Psalm 27:14). God has His own times at hand. He is never late, nor is He ever early; He is always on time. Thus we need never fear. God will undertake for us at His chosen moment.

Further Job accuses God, saying, He "hath vexed my soul." Job is charging that God not only failed to appear to justify him in the presence of his companions, but He failed to relieve him of the suffering and affliction he bore, creating mental anguish and sorrow. We are so quick to blame God for things. Job was no different. Had he been willing to examine his own heart in his affliction, he would have discovered that, because of his failure to trust God fully, he was responsible for his own anguish. We bring so much sorrow upon ourselves because we do not believe God and take Him at His Word.

"All the while my breath is in me, and the spirit of God is in my nostrils," Job says. God's servant gives due honor and respect to Him who is the Giver of Life. The phrase, "the spirit of God is in my nostrils," means that Job was alive at this moment because of the grace of God.

Notice the important statement in verse 4, "My lips shall not speak wickedness, nor my tongue utter deceit." How vital this is. You and I should keep this thought before our eyes daily: "My lips shall not speak wickedness, nor my tongue utter deceit." The word "wickedness" is really "untruth." What Job was saying was, "Regardless of what you three men say about me, I will speak the truth." How important that we ask the Holy Spirit to guard our lips, that we speak only those things that honor and glorify God. The Lord Jesus said, as recorded in Matthew 12:36-37, "But I say unto you, That every idle word that men shall speak, they shall give account thereof in the day of judgment. For by thy words thou shalt be justified, and by thy words thou shalt be condemned." Someone has declared that "in America we can say what we think, and even if we cannot think, we say it anyway." How frequently we speak without thinking. What grief we cause simply because we do not let the Lord guard our lips. We accuse, injure, destroy, and produce endless sorrow because we do not speak the truth in love. Job vows that he will not be guilty of such wickedness.

Further he says, "God forbid that I should justify you: till I die I will not remove mine integrity from me." In his use of the word "justify," Job meant that he would not give in to the arguments of his friends claiming him to be a hypocrite. He knew his own heart and refused to bow to the groundless arguments of his opponents. He resolved that until the day of his death he would continue to live and speak the truth. What he said here was a reaffirmation of what he already said in chapter 13:15, "Though He slay me, yet will I trust in Him." I admire Job's determination to walk with God. He had trouble within and persecution and temptation without, but with bold confidence he could say, "Till I die I will not remove mine integrity from me."

Further he says, "My righteousness I hold fast, and will not let it go: my heart shall not reproach me so long as I live." Job desired to hold fast his integrity. This was the honest expression of his heart, suggesting his determination to walk with the Lord in spite of his environment. God's people need this same determination in our day. There are so many crowd-followers, so many Christians who walk with the Lord about an hour a week, when they are in church. We read in 1 Peter 2:21, "For even hereunto were ye called: because Christ also suffered for us, leaving us an example, that ye should follow His steps." There was never a time in the life of our Lord when He did not walk according to the will of the Father. We are to follow in these same steps. It is not always easy, but as one does, he enjoys the blessing of God.

In a certain Sunday school, the superintendent of the junior department was surprised to find that the offering, which was placed outside the door of the department room, had not been reaching the treasurer. A little checking revealed that one boy had been slipping out of the door and pocketing the offering. The same boy just a few months before had won the award for learning the greatest number of Bible verses, including the Ten Commandments. When he was confronted with his wrong-doing, he saw no relationship between taking the offerings and the commandments he had memorized. What was this boy's trouble? He had memorized the commandments, but he had never *learned* them.

Are there not many who say they know Christ, but what they mean is they know about Him. They have never really met Him. How do we know? Their lives prove it. When a person is truly saved, when he sincerely believes on the Lord Jesus, the result will be a heart transformation. He will become a new creature in Christ. He will be able to say with Job, "My righteousness I hold fast, and will not let it go: my heart shall not reproach me so long as I live."

Job continues by saying, "Let mine enemy be as the wicked, and he that riseth up against me as the unrighteous." This verse does not mean that it was Job's desire that his enemies be treated as the wicked. He is justifying himself in this verse and the remaining verses of the chapter by comparing himself with the wicked. He is not invoking a curse on his enemies; rather, he is suggesting that if they cannot comprehend his desire for righteousness, then they must be wicked, and as wicked men they must suffer the results of wickedness.

Next he gives us the reasons for his earnest desire to be a righteous man. "For what is the hope of the hypocrite, though he hath gained, when God taketh away his soul?" Bildad had condemned hypocrisy; Job likewise concurs with him: the hypo-crite will perish in his sin. For this reason Job wants nothing to do with hypocrisy. The hypocrite is without hope, "For what is the hope of the hypocrite, though he hath gained, when God taketh away his soul?" The hypocrite may gain in various ways. Since his hypocrisy is unknown to many, he often gains the favor of the crowd. He is well spoken of by his friends, who do not know his sinfulness. Frequently he gains in wealth, and by his lies and acts of deceit he accumulates much money.

But of what value are these things? Job asks, "Will God hear his cry when trouble cometh upon him?" This is the second reason why Job wants nothing of hypocrisy. The hypocrite's prayer will not be heard. Of course, if he repents and turns to the Lord, God will hear. The invitation of Isaiah 1:18 still holds good: "Come now, and let us reason together, saith the LORD; though your sins be as scarlet, they shall be as white as snow; though they be red like crimson, they shall be as wool." But very often the hypocrite is mastered by his sin and his heart is hardened to the extent that he will not turn to God. When troubles come, he may pray, but he refuses to repent. He will expect God to help him in his calamity, but God will be silent until there is genuine heart repentance. The hypocrite will not receive answers to his prayers, for God refuses to do anything *for* one until that one lets God do something *in* him.

The hypocrite uses God for a convenience only. This is Job's third reason as to why he will have nothing to do with hypocrisy. "Will he delight himself in the Almighty? will he always call upon God?" The hypocrite finds no favor with God. He only wants God to help in times of need. When the hypocrite is without resources, he expects God to come to his rescue. In other words, he uses God for his own selfishness. He finds no joy in daily communion and fellowship with the Lord. To him, refuge in God is purely an emergency measure.

This might be a good time to pause and consider your own state before God. Do you really know Him? If you have repented of your sin and believed on Him, is Christ everything to you? Do you find joy in communing with Him daily and feeding upon His blessed Word? We need to beware of hypocrisy, the well-used tool of Satan.

Beginning with verse 11 through to the end of the chapter, what Job says seems to be contrary to what he had already stated in chapter 21, verses 22-23 and chapter 24, verses 22-25. He appears now to state what Zophar would have said, had he taken his turn following chapter 26. Zophar has nothing more to say in the book. Possibly in disgust, he has given up. If you will compare verse 13 with verse 29 of chapter 20, you will see that what Job says in verse 13 is really Zophar's argument rather than Job's. It looks as though Job's purpose in restating Zophar's argument is that, though Zophar's statement was true, it should not have been used to incriminate Job.

With this brief explanation, let us consider what Job has to say in the remainder of the chapter. In verses 11 and 12 he declares, "I will teach you by the hand of God: that which is with the Almighty will I not conceal. Behold, all ye yourselves have seen it; why then are ye thus altogether vain?" God's servant attempts to put his critics straight concerning God's judgment on the wicked. Job cannot conceal this truth. What God has revealed, no one has any right to conceal. He affirms that his friends know these facts; thus he asks, "Why then are ye altogether vain?" What right had they to condemn him as a wicked man simply because he was afflicted? Job is getting at the heart of the matter, which we have seen thus far throughout the book, his being criticized unjustly by his friends.

How we must be on our guard constantly against this evil of criticism. Usually we criticize others because of our faulty understanding of their circumstances. If we could see their hearts and lives as God does, doubtless our attitude would be different. We need to pray daily that the Lord will keep us from the satanic evil of criticism.

Perhaps you recall the occasion when some of the friends of the Lord Jesus criticized Him severely, saying, "He is beside Himself" (Mark 3:21). How regrettable that these evil men could not understand the words and works of the Son of God. Their reaction was, He is out of His mind. They criticized because they did not know. Oh, beware of this sin that brings sadness and sorrow to so many. Learn the facts; be slow to speak words that will damage and destroy. God says in Isaiah 29:20-21, "All that watch for iniquity are cut off: That make a man an offender for a word, and lay a snare for him that reproveth in the gate, and turn aside the just for a thing of nought." A fault-finding, criticizing habit is fatal to all that is excellent. Nothing will stifle growth quicker than a tendency to hunt for flaws, to rejoice in the unlovely like a hog which always has its nose in the mud and rarely looks up. The direction in which one looks indicates his life aim. People who are always looking for something to criticize, for the crooked and ugly, who are always suspicious, who invariably look at the worst side of others, are but giving the world a picture of themselves. Will you ask God to remove every trace of criticism from your heart, that you might be a holy man of God, filled with the Spirit, speaking praises rather than condemning those who need help?

In verse 13 Job says, "This is the portion of a wicked man with God, and the heritage of oppressors, which they shall receive of the Almighty." Though the portion of some men seems to be wealth and prestige, Job informs us that before God such a portion will result in ultimate ruin and misery. Though they may have escaped the judgment of men, rightly deserved because of their oppression, they will never escape the judgment of God.

Next Job declares the state of the children of the wicked. "If his children be multiplied, it is for the sword; and his offspring shall not be satisfied with bread." The wicked man, though wealthy and prosperous, may provide for his children. Very often this prosperity, received without work, results in irresponsible living. Those who receive things easily rarely appreciate them. Thus wealth may react as a slow poison, bringing sure death upon its victims. Though they have much, the children of the wicked rarely find satisfaction. They "shall not be satisfied with bread." They are like those of whom we read in Haggai 1:6, "Ye have sown much, and bring in little; ye eat, but ye have not enough; ye drink, but ye are not filled with drink; ye clothe you, but there is none warm; and he that earneth wages earneth wages to put it into a bag with holes."

The children of the wicked are very often like their wicked parents: when they die they will not be missed. Job says, "Those that remain of him shall be buried in death: and his widows shall not weep." Very often they are selfish and inconsiderate of others. Their easily-gained wealth has turned their faces from the important things of life.

The prosperity of the wicked is for a brief season only. "Though he heap up silver as the dust, and prepare raiment as the clay; He may prepare it, but the just shall put it on, and the innocent shall divide the silver." In the providence of God, very often the righteous are rewarded with the wicked man's wealth. After death stamps out the oppressor, there are occasions when his wealth will go to the oppressed. But even greater is the spiritual blessing known by the oppressed, never experienced by the wicked: to have the blessed assurance that God will provide every need—physical, spiritual, and mental; to know that He will undertake for every problem is far greater than the accumulation of all the wealth anyone could desire. Such blessing is not temporary but eternal in the Lord.

The wicked man "buildeth his house as a moth, and as a booth that the keeper maketh." The "booth" referred to here was prepared by the watchman to be used for a single season in the vineyard. It was only a temporary shelter. The wicked man who prepares his own covering will soon discover its worthlessness. How wonderful to be covered by the blood of Christ, with the assurance of everlasting life. Jesus declared in John 10:27-29: "My sheep hear My voice, and I know them, and they follow Me: And I give unto them eternal life; and they shall never perish, neither shall any man pluck them out of My hand. My Father, which gave them Me, is greater than all; and no man is able to pluck them out of My Father's hand." What could be more wonderful than this—the assurance of eternal life through Christ! The wicked man knows nothing of this confidence. He can know if he repents and turns to Christ, but apart from Christ, he possesses no hope of life eternal. Only a brief span on this earth, then comes his lot—eternal perdition.

"The rich man shall lie down, but he shall not be gathered: he openeth his eyes, and he is not." He lies down in his wealth, thinking he has security, but all too soon he hears the voice of doom, "Thou fool, this night thy soul shall be required of thee: then whose shall those things be which thou hast provided?" (Luke 12:20) The prosperity of the wicked is brief. It is as a sleep—only a few hours, and then all is done. But the wicked man cannot sleep. His conscience will not let him sleep. Job says, "Terrors take hold on him as waters, a tempest stealeth him away in the night. The east wind carrieth him away, and he departeth: and as a storm hurleth him out of his place." Here is a picture of the grim enemy death attacking the man who has done without God. It is bad enough to try to live without the Lord, but it is far worse when one must stand before God in judgment. What will be the result? Job says, "For God shall cast upon him, and not spare: he would fain flee out of His hand." While he lived, the wicked man, though trapped in tight spots, always managed to buy his way out. But now he has been stripped of all his wealth; he stands empty-handed before God. Who will plead his case? Who will help him now? There is no one, "he would fain flee out of the hand of God," but he cannot. "The soul that sinneth, it shall die" (Ezekiel 18:20).

There is great rejoicing on earth when the wicked are gone: "Men shall clap their hands at him, and shall hiss him out of his place." Hissing was a common oriental token of scorn. The man who lived for himself, at the expense of others, will not be missed by those who were oppressed. They shall rejoice in his departure.

What is the lesson for you and for me? Simply this: are we a blessing or a reproach to our fellowmen? Are we helping them or hindering their progress? Are we living for self or for Christ? Is the Son of God the Lord of all? It may be you have never taken time for Him. You have been so busy living for this world and the things this world has to offer that you have neglected the really important things of life. Before it is too late, come to God. Get right with Christ. The Word of God is true, "It is appointed unto men once to die, but after this the judgment" (Hebrews 9:27). The day is coming when we must face God. Are you ready? Have you taken Christ into your life? If not, I hope you will at this very moment.

JOB 28:1-28

Job HAD ADMITTED that what his friends had said about God's judgment of the wicked was true. Yet he seems to be perplexed still with the question, "Why does God afflict the righteous?" Now he tells us that though men may delve into the depths of the earth and discover the treasures of God, yet they cannot comprehend the mysteries of His providence. One may look into the heart of the earth and clearly see and understand God's mighty works, but apart from divine insight, no one is permitted to look into the counsels of Heaven.

In verse 1 Job says, "Surely there is a vein for the silver, and a place for gold where they find it." Job has been telling us about the wicked man who gloried in his riches. Now he tells us of the true source of those riches: they come from God, created by Him and deposited in the earth. No man has any right to boast. "Iron is taken out of the earth, and brass is molten out of the stone." The brass of which he spoke here is really copper. Iron and copper are less costly than silver and gold but they are most essential. God, recognizing the needs of mankind, deposited in the earth those things which would be most vital to living.

Job informs us further that these metals must be searched out from the earth: "He setteth an end to darkness, and searcheth out all perfection: the stones of darkness, and the shadow of death." Man must determine ways to find these precious metals, so he sets out with his lamps amidst the darkness to search and labor for that which God has hidden in the earth. The way of the miner is not always an easy one, we are told. "The flood breaketh out from the inhabitant; even the waters forgotten of the foot: they are dried up, they are gone away from men." The search is frequently hampered by subterraneous waters. The word "inhabitant" is really "stranger." Man, who is a stranger in the depths of the earth, will be surprised suddenly to find a stream breaking forth beside him. But, says Job, "They are dried up, they are gone away from men." Soon the pumps are at work and the water is cleared away so that further efforts will not be hampered. Thus God has made this provision for man, that life may be sustained.

Job continues by saying, "As for the earth, out of it cometh bread; and under it is turned up as it were fire." Many make their living by what they find in the depths of the earth. From these treasures they buy food for the body. Also, from them they get their fuel, "as it were fire," to prepare the food.

Not only has God placed certain essentials for life in the earth, but even the luxuries. Job tells us that "the stones of it are the place of sapphires: and it hath dust of gold." For some it would be far better if these valuable treasures were left in the earth, that covetous hearts might not search for security in uncertain riches.

Notice, too, from verse 7, that God has given man wisdom that He has not endowed to the lesser forms of life. "There is a path which no fowl knoweth, and which the vulture's eye hath not seen." The word "fowl" probably refers to the eagle, which is more sharp-sighted than any other bird. Even though the eagle can see its prey at an amazing distance, only man has the ability to search out God's hidden treasures in the earth. Even the king of the beasts, the lion, knows nothing of the wealth buried in the earth. "The lion's whelps have not trodden it, nor the fierce lion passed by it."

Thus with his God-given knowledge, man turns to his task of uncovering the hidden treasures. "He putteth forth his hand upon the rock; he overturneth the mountain by the roots. He cutteth out rivers among the rocks; and his eye seeth every precious thing. He bindeth the floods from overflowing; and the thing that is hid bringeth he forth to light." His search is rewarded by great treasures.

When we pause to consider the wealth and treasure that are buried in the earth, who could begin to estimate the value of such deposits? Oh, the grace of God, that He should provide this for sinful man. Those of us who have been privileged to become partakers of these treasures should never forget their true ownership. God says in Psalm 50:12, "If I were hungry, I would not tell thee: for the world is Mine, and the fulness thereof."

As we think of the precious stones hidden away under the earth's surface, there is something far more valuable than these in the sight of God. Do you know what it is? His jewels! Speaking of His own people, the Lord said in Malachi 3:17: "And they shall be Mine, saith the Lord of hosts, in that day when I make up My jewels; and I will spare them, as a man spareth his own son that serveth him." More precious to God than diamonds, rubies, and sapphires are those who have believed on the Lord Jesus Christ. Though the treasures under the earth are hidden from the eye of man, every one is known to God. You may be sure that every one of His own people is known to Him, as well. Sometimes we feel forsaken and forgotten. It is true that even dearest friends and loved ones may forsake us, but God never will. We are His precious jewels if we are in Christ. Child of God, we have nothing to fear, for we are precious in His sight.

Alexander Maclaren was just sixteen when he accepted his first job in Glasgow, six miles from home. Between home and the city was a deep ravine, supposedly haunted. He was afraid to go through there, even in the daytime.

"Come home as fast as you can, when you get off on Saturday night," were his father's parting words on Monday morning. Thinking of the deep ravine, he said, "I will come home early Sunday morning."

"No, Alec, come home Saturday night."

All the week Alec worried about the ravine. On Saturday night he came to the edge of the ravine. Looking into the inky blackness, he could not move. Tears came. Then suddenly he heard footsteps. Out of the darkness came the grandest man on earth.

"Alec, I came to meet you." Together they went into the valley and Alec was not afraid of anything that night.

As that son was precious to his father, so every son of God is precious to our wonderful Lord. For this reason He promises in Hebrews 13:5, "I will never leave thee, nor forsake thee." What is your need at this moment? What is your problem? Look up to the Lord! Look into His blessed face, hear His words of comfort and peace. He will not fail you; you are one of His jewels, more precious than all the wealth hidden below the earth.

Job continues by speaking of a greater treasure than that which man can hold in his hand; it is that which he receives into his heart. "But where shall wisdom be found? and where is the place of understanding?" Can the eye of man see divine wisdom as he has been able to see the treasures of the earth? Most surely not. Divine wisdom cannot be seen at the moment. For divine wisdom is a Person—that Person is the Son of the Living God. Someday He will be seen, for the Scriptures are clear, "Behold, He cometh with clouds; and every eye shall see Him, and they also which pierced Him: and all kindreds of the earth shall wail because of Him" (Revelation 1:7). But presently He cannot be seen with the human eye—only with the eye of faith, as the Apostle Paul tells us, "Whom having not seen, ye love; in whom, though now ye see Him not, yet believing, ye rejoice with joy unspeakable and full of glory" (1 Peter 1:8).

Concerning divine wisdom, Job says, "Man knoweth not the price thereof; neither is it found in the land of the living." Who could begin to put a price on all we have received by receiving Christ into the heart? Who could estimate the value of such an experience? It is impossible, for there is nothing on earth to which this most wonderful experience can be compared. Nothing like it is found in this world. Even all the wealth of the world could not begin to compare to the importance of knowing Christ as Saviour and Lord. God says in Mark 8:36-37, "For what shall it profit a man, if he shall gain the whole world, and lose his own soul? Or what shall a man give in exchange for his soul?" The most essential and vital experience in life is to receive Christ into one's heart.

Job goes on, "The depth saith, It is not in me: and the sea saith, It is not with me." Ask the miners; they will tell you that wisdom is not found in the depths of the earth. They have gone into the innermost recesses of the darkness of the earth, but the wisdom of God was not there. Ask the sailors; they will tell you it is not on the sea.

Further Job states that "it cannot be gotten for gold, neither shall silver be weighed for the price thereof." I suppose, if salvation were offered for a specified sum of money, many would respond more readily. But "it cannot be gotten for gold." We read in 1 Peter 1:18-19, "Forasmuch as ye know that ye were not redeemed with corruptible things, as silver and gold, from your vain conversation received by tradition from your fathers; But with the precious blood of Christ, as of a

lamb without blemish and without spot." The wisdom of God
is a gift. Neither little money nor much can obtain this precious
gift, it can be received only by faith through the grace and
mercy of God. It is as we read in Romans 3:24, "Being justified
freely by His grace through the redemption that is in Christ
Jesus."

Next we are told, "It cannot be valued with the gold of
Ophir, with the precious onyx, or the sapphire. The gold and
the crystal cannot equal it: and the exchange of it shall not be
for jewels of fine gold." The gold of Ophir was known as the
most precious. The onyx and crystal were extremely valuable
in Job's day. But what were these in comparison to the wisdom
of God? "To whom then will ye liken God? or what likeness
will ye compare unto Him?" (Isaiah 40:18) To know the Lord,
and to have Him as one's possession, is to have more than
all that the wealth in the world could provide. The value of
wisdom, the assurance of salvation, is far beyond and above
anything money can buy.

Job continues by saying, "No mention shall be made of coral,
or of pearls: for the price of wisdom is above rubies. The topaz
of Ethiopia shall not equal it, neither shall it be valued with
pure gold." Yes, far above the price of rubies is the wisdom of
God manifested in His beloved Son, Jesus Christ. Many who
have all that money can buy are devoid of peace and lasting
happiness, for these are not found in earth's treasures. They
are known only in heavenly wisdom — the wisdom of God —
Christ the Son of God.

How delusive riches are. Thousands on every hand are
clamoring to get more and more of that which appears to be of
greatest value, but soon these earthly treasures will crumble
into dust. God says, "Lay not up for yourselves treasures upon
earth, where moth and rust doth corrupt, and where thieves
break through and steal: But lay up for yourselves treasures
in heaven, where neither moth nor rust doth corrupt, and where

thieves do not break through nor steal: For where your treasure is, there will your heart be also" (Matthew 6:19-21).

Are you laying up treasures for eternity? Only what is done for Christ will last. Do you really know Christ? Is He your Saviour and Lord? Then live for Him, tell others about Him. All around you there are those who know not the gift of God, the Heavenly Treasure. The burden falls upon those of us who have received Him to tell these helpless, struggling souls about Him who is the wisdom of God. If, while digging in the earth, you were to find a precious stone of inestimable worth, would you not tell others about your discovery? Surely you would. If you have found Him whose price is far above rubies, share Him with others. If Christ is in your heart, let His Words be on your lips. The Bible says in Matthew 12:34, "Out of the abundance of the heart the mouth speaketh." If you know Christ, you have found a wonderful treasure. Tell others about Him!

Job asks several questions: "Whence then cometh wisdom? and where is the place of understanding?" He had previously asked these questions in verse 12. Repetition in the Bible is usually indicative of something of utmost importance. It is well that we consider the answers to these questions. Do you know the answers? Job makes it clear that God's wisdom is twofold. There is that part of His wisdom known by Himself only, not to be known by us. On the other hand, there is the revealed wisdom of God, which is for all who trust in Him. God tells us that "the secret things belong unto the LORD our God: but those things which are revealed belong unto us and to our children for ever, that we may do all the words of this law" (Deuteronomy 29:29).

First, Job speaks of the hidden wisdom: "Seeing it is hid from the eyes of all living, and kept close from the fowls of the air." Even the great philosophers and scientists, who delve into the mysteries of the world, cannot attempt to explore this wis-

dom. It is known only to God, having to do with His will and
providence. Even dearest saints have no authority to expect
knowledge of the unrevealed unless God in His mercy desires
to make it known. So often God's people ask that age-old question, "Why? Why did God do this to me? Why did God permit
this tragedy to enter into my home?" Do not ask God why, for
you are trying to peer into that portion of His plan that cannot
possibly be known until we see Him face to face. Death is the
door through which we pass into the wisdom unknown to the
living.

Job continues by saying, "Destruction and death say, We
have heard the fame thereof with our ears." Death for the believer in Christ is not a cold, lifeless state. Those who have
died in the Lord can say, as did Job, "We have heard." They
have heard the voice of the Lord. Though they were confused
and perplexed throughout life, death made all things different.
The unknown became known and understandable. The scales
have been removed from once-blinded eyes, and now they can
see as never before. "Now we see through a glass, darkly; but
then face to face: now I know in part; but then shall I know
even as also I am known" (1 Corinthians 13:12).

Look at verses 23 and 24: "God understandeth the way
thereof, and He knoweth the place thereof. For He looketh
to the ends of the earth, and seeth under the whole heaven."
Because you and I cannot understand why we must face confusing and disturbing trials, it is not to be said that God cannot
understand. Job assures us that "God understandeth the way
thereof."

It is very possible at this moment that the circumstances in
which you find yourself appear to be extremely bewildering.
Trust God! Has He failed you even once in the past? Of course
not! Nor will He fail you now. Though the reason for your trial
is unknown to you, remember it is perfectly understandable to
God, for He sees all things. "He looketh to the ends of the
earth," Job says. The eyes of the Lord are in every place. Not

once has He removed His gaze from you. "The eyes of the LORD run to and fro throughout the whole earth, to show Himself strong in the behalf of them whose heart is perfect toward Him" (2 Chronicles 16:9). The wonderful thing about it all is that, not only does God see us and understand fully why we are in certain circumstances, but He is in a position to help us. Job says that God is able "To make the weight for the winds; and He weigheth the waters by measure."

What do we know about the wind? "Thou hearest the sound thereof, but canst not tell whence it cometh, and whither it goeth" (John 3:8). God knows all about the wind. In fact, He controls it. How wonderful that we worship such a God! He is the Creator and the Master of all the elements. Job says, "When He made a decree for the rain, and a way for the lightning of the thunder: Then did He see it, and declare it; He prepared it, yea, and searched it out." There is much no man has ever been able to learn about the elements and about creation, but God the Creator knows all things.

Not all of God's wisdom is hidden from the eye of the earnest seeker, for Job tells us that God said, "Behold, the fear of the Lord, that is wisdom; and to depart from evil is understanding." Here is wisdom within our reach. Let us not be concerned about the things God has not revealed. It is futile to try to comprehend those things God has kept unto Himself. Rather, let us fear the Lord and turn from evil. Let us turn unto Him who is wisdom—Christ, the Son of God. In turning unto Him, let us turn away from sin, that we might follow Him and obey Him. Would you be wise? Then heed the Word of God. Christ is the revealed wisdom of God. In holy awe, bow before Him and acknowledge Him as Lord of your life. Then trust Him for all things. There will be no need to fear the future nor those things that would harass us in the present. We shall be able to say with David, "The LORD is my rock, and my fortress, and my deliverer; my God, my strength, in whom I will trust; my buckler, and the horn of my salvation, and my high tower. I will call upon the LORD, who is worthy to be praised: so shall I be saved from mine enemies" (Psalm 18:2-3). You may be surrounded by enemies—the enemies of doubt, fear, nervousness, uncertainty, or many others. Do not look to your enemies; look to your Mighty Conqueror, the Lord of all. He will not fail you.

JOB 29:1-25

At the close of his previous discourse Job paused, waiting for a reply. But since there was none, he proceeded to illustrate from his own personal experience some of God's mysterious dealings, which he had discussed in his last address. Looking at things retrospectively, he cried out, "Oh that I were as in months past." There is a tendency in the midst of trial to compare the present calamity with former days of prosperity and blessing. Such a procedure can be very dangerous, for it usually provokes self-pity. The Apostle Paul refused to permit himself to fall into this grave error. He declared, "Forgetting those things which are behind, and reaching forth unto those things which are before, I press toward the mark for the prize of the high calling of God in Christ Jesus" (Philippians 3:13-14). He was through with the past. Looking to the future he knew that whatever his situation, it was because of God's providence. Keeping his eyes fixed on the Lord Jesus, he would not permit himself to look back. Doubtless this was one of the reasons for his life of overflowing joy.

"Oh that I were as in months past," exclaimed Job. Then he

added, "as in the days when God preserved me"—that is, the days when God preserved him from calamity, when he went about at liberty with no physical limitations to retard the full enjoyment of life. Further describing this time he says, "When His candle shined upon my head, and when by His light I walked through darkness." The candle shining upon his head refers to the enjoyment of God's favor. Job recalls the days when he walked through the uncertain paths of life with the confidence that no serious ill could harm him because the Lord was with him. It would seem from some of these statements that Job had almost forgotten about the Lord's sovereign and unchangeable care.

Job continues by telling us that the happy days filled with God's care and blessing, of which he is speaking, were "in the days of my youth, when the secret of God was upon my tabernacle." Young people are usually carefree and give little thought to the future. In the days of his youth Job did not foresee the severe testing and trial of his later years. But whether young or old, who knows what the future will bring? How important that we are right with God and live in fellowship with Him at all times.

In describing the days of his youth, Job speaks of them as days when "the secret of God was upon my tabernacle." What is the secret of God? In Psalm 25:14 we read, "The secret of the LORD is with them that fear Him; and He will show them His covenant." The secret of the Lord is the intimate fellowship and friendship we have with God when we are walking in the light, as He is in the light. Job knew this wonderful fellowship in the days of his youth. But later, when subdued by his trials, he appears to have lost this valuable possession. If ever there was a time when intimate and close fellowship with the Lord is needed, it is in seasons of adversity. If we are willing fully to trust the Lord for His divine wisdom and help, He will guide us safely through any of the storms of life. But the Psalmist makes it clear that we must fear God, that is, we must revere and respect Him, permitting Him to have us as His complete possession.

I am sure many of us, like Job, have been guilty of looking back to those days in which we seemed to be more prosperous in spiritual things. We might even think that God has changed. Be assured, He never changes: He is "the same yesterday, and to day, and for ever" (Hebrews 13:8). It is we who change. While all is running smoothly and going well, it is easy to rejoice in the Lord. But the crucial test comes when we are thrust into the throes of some disturbing perplexity of life. It is then that we are often miserable simply because we are not fully committed to Christ.

Police in Philadelphia arrested a forty-year-old man for stealing cement. The officers reported that Angelo Grisolia spent several hours loading over 6,000 pounds of cement into a borrowed truck. When he tried to drive the truck from the scene, it would not move, for it was stuck in the sand with the overload.

How many Christians there are who have lost the blessing and joy in the Lord they once knew, simply because they overloaded their lives with the things that appeal to the flesh, instead of living in complete dependence on God. Such a practice cannot possibly please the Lord, for He said in Luke 6:46, "Why call ye Me, Lord, Lord, and do not the things which I say?"

So we see that Job lost the joy and blessing he once knew in his youth simply because he depended upon himself rather than upon the Lord. I wonder if there is any trace of this same failure within you? Is Christ Lord of all in your life at this moment? It may be that you, too, like Job, knew better days some time in the past. Again I say, the fault lies not with God, but with you. Somewhere at some time you changed in your attitude toward Him. Can you truly say at this moment that He is Lord of all? If so, you will prove this by your ready obedience to His revealed will.

Ye call Me Master and obey Me not;
Ye call Me Light and see Me not;
Ye call Me Way and walk Me not;
Ye call Me Life and desire Me not;
Ye call Me Rich and ask Me not;
Ye call Me Eternal and seek Me not;
Ye call Me Gracious and trust Me not;
Ye call Me Noble and serve Me not;
Ye call Me God and fear Me not;
If I condemn you—blame Me not.

How important that we make our profession real, that we are sincere, that the words that come from our lips are supported by sincere actions from the heart.

Job informs us next that his days of prosperity and enjoyment were largely made possible because he still had his children, which had since been taken from him. "When the Almighty was yet with me, when my children were about me." Indeed, it is true that children by their presence help provide joy for any occasion. But now even Job's children were gone. Further he says, "When I washed my steps with butter, and the rock poured me out rivers of oil." Here he has in mind his great wealth. His supply of dairy products was so bountiful that after everyone had been fed, if need be he could wash his steps with the remainder. Likewise, the olive oil which was used for food, lighting, anointing, and medicine abounded to the extent that it was as though he possessed rivers of oil. Job had been extremely wealthy, but now stripped of it all, he is heavyhearted, gloomy, and sad.

Could it be that this suffering saint placed too much emphasis on "things" and not enough upon the importance of complete and full commitment to God? This could be true of us. It is very possible, in this materialistic age in which we are now living, to set our affections on things below rather than on things above. We need to turn our eyes upon Jesus; daily we must walk with Him. Let us not look back; our greatest days are yet to come. Thus we must lean on Christ.

In speaking further of the past, Job reminds us of the mighty influence he had upon people of all ages. He says, "The young men saw me, and hid themselves." The word "hid" literally means that they stepped back in respect and reverence. Likewise, the aged gave Job due recognition. "The aged arose, and stood up." Those of special prominence had respect for Job: "The princes refrained talking, and laid their hand on their mouth." In the midst of a speech, they would pause to give due honor to Job, for he was well recognized as a man of wisdom and integrity. "The nobles held their peace, and their tongue cleaved to the roof of their mouth." Many were fearful to speak in the presence of Job, for what he had to say seemed to be so much more profound. When he opened his mouth, he had something to say, for he was a man who walked with God and who kept in touch with God. Job says further, "When the ear heard me, then it blessed me; and when the eye saw me, it gave witness to me." Wherever Job went he was praised as a man of men, one who stood far above his fellows in holiness of character and obedience to God's purpose.

Job proceeds to tell us of the grounds on which he was praised and honored. First, he says, "Because I delivered the poor that cried, and the fatherless, and him that had none to help him. The blessing of him that was ready to perish came upon me: and I caused the widow's heart to sing for joy." He was benevolent, ever ready to help those in need. If the poor were worthy of help, he provided for them. He protected them from unjust men and gave them wise counsel amidst their manifold problems. He cared for the fatherless children and helpless, struggling widows. He had a heart of gold that knew nothing of selfishness, when it came to helping others.

Is this not something of the true religion of which Jesus speaks? "Pure religion and undefiled before God and the Father is this, To visit the fatherless and widows in their affliction, and to keep himself unspotted from the world" (James 1:27). If one is truly a child of God, his vision will go far beyond the walls of his own home. He will be concerned and interested in the needs of others. To do this, he must keep himself unspotted from the world. For what is worldliness? Basically, it is selfishness. Selfishness is the root evil of saved and unsaved alike. How important then that we claim daily victory over this destructive evil.

When Frances Willard was a student in Northwestern College for Women, she wrote in her journal, "Doctor Foster closed the Bible after his discourse at the university chapel yesterday with these words, 'With most men, life is a failure.' These words impressed me deeply. There is sorrow in the thought, and tears and agony are wrapped up in it. Oh, Thou who rulest above, help me, that my life may be valuable, that some human being shall yet thank Thee that I have lived and toiled." From that time on, Frances Willard was used of God to help others. She gave her life to this high and noble purpose. Victory had been won over the evil of self.

What about you? Have you come to the place whereby self is crucified and Christ is alive? "He died for all, that they which live should not henceforth live unto themselves, but unto Him which died for them, and rose again" (2 Corinthians 5:15). God is looking to you to help the poor, the fatherless, the widows, the hungry, and the needy. Greatest of all, if you are a child of God, He is looking to you to give them the Bread of Life, that they might not perish in spiritual hunger. How great is the task, far too great for any of us. But remember, our God is a mighty God. We are insignificant and worthless, but there is no limit to His power. Let Him live through you, that He might use you, even as Job was used. Pour out yourself to provide for and help those who are so greatly in need. Some seem to have the mistaken notion that service for the Lord is to be done only by preachers and missionaries. *Everyone* who has believed on Christ is called to serve. We are to be ambassadors of kindness and good will.

On occasion I have heard people say, "I once had a call to be a missionary," or, "I once felt that I should be a preacher."

Do these people not know that they *are* missionaries and preachers? *Everyone* who has been born again has a distinct call from God to serve Him immediately. It is not a question of taking ordination vows. Our ordination, our commission, comes from Jesus Christ. God expects us to be shining lights to spread the sunshine of His grace and love right where we are. This takes courage. It takes very little courage to withdraw, but much to stay put and let your light shine where you are. But as long as we are mastered by the self-life, we shall never do this. We shall not see others in their misery and grief, but only our own needs and wants. Oh, what a horrible way to live—for self only. Yet many Christians live this way, forgetting their God-given call.

Look around, child of God. See your neighbors and friends in their grief—and then do something about it. One of the best ways to achieve the mastery over the subtle enemy of self is to reach into the lives of others with God's loving kindness. Remember your call as a saint of God—to live not for self but for the Lord.

Job was well respected and honored by every level and age of society. Much of this honor was due to his holy life and character, as well as his benevolence in providing for the needy. Job's benevolence ran deeper than a generous heart. The real secret is revealed in his words, "I put on righteousness, and it clothed me." One may be benevolent out of a selfish heart. Countless numbers of socially-minded individuals are benevolent with the intent of gaining the praise of men. Job's benevolence was the result of God's righteousness.

Every true believer is the possessor of the righteousness of God. Paul says in Ephesians 4:24, "And that ye put on the new man, which after God is created in righteousness and true holiness." The result of this righteousness should be justice. Job said, "My judgment was as a robe and a diadem." The word "judgment" used here is really "justice." "Robe and diadem" suggest the high priest's dress. The high priest represented the people before God, and God before the people. Thus when one receives the righteousness of God, he receives a new heart that normally will be burdened and concerned about the needs of others.

Job said further, "I was eyes to the blind, and feet was I to the lame." Because his heart was filled with the love of God, he helped the blind to see and the lame to walk. I am sure this has a deeper meaning. Doubtless he helped the spiritually blind to see by telling them of the Lord. Perhaps, too, he helped the lame to walk, that is, the weaker brother who was stumbling about because of some besetting sin.

You and I are called to do the same. We must help the millions who are spiritually blind to see. We read in 2 Corinthians 4:3-4, "But if our gospel be hid, it is hid to them that are lost: In whom the god of this world hath blinded the minds of them which believe not, lest the light of the glorious gospel of Christ, who is the image of God, should shine unto them." Multitudes are groping about in spiritual blindness. They need to hear of the Lord Jesus who can touch blinded eyes and give sight. At the same time, there are many of God's people bogged down by besetting sins. They need to realize that there is deliverance and power in Christ. You and I must help them. "Ye which are spiritual," God says, "restore such an one in the spirit of meekness; considering thyself, lest thou also be tempted" (Galatians 6:1).

A wonderful thing about Job was that he was a man who believed in salvation not *by* works, but in a salvation that *produced* works. You may be sure this is the kind of salvation the Bible teaches, for God makes it clear in James 2:17 that true, saving faith demands works. "Even so faith, if it hath not works, is dead, being alone." For one to declare belief in the Lord without giving evidence of belief through a life of holiness and benevolence is unscriptural.

Job did much for the poor, but he makes a statement here that is worthy of note. "I was a father to the poor: and the cause which I knew not I searched out." Some among the poor are mere deceivers, lazy, refusing to work. Job makes it clear in this verse that he investigated the reason for one's poverty before giving to him. This is so important.

Next Job says, "And I brake the jaws of the wicked, and plucked the spoil out of his teeth." Not only did Job prove himself to be a champion in caring for the needy, he was willing to stand for light and truth in the face of injustice. He never turned his face from the sight of wrongdoing. He was not a visionary but a realist when facing sin.

Is it not true that often pastors and church boards gloss over sin and ignore the commandments of God in order to refrain from hurting or embarrassing anyone? We must be bold in facing the matter of sin. God will accept no substitutes. Sin must be dealt with or judgment will be the result. But before we are in a position to deal with someone else's sin, we must be absolutely certain that we have dealt with our own. What about it? Is there any trace of evil in your heart? Are you right with God? It could be that your own personal sin is provoking someone else to wrath. Remember, before you take the outward look, be sure you have taken the inward look. Pray, "Search me, O God, and know my heart: try me, and know my thoughts: And see if there be any wicked way in me, and lead me in the way everlasting" (Psalm 139:23-24). Wealth provides many temptations to the godly as well as to the ungodly. Job reminds us of these temptations. When he had everything, he said, "I shall die in my nest, and I shall multiply my days as the sand." In the midst of his riches it was hard for him to foresee poverty. Likewise, he was so well off he could not visualize dying. His days, he thought, were innumerable, as are the grains of sand on the beach. But in his misery he thought altogether differently.

Further he says, "My root was spread out by the waters, and the dew lay all night upon my branch." He felt that he was like a tree that grew and abounded plentifully because its roots spread out into the sustaining waters. The phrase, "the dew lay all night upon my branch," suggests God's care and providence for him. It means to live in plenty, without any want. He was mighty as a conqueror and needed not to fear his enemies: "My glory was fresh in me, and my bow was renewed in my hand." Though strong, Job became ever stronger, so that even the great and mighty were fearful of him. Now he reverts again to his remembrance of respect that all men gave him, saying, "Unto me men gave ear, and waited, and kept silence at my counsel." His advice was well received and recognized as the oracles of God. "After my words they spake not again; and my speech dropped upon them." What Job said was received as final, the word of the Lord. "And they waited for me as for the rain; and they opened their mouth wide as for the latter rain." This suggests the appreciation they had for Job's counsel. "If I laughed on them, they believed it not; and the light of my countenance they cast not down." Job was not given to frivolity. He was grave and serious. On the other hand, he was known for his genial and joyous spirit. He was not so holy that he could not smile, nor so serene he could not see the lighter side of life. In other words, though a man of God with a deep hold on the Lord, he was still human.

Finally Job says, "I chose out their way, and sat chief, and dwelt as a king in the army, as one that comforteth the mourners." Throughout the chapter there seems to be many statements that suggest that Job foreshadowed Christ, but this twenty-fifth verse seems to excel them all. How beautifully Christ is pictured here. What Job was to his people, Christ is to us. He chooses out our way, He leads us step by step, He is Lord of all. He is the King in the army, to fight our battles for us. And surely He provides comfort in every hour of need. Is it not true that we need to depend upon Him more strongly?

Whatever your need at this moment, recognize that you have a great God, unfailing in His love and care. Trust Him! Believe Him! And should it be that you have never received the Lord Jesus into your heart, I hope you will just now. It is difficult to try to live without Christ. Let Him become your Lord as you humbly bow at His feet: acknowledge Him as the One who died for your sins and rose again.

JOB 30:1-31

JOB LAMENTS HIS SAD PLIGHT, not simply from the view of the physical suffering involved, but because of the mental anguish resulting from the attitude of those who should have known better. Those who had been inferior to him in his days of prosperity now looked upon him and treated him as their inferior.

First he tells us that some of the youth had little respect for him. "But now they that are younger than I have me in derision, whose fathers I would have disdained to have set with the dogs of my flock." If for nothing more, the young people should have respected him for his age and righteous character. But even they made fun of him. The fathers of these young people were men who lived on an extremely low plane of life morally and spiritually. They deserved only to be placed with the dogs that attended the shepherds and watched over the flocks. In the East, dogs were not permitted to come into the house. They were looked upon as unclean. Job did not treat these men as dogs, but he could have, because of his position.

On the contrary, he was kind and benevolent to them. In return, they treated him with ridicule and scorn.

Further he informs us that these men were much too old to be of any employment value. "Yea, whereto might the strength of their hands profit me, in whom old age was perished?" Their labors were not worth their pay. The phrase, "in whom old age was perished," suggests that they were in their second childhood and not to be depended upon in positions of responsibility demanding vigor and activity.

These men were extremely poor, but in spite of this they refused to work. "For want and famine they were solitary; fleeing into the wilderness in former time desolate and waste. Who cut up mallows by the bushes, and juniper roots for their meat." They were the castoffs of society who did not want to work. At the same time, they were too proud to ask alms. Because of their attitude, no one wanted to help them. Thus they fled to the desert places for food and shelter.

Certainly it is not sinful to be poor. There are many in the world who have no control over their plight, and are without food and shelter. But unlike these described in our text, they are the unfortunate products of their circumstances. They deserve to be helped. These of whom Job speaks were the lowest and most degraded kind of persons.

Job informs us further, "They were driven forth from among men, (they cried after them as after a thief;) To dwell in the cliffs of the valleys, in caves of the earth, and in the rocks." This suggests the low, despicable characters these men possessed. They were thieves, scoundrels, the scum of the earth. Too lazy to build themselves shelters, they lived amidst the trees. "Among the bushes they brayed; under the nettles they were gathered together." They congregated in little groups here and there among the bushes and trees, existing in their low estate. "They were children of fools, yea, children of base men: they were viler than the earth." The phrase, "viler than the earth," really means that these wicked and profane men were

driven out of the cities and off the land by those who had respect for the higher things of life. Probably humans could go
no lower than these men had gone. Living in sin, given to
stealing and plundering, with no concern for earning an honest day's wage, they had degenerated to about the lowest level
of humanity.

But they are typical of us all! In the sight of God, until a
man or woman is converted, he or she is no better than the
despised and unwanted outcasts of society. Though there are
degrees of sin, God cannot under any circumstances condone
sin. All sin is abominable in His sight. No matter how good a
person may think he is, before the Lord he is a condemned
sinner. We read in Galatians 3:22, "The scripture hath concluded all under sin." There are no exceptions. But the Bible
offers good news—there is forgiveness for sin so that anyone
might be right with God. In Psalm 86:5 we have these wonderful words, "For Thou, LORD, art good, and ready to forgive;
and plenteous in mercy unto all them that call upon Thee."
Are you a forgiven sinner or a condemned sinner? If you have
trusted in Jesus Christ, you are a forgiven sinner. If you have
not trusted in Christ, you are a condemned sinner; and should
you die in your present state, you will be separated forever from
the love and mercy of God.

Why be a slave to sin when you might be set free by the
Lord Jesus Christ? A preacher in Uganda recently illustrated
this great truth with a homely but very practical illustration. A
brother and sister were left at home by their parents. The
brother had a new slingshot, and seeing his father's chicken
walking around, he aimed at it and killed it. The sister said,
"What will Father say? Let us bury the chicken quickly." They
did. When the father returned home he searched everywhere
for the chicken and finally asked the children if they had seen
it.

"No," was the answer they both gave. From then on, each
day when work needed to be done around their home, the sister

said to her brother, "You must do this work or I will tell Father what happened to the chicken." So the boy virtually became her slave; but he soon tired of this and thought, "Why should I be a slave when I can be free?" That evening when his father returned to the village he ran to meet him and said, "Father, I killed that chicken with my slingshot and I am sorry." Of course, his father forgave him. How happy the boy was! Now his sister could not demand that he do her work. He was no longer a slave.

Could it be that you have been a slave to sin? Look to the Lord Jesus, and confess to Him. Receive Christ into your life, and enter at once into the freedom and liberty that He gives. In John 8:36 God says, "If the Son therefore shall make you free, ye shall be free indeed." How wonderful that He has provided deliverance from the penalty and power of sin through Jesus Christ, His beloved Son. No matter how far down one has gone in sin, Christ can lift him up.

Job continues by telling us that those he has described in the first eight verses of chapter 30 were ridiculing and mocking him. "And now am I their song, yea, I am their byword. They abhor me, they flee far from me, and spare not to spit in my face." Even to spit in the presence of another in the East was insulting. Thus the action of these men toward Job revealed their scorn and indignation. They had no restraint in expressing their hatred toward God's servant.

With cursing also they expressed their bitterness. Job says, "Because He hath loosed my cord, and afflicted me, they have also let loose the bridle before me." They said and did what they pleased to Job. They showed him no respect whatsoever. Notice how they jostled him about, knocking him down, and kicking him. "Upon my right hand rise the youth; they push away my feet, and they raise up against me the ways of their destruction." The word "youth" here refers to a "low brood." This is just another expression describing these beastlike characters who joined the multitudes in pouring their reproach upon Job. Not only did they make a jest of Job but they made a prey of him, pouring out their wrath upon him. They blamed him for their horrible state of affairs. Though he was innocent, they gave no regard to him. They had to blame someone; thus they chose Job.

"They mar my path, they set forward my calamity, they have no helper," Job declares. The "marring of the path" means that they accused him falsely. Job had treated these people justly; but, probably inspired by the speeches of Job's three friends, they claimed that he had been unjust. Though they falsely accused Job, they had no satisfactory evidence for their accusations. "They set forward my calamity," Job says, "but they have no helper." They cannot get support for their lies.

Further, those who treated Job in this manner were many in number. "They came upon me as a wide breaking in of waters: in the desolation they rolled themselves upon me." As the flood waters roll unmercifully, bringing destruction in their path, so these ungodly men had brought misery into Job's life.

In summing up their attitude Job says, "Terrors are turned upon me: they pursue my soul as the wind: and my welfare passeth away as a cloud." The word "soul" could also be translated "dignity." These enemies of God's servant sought to destroy the favorable and respected position among men which Job once knew.

All of this had its effect upon Job. It is quite obvious that it even affected his mind. The next several verses suggest strongly that his suffering was not only physical but also mental: "And now my soul is poured out upon me; the days of affliction have taken hold upon me." "The days of affliction" had taken hold of him in the sense that day and night his mind was greatly disturbed by his calamities. His physical pain was continuous, there was no relief either in the night or in the day. As Job says, "My bones are pierced in me in the night season: and my sinews take no rest." It is quite obvious that Job found it most difficult to sleep because of his extreme suffering.

You will recall that Job's body was covered with sores. Now he tells us of the effects of these sores: "By the great force of my disease is my garment changed: it bindeth me about as the collar of my coat." The soft clothing he used to wear had become stiff as his collar from the continuous running of the open sores. Being without a change of garment, his clothing added more to his grief and misery. What a pitiful condition Job was in. He seemed disturbed that God did not intervene. In fact, he even expressed the feeling that God had cast him off. "He hath cast me into the mire, and I am become like dust and ashes." Prayer seemed to be of no avail. "I cry unto Thee, and Thou dost not hear me: I stand up, and Thou regardest me not." The standing position was always assumed as one stood before a king. Job stood up as a sign of respect before God, and prayed. But regardless, there was no change in his condition. He thought he was utterly forsaken: "Thou art become cruel to me: with Thy strong hand Thou opposest Thyself against me."

God would not assume such an attitude toward His servant: it only seemed this way to Job because there appeared to be no release from his misery. Nevertheless, Job accused God for his present circumstances: "Thou liftest me up to the wind; Thou causest me to ride upon it, and dissolvest my substance. For I know that Thou wilt bring me to death, and to the house appointed for all living. Howbeit he will not stretch out his hand to the grave, though they cry in his destruction."

We must not be too critical of Job, for, if we were in his circumstances, I am sure many of us would act in a similar manner. Can it not be said that Job's besetting sin at this time seemed to be that of unbelief? Earlier he had declared, "Though He slay me, yet will I trust in Him." He seemed to have lost his confidence in God. Is it not true, however, that though our lot has not been as severe as Job's, even in circumstances of lesser severity we have failed to trust the Lord as we should?

In Psalm 31:24 we have this marvelous promise: "Be of good courage, and He shall strengthen your heart, all ye that hope in the LORD." To hope in the Lord is to trust in the Lord. If we fully trust Him, He promises that He will undertake. Do not look to yourself; do not look to your own resources. Lean wholly on the Lord.

A Scottish saint, while suffering terrible agonies, was kept in perfect peace.

"Do not be afraid of death," he said, "for Christ has borne the substance. All that remains for His people is a shadow, and no one need be afraid of a shadow."

"It is his Scotch determination," said one who visited him, "that enables him to endure."

"Tell that friend," said he, "that, if all the grit to be found in Scotland be centered in one man, it would not enable him to endure these pains for one hour. I seem to rest on the crest of a mountain. Below in the valley a storm is raging—that is my disease. But on the mountaintop I rest in peace through the grace of God."

How true! The Lord will never fail us; He cannot fail. Thus we must trust Him implicitly. "He giveth power to the faint; and to them that have no might He increaseth strength" (Isaiah 40:29). But it may be that you do not know the Lord. You cannot endure your trial alone. No man is sufficient for these burdens that befall all of us. You need Christ in your life.

Like most of us have done on occasion, Job now points to his good works in the hope that God will be lenient because of these. "Did not I weep for him that was in trouble? was not my soul grieved for the poor?" It would seem that Job is trying to reason with God by suggesting that, because he had been considerate and helpful to those who were in need, God ought to help him. Any such feeling would be an infringement of the authority and sovereignty of God. The Lord's attitude toward us is never shaped or directed by what we do or do not do. God does not love us more when we do things that please Him. His love is not objective but subjective. He loves us with an unfathomable, inexhaustible love that is not dependent upon our few paltry good works. Often we try to interpret God from a mere human viewpoint; this is impossible. We must, by faith, accept Him as He is.

Job says further, "When I looked for good, then evil came unto me: and when I waited for light, there came darkness." Probably Job looked for good because he had done good things and expected to be rewarded. Again I say, God's goodness toward us is not based upon our goodness toward Him. Constantly the Lord is pouring out His undeserved and unearned goodness upon us. The few hours, comparatively speaking, of suffering and misery we experience are far less than we deserve.

Affliction and trial are not always the results of wrongdoing on our part. In various parts of the world there are saints of God who have been bedridden for years. Many of these have been a benediction to scores of people who have visited their bedside. Can we say that these saints are suffering for their wrongdoings? Not necessarily! In fact, in many cases there is no adequate answer on the human side. Someday we shall understand, but presently we realize that the will of God is being done. We cannot ask, "Why?" but simply rely on the truth of Proverbs 25:2, "It is the glory of God to conceal a thing." God understands and someday He will make all things clear.

Job reminds us again of the deep-seated turmoil in his heart. "My bowels boiled, and rested not: the days of affliction prevented me." "Bowels" refers to the deep feelings within his heart. The word "prevented" means that his afflictions came with surprise to him, they came unexpectedly. Job's lot was one of constant misery. He says, "I went mourning without the sun: I stood up, and I cried in the congregation." He walked about in dark places lamenting his sorrowful state. If he joined the congregation of worshipers, he stood and cried throughout, realizing his pitiful condition. Oftentimes the pain was so great that he cried aloud, sounding as the beasts of the field or the fowl of the air. "I am a brother to dragons, and a companion to owls," he laments.

Job's appearance must have been awfully depressing, for he said, "My skin is black upon me, and my bones are burned with heat." The idea expressed by the original here is that his skin was falling from him. Amidst the oozing and running of the sores, his skin was peeling off constantly. His body burned with fever. And then, to top it all, he had lost the joy of the Lord; the song he once had in his heart disappeared. "My harp also is turned to mourning, and my organ into the voice of them that weep." Job was depressed, and surely he had reason to be so. But be assured, it is not God's will for the believer to lose his song. Amidst the worst calamities of life, the one who truly believes on the Lord can "rejoice with joy unspeakable and full of glory." If the believer loses his joy, the devil has won a great victory. We may lose our health, our money, our loved ones, but God never intends that His people lose the joy that Christ gives. In fact, if we are to face the uncertainties of life, we need this joy. As declared in Nehemiah 8:10, "The joy of the LORD is your strength." One may be in most distressing circumstances and still look up with praise to God because of the joy of the Lord that floods his soul. If you really know the Lord Jesus in your heart, regardless of your sorrow you should have His joy within.

Have you noticed the relationship between chapter 53 and chapter 54 of Isaiah? Isaiah 53 tells of the sacrifice of Christ for our redemption. Now consider the first word in chapter 54 —"Sing." There is no song apart from the sacrifice of Christ. If you have Christ in your heart, you are privileged to have an everlasting song. If you have no song, the reason may be that you do not really know the Lord. If this is your case, I urge you to receive the Lord Jesus into your heart. With Him you will be able to face any of the disturbing experiences of life with the joy of the Lord flooding your soul.

JOB 31:1-40

REPEATEDLY, Job's three friends have condemned him as a sinner who justly deserves his present sufferings. Now Job justifies himself, not as a perfect man, but as one anxious and desirous of pleasing God. He begins by saying, "I made a covenant with mine eyes; why then should I think upon a maid?" "Think" as used here means "to cast a lustful look." Job guarded against lust by taking the first and most important step against it: he refused to look upon anything that might suggest evil, thus protecting himself from wicked thoughts. The eye is the gate through which lust often enters the soul. In 1 John 2:16 we read of "the lust of the eyes." If one is given to sexual passions, it is well for him to refrain from looking at anything that might stimulate unholy desires. Thus, Job made a covenant with his eyes, refusing to look at those of the opposite sex, that he might not stimulate the desires of the flesh. Had David done this, he might not have fallen into heinous sin.

In Matthew 5:28 our Lord informs us that the impure look is quite as bad as the impure act. "Whosoever looketh on a woman to lust after her hath committed adultery with her al-

ready in his heart." It is of utmost importance that every believer, like Job, covenant with his eyes that he will not look
upon anything that will turn his attention from the holiness of
God.

Had Job not sought to bridle his passions, he could not have
expected any help whatsoever from God. "For what portion of
God is there from above? and what inheritance of the Almighty
from on high?" God can never condone or bless sin. If one
persists in choosing sin, then let him not expect to look for the
Lord's guidance and care. Actually, verse 3 is the answer to
verse 2, "Is not destruction to the wicked? and a strange punishment to the workers of iniquity?" In place of the grace of
God, the one who continues in evil will experience the judgment of God.

Job realized that all man's ways are known by the Lord.
"Doth not He see my ways, and count all my steps?" No sin
goes unnoticed by the eye of the Almighty. David said in
Psalm 44:21, "He knoweth the secrets of the heart." Yes, the
Lord knows every thought that passes through the mind. We
cannot escape His eye. Thus Job argues, "If I have walked with
vanity, or if my foot hath hasted to deceit; Let me be weighed
in an even balance, that God may know mine integrity." This
word "vanity" is really "falsehood." Job declares that he has
been righteous before God, that there is no trace of falsehood
or deceit in what he is saying. To this end, he asks that he
might be placed in the balance of God's justice, that what he
has said might be proved. If it were not true, he was willing
and ready to suffer the judgment God has promised to sinners.
"If my step hath turned out of the way, and mine heart walked
after mine eyes, and if any blot hath cleaved to mine hands;
Then let me sow, and let another eat; yea, let my offspring be
rooted out." Of course, no one but God can see man's heart as
it really is. Job argued that he had not yielded to the temptations that had come through his eyes. If this is not true, he
longs for God to pour out judgment upon him.

Further, God's suffering servant avowed his innocence of adultery. "If mine heart have been deceived by a woman, or if I have laid wait at my neighbour's door; Then let my wife grind unto another, and let other bow down upon her." "Deceived" as used here expresses the meaning of being seduced. Job had not been seduced by women, nor had he "laid wait" close by his neighbor's door until the husband went out. If this is not the truth, he is willing that his wife become a slave, grinding at the mill for others, serving them as a slave night and day. Nothing could be more humiliating to one in the East than to have one's wife forced to slavery. If there was any deceit in what he was saying, Job was willing that his wife, whom he loved, be subjected to this shame.

Pointing out the seriousness of the offense of adultery, Job says, "For this is a heinous crime; yea, it is an iniquity to be punished by the judges. For it is a fire that consumeth to destruction, and would root out all mine increase." Adultery is a sin that affects the community. Not only are those involved defiled, but many others are drawn into the sin. It was a serious offense in Job's day, often punishable by death. But even worse is the judgment of God upon sex sins: "It is a fire that consumeth to destruction." How important it is that believers practice the purity of God.

In this day, when Satan has capitalized upon the eye as a means for enticing even the people of God into gross sin, like Job we need to covenant with our eyes, that we will refuse to look upon anything or anyone that will arouse our passions and may lead into worse sin. Of course, in ourselves we cannot do this, but as we look to the Lord for His moment-by-moment help through the indwelling Holy Spirit, we shall reap the blessings of constant victory. You and I must say, as David declared in Psalm 124:8, "Our help is in the name of the LORD, who made heaven and earth." The same God, who called the world into existence, offers all the power needed to overcome temptation. We must, however, lean upon Him constantly, recognizing the many weaknesses of the flesh. Do not trust yourself for a moment. Let your dependence be upon God; He will give you the strength and the power to overcome any sin. We read in 1 John 5:4-5, "For whatsoever is born of God overcometh the world: and this is the victory that overcometh the world, even our faith. Who is he that overcometh the world, but he that believeth that Jesus is the Son of God?" Here is the promise of an everlasting victory through Christ.

Job had been accused of unfairness in his treatment of his servants. He points out that, not only is this ungrounded, but unreasonable. "If I did despise the cause of my manservant or of my maidservant, when they contended with me; What then shall I do when God riseth up? and when He visiteth, what shall I answer Him?" One may be successful in oppressing those of a lower plane of life, but only temporarily. There are no low planes in God's sight. He who oppresses his neighbor must eventually suffer the judgment of God. Job knew this. Thus he argues that it would be foolish to ignore the rights of his employees and bring upon himself further trouble.

No human is without God-given rights, for Job asks, "Did not He that made me in the womb make him? and did not one fashion us in the womb?" Everyone born into this world has certain inalienable rights, and on these rights no one can transgress without sinning against God.

God's servant argued further that he had never failed to minister to the needs of the poor. "If I have withheld the poor from their desire, or have caused the eyes of the widow to fail; Or have eaten my morsel myself alone, and the fatherless hath not eaten thereof; (For from my youth he was brought up with me, as with a father, and I have guided her from my mother's womb)." The orphans Job helped were brought up as though he were their father, and the widows for whom he cared were treated as though they were his sisters. "If I have seen any perish for want of clothing, or any poor without covering; If his loins have not blessed me, and if he were not warmed with the fleece of my sheep." Here the parts of the body that were benefited by Job's gifts are poetically expressed as thanking him. "If I have lifted up my hand against the fatherless, when I saw my help in the gate." "The help in the gate" he might get would be from corrupt judges who would bow to the wealthy and fulfill their desires for money. Thus, if an orphan were to declare to the judges that he was being maltreated, his wealthy master would be declared just by the bribed court. If Job had done any of these things, he was ready and willing to receive immediate judgment. "Then let mine arm fall from my shoulder blade, and mine arm be broken from the bone." He was willing to suffer physical punishment for any evil that he might have committed. The reason he did not do these things was his fear of God. "For destruction from God was a terror to me, and by reason of His highness I could not endure." Job was a man of integrity. What he did was performed in the light of God's plan and will. Had he oppressed the poor and needy, he knew all too well that God's judgment would be upon him, for no one can abuse his brother without the punishment of God.

Now Job begins his third argument. He has argued for his integrity, first of all, on the grounds that he refrained from sin by guarding his eyes; secondly, by the fact that he did not oppress the poor and needy; and now, thirdly, that he has not trusted in money. "If I have made gold my hope, or have said to the fine gold, Thou art my confidence; If I rejoiced because my wealth was great, and because mine hand had gotten much." Job was not guilty of the sin of covetousness, as many are. This is a very wicked sin, for it turns the eyes of the guilty one from God to man. Frequently the wealthy man is self-dependent; he feels that he does not need the Lord. How deluded he is, thinking that he has everything because he has money. Job was not guilty of this sorrowful evil.

Further, God's servant suggests that the worship of money is an act of idolatry, as wicked as the worship of the sun or the moon. "If I beheld the sun when it shined, or the moon walking in brightness; And my heart hath been secretly enticed, or my mouth hath kissed my hand." By the worship of money one may be "enticed" into the sin of idolatry. The heathen bows and kisses his god of wood or stone. Job feels that if he were guilty of the idolatrous sin of covetousness, he might just as well kiss his own hand, for actually he would be worshiping himself.

He concludes this argument by saying, "This also were an iniquity to be punished by the judge: for I should have denied the God that is above." For one to depend upon his money and to fail to look to the Lord is a sin that results in the judgment of God. How common this sin is in our day. Jesus warned of this evil in Luke 12:15: "Take heed, and beware of covetousness: for a man's life consisteth not in the abundance of the things which he possesseth." How many there are clamoring for money, and the things money can buy, to the exclusion of God and their need of a personal relationship with Him. There are some who think they have made a success in life, when all they have made is money. Money does not necessarily mean success. A man may have money and be miserably wretched in his own existence. Someone has said, "Money is the universal passport for everywhere except Heaven, and the universal provider for everything except happiness."

Did you ever see a tombstone with a dollar sign on it? Neither did I. I have known hundreds of men who lived as though their only ambition was to accumulate money. But I have never known one who wanted a final judgment on himself to be based on what he got. A man does not want people to read in his obituary a balance sheet of his wealth, but a story of his service to humanity. If he has lived for himself and the flesh, there will not be much of a story to tell.

There is no sin in being rich, of course; the sin comes when we use our riches for ourselves and ignore God. Money is not the root of all evil, but the love of money is. When one loves his money, he worships his money. Job was not guilty of this sin. How about you? Do you think money would be the answer to all your problems? I assure you that it would not. Christ is the answer. Trust Him for all things, for only He can provide all things. We read in Philippians 4:19, "But my God shall supply all your need according to His riches in glory by Christ Jesus." Put Christ first and everything else will take its rightful order.

Coming now to verse 29 of chapter 31, we see Job arguing for his integrity on the ground of his attitude toward his enemies. In Matthew 5:44 the Lord Jesus says, "But I say unto you, Love your enemies, bless them that curse you, do good to them that hate you, and pray for them which despitefully use you, and persecute you." It is quite obvious that Job respected his enemies in this manner. He says, "If I rejoiced at the destruction of him that hated me, or lifted up myself when evil found him: Neither have I suffered my mouth to sin by wishing a curse to his soul." Job did not triumph when his enemies were trapped in sin, nor did he speak evil of his enemies. Surely he is to be commended for this splendid spirit.

How greatly we need this attitude of love in the Church of Christ today. There is so much hatred evidenced among those who profess to be Christians. Though the Bible declares that "we are one in Christ," it is difficult to find this unanimity among believers. Is this a problem with you? Is there any trace of dislike or hatred toward a Christian brother in your heart?

Whenever you are tempted to think unkind thoughts of others, say to yourself, "The Son of God loves me." Think on those words for a few minutes—"The Son of God loves me." That is the marvel of all history. You, the worthless being that you are, loved by the Son of God! I, a hell-deserving sinner, loved by the Son of God! There is not a single thing in any of us to draw out the love of God. He has every reason to despise us. But He loves us. The Word of God tells us so in Ephesians 5:2, "Christ also hath loved us, and hath given Himself for us." Maybe someone has been unkind to you. Is that any worse than what you have been to God? Most certainly not! The next time you are tempted to think evil thoughts about someone, say to yourself, "The Son of God loved me . . . the Son of God loved me."

Job was kind to all, not only those who were kind to him, but those who were unkind. He never turned a stranger away. He never failed to care for a traveler. "If the men of my tabernacle said not, Oh that we had of his flesh! we cannot be satisfied. The stranger did not lodge in the street: but I opened my doors to the traveller." Job was ready to help everyone.

Job says further, "If I covered my transgressions as Adam, by hiding mine iniquity in my bosom: Did I fear a great multitude, or did the contempt of families terrify me, that I kept silence, and went not out of the door?" Job was not like Adam, who, after he had sinned, hid from God. Job could look anyone in the eye. He did not need to hide because of anything he had done; he had been just before God and just before men. Like Paul he could say, "Herein do I exercise myself, to have always a conscience void of offence toward God, and toward men" (Acts 24:16). What a wonderful way to live. Job was not like the thief who must constantly be wary of the eye of the police. He had nothing to hide.

It is amazing how many do their best to be respectable and law-abiding as far as the eye of men is concerned, but give no regard to the eye of God. Important as it is to keep the laws of men, it is of greater importance that we obey the laws of God. Those who obey the laws of God will respect and keep the laws of men. But never forget, our first duty and obligation is to the God who created us. He demands that we come to Him by believing on His Son, His only begotten Son, who died on the cross for our sins.

Job pleads further that his arguments might be heard and that the critics might be silenced. "Oh that one would hear me! behold, my desire is, that the Almighty would answer me, and that mine adversary had written a book." Job desires that his accusers write all of their accusations in a book. This, he says, he would carry everywhere he went: "Surely I would take it upon my shoulder, and bind it as a crown to me." With the book opened to the eyes of men and with the accusations boldly displayed, Job would do his best to justify himself by living in a manner that would forever prove the accusations to be wrong. "I would declare unto Him the number of my steps; as a prince would I go near unto Him."

Job had been a great landowner. As a wealthy employer he had employed many men to work for him in the fields. He had been criticized by his enemies as being unfair to his laborers. If this were true, Job was willing to receive his just reward. "If my land cry against me, or that the furrows likewise thereof complain; If I have eaten the fruits thereof without money, or have caused the owners thereof to lose their life: Let thistles grow instead of wheat, and cockle instead of barley." The punishment he chose for himself was to receive, as the fruits of his huge investment of wealth and labor, only bramble and weeds. He said this because he was so certain that his accusers were lying.

The chapter closes with the statement, "The words of Job are ended." This does not mean that he speaks no more in the book, but rather that he has nothing further to say to his three friends about these matters. He has offered them his concluding argument. He has nothing more to say by way of self-defense and vindication. If what he has said does not suffice, he chooses to keep quiet.

Job was a wise man. Sometimes it is far better to remain silent. Job had said, "How forcible are right words! but what doth your arguing reprove?" (Job 6:25) There comes a time when we might just as well cease from speaking, for very often words stir up anger and turmoil. Recall the incident of Jesus before Herod. Herod asked many questions and made several accusations. But what do we read about Jesus? "He answered him nothing" (Luke 23:9). Indeed, there are many occasions when silence is golden. Much that is said might better be left unsaid. Let us learn the lesson of silence when it would glorify and honor God. On other occasions, when we must speak, let us ask God for wisdom, that we shall speak words that will edify and help.

JOB 32:1-22

JOB FINISHED HIS SPEECH but there was no reply from his three friends. They who had been so quick to speak in the past suddenly became silent. The reason they gave was that Job "was righteous in his own eyes." They concluded that, if a man were as strongly opinionated as Job, there would be no use wasting words. But these three friends were wrong. They could not see Job's heart. Man is a poor judge. In fact, we read in Psalm 75:7, "But God is the judge: He putteth down one, and setteth up another." It is far better to leave the task of judging with God rather than trying to assume the role ourselves. How many Christians are guilty of this destructive evil of criticizing other Christians. Usually it is because we do not fully understand the facts. If we were living in the circumstances of those we criticize, we should have nothing to say, for we would fully understand the promptings of their actions. If we knew each other as God knows us, we should certainly be more considerate and less critical.

The story is told of the man trying to get to sleep in his berth in a Pullman. After listening for an hour or more to a screaming baby, he called out to the man who was walking up and down the aisle with it, "Take that kid to its mother." The man replied with a tearful voice, "I would gladly do so, my friend, but this baby's mother is in a casket in the baggage car." How we need to pray that God will help us speak words that edify and help others rather than words that destroy and produce sorrow.

Now we see a fourth friend entering the picture. He begins a speech which continues through chapter 37. Someone had to intervene, for the discussion between Job and his friends was getting more heated all the time. Thus Elihu appears as a moderator. Spiritually he was well qualified for this position, for his name meant, "My God is He." From the start Elihu evidenced a very worthy characteristic. He had been listening to the discussion between Job and his friends. Though tempted to speak, he remained silent until he was certain he had something to say. Rather than going to others and telling what was on his heart, he spoke to the guilty ones. He was not a gossiper; he faced his adversary with the facts.

First, he was disturbed by Job because Job "justified himself rather than God." According to Elihu, Job was more concerned about speaking of himself and his own righteous character than he was of the holiness of God. Elihu saw no reason for this self-justification, but certainly he recognized the importance of exalting the Lord. This is indeed most worthy, for if God is lifted up and honored, we shall have nothing to fear.

Elihu was also angry with Job's friends, "because they had found no answer, and yet had condemned Job." They had condemned him as a hypocrite, though they had found no reasonable foundation for their arguments. Repeatedly they affirmed that he was a hypocrite. Listening to Job's arguments, they did not respect them. In fact, they practically ignored them.

We should note that Elihu was extremely courteous and respectful. He had remained silent until now for two reasons. First, he waited until Job had spoken. He felt that one who was under the fire of the words of his would-be comforters, such as

Job, should be permitted to say all he had to say. Secondly, he refused to interrupt the three friends because they were older than he. But now they have nothing more to say. Job seems to have finished. Thus Elihu grasps the opportunity to speak.

We can learn a very important lesson from Elihu. I am sure as he heard caustic and disturbing words flying back and forth between Job and the three friends, he had been ready to speak many times. But giving all due respect to God's suffering servant and the seniority of the friends, he remained silent. How commendable! There are occasions when all of us should remain silent. Have we not been sorry for words we have spoken when we should have kept quiet?

Dr. William Osler has said, "To know when to keep silent is one of the finest arts. The atmosphere of life is darkened by the mourning of men and women over the nonessentials, the trifles that are inevitably incident to the day's routine. Things cannot always go our way. Learn to accept in silence the minor aggravations. Cultivate the gift of taciturnity and consume your own smoke with an extra draught of hard work so that those about you may not be annoyed with the dust and soot of your complaints."

Well did David pray in Psalm 19:14, "Let the words of my mouth, and the meditation of my heart, be acceptable in Thy sight, O Lord, my strength, and my redeemer." Words must be carefully weighed before spoken, that they might be God-honoring and God-exalting words. If they are not, it is far better that we do not speak. In Colossians 4:6 God says, "Let your speech be alway with grace, seasoned with salt." Oh, that we might speak in a manner that will glorify the Christ who saved us. Of course, until one has really met Him as Saviour and Lord, he will not have Him to control his speech. Only Christ can control an unruly tongue. He does this by controlling the heart. When He is received into the heart and acknowledged as Lord, our words will honor Him because we have His strength to enable us to obey Him.

Elihu was greatly disturbed because the three friends remained silent when they should have spoken. This sin can be equally as dangerous as the one of speaking when we should be silent. Sometimes silence is golden; on other occasions it is cowardly. Thus Elihu is incensed because "there was no answer in the mouth of these three men."

Elihu continues by saying, "I am young, and ye are very old; wherefore I was afraid, and durst not shew you mine opinion." Here we see another wonderful characteristic in Elihu. Though he was young and had unusual ability, he was not arrogant or boastful. He was a humble man, refraining from speaking in the audience of those of greater experience. He must have been like Moses in this respect, a man of tremendous competency. Yet we read of Moses in Numbers 12:3, "Now the man Moses was very meek, above all the men which were upon the face of the earth." Elihu, too, must have been a meek and humble man.

How relatively easy it is to talk of our own exploits and accomplishments. Yet God has declared in Proverbs 27:2, "Let another man praise thee, and not thine own mouth; a stranger, and not thine own lips." If our work is worthy it will not be necessary to tell of it to others, for our works will declare their own worthiness. Bishop Berry once said, "Fame is a bubble and it often comes from blowing your own horn."

Dr. Harry A. Ironside used to tell of an occasion when he was in London. While walking home from a meeting, he was accompanied part of the way by the Marquis of Aberdeen, who had presided, and the Lord Bishop of Norwich, who had been one of the speakers. Being an American and unaccustomed to titles, Dr. Ironside felt embarrassed as to how to address men of their position. He expressed his perplexity, and the marquis replied, "My dear brother, just address us as your brethren in Christ. We could have no higher honor than that."

Elihu suggests that age and experience should qualify one to be wise, as he says, "Days should speak, and multitude of years should teach wisdom." As we grow older we should profit more and more by every experience of life, that we might be better prepared to help others; otherwise, old age will be a reproach. But more important than the wisdom that comes with age is the divine wisdom that comes through inspiration. Elihu tells us, "But there is a spirit in man: and the inspiration of the Almighty giveth them understanding." Without question, Elihu was a child of God. Though living many years before it was written, he evidenced the truth of 1 John 2:20,27, "But ye have an unction from the Holy One, and ye know all things. . . . But the anointing which ye have received of Him abideth in you, and ye need not that any man teach you: but as the same anointing teacheth you of all things, and is truth, and is no lie, and even as it hath taught you, ye shall abide in Him." Many live to a ripe old age but are wise only after the flesh. But if one has been born again, possessing the Holy Spirit through belief in Christ, he has divine wisdom which is absolutely essential to face the problems and conflicts of life.

Mere human wisdom is grossly incompetent to see us through confusion and turmoil, for "Great men are not always wise: neither do the aged understand judgment." A man may have reached the top in his field, but though he has been thoroughly trained and though he is well qualified for his work, he may be woefully ignorant when it comes to recognizing the really important things of life. How many intellectuals stumble at the simplicity of the gospel — salvation through the shed blood of Christ. Though possessing almost unlimited intelligence, able to wrestle with profound problems, they are unable to receive by faith the truth of Christ and His saving grace. Many aged men and women are the same way. Having spent years on this earth accumulating the wisdom of the world, in spite of their years they cannot grasp the simple truths of the gospel story. Who is a truly wise man? In Proverbs 9:10 God says, "The fear of the LORD is the beginning of wisdom." If one is to be wise, he must know the Lord through a personal acceptance of Jesus Christ as Saviour.

Elihu pleads for his listeners to give attention to what he has to say: "I also will show mine opinion." "Opinion" used here is the word "knowledge." The knowledge he proffers is not of his own but that given by the Spirit through inspiration, as he has already told us in verse 8. Thus he claims inspiration for what he is about to say.

"Behold, I waited for your words; I gave ear to your reasons, whilst ye searched out what to say." Here Elihu is speaking specifically to the three friends of Job. He informs them that he had been listening carefully to everything they had to say to be sure that he thoroughly understood them before he spoke. After listening carefully, he concludes that their arguments evaded the issue at hand: "Yea, I attended unto you, and, behold, there was none of you that convinced Job, or that answered his words." Elihu further informs the three friends that he must speak, "Lest ye should say, We have found out wisdom: God thrusteth him down, not man." The three friends have declared repeatedly that Job was suffering because of his sin, and God was judging him because of his lack of repentance. They posed as wise men, offering their counsel. With this Elihu disagreed strongly. Having listened to the three accusers take advantage of Job, Elihu must stand and speak for the truth.

It is without prejudice that Elihu offers his counsel. Both Job and his three friends on occasion became bitter in their speeches because the words each spoke disturbed the other. Elihu informed them that he could be impartial in his remarks since the arguments of Job and his friends were not directed against him. He had no account to settle and could speak objectively. Thus this man of God enters the scene unhindered by personalities, filled with the Holy Spirit, to offer counsel according to the wisdom of God.

How wonderful it is to find a friend like this in the hour of need, someone who has a hold on the Lord, who will not take sides, but who offers counsel pure and sanctified. It would be well for all of us when we need help to seek out one of this caliber, a spiritual man, a man who is walking with God. Of course, every Christian should be this kind of person. Before God we ought to ask Him to examine our own hearts to be sure that we are spiritual men and women.

Because the three friends were silent, Elihu felt that this was his cue to speak. "They were amazed, they answered no more: they left off speaking. When I had waited, (for they spake not, but stood still, and answered no more;) I said, I will answer also my part; I also will shew mine opinion." Job's three friends kept quiet, expecting possibly that someone in the listening audience would praise them for their seemingly wise advice. How surprised they must have been as Elihu proceeded to rebuke them. This they least expected.

Elihu claims to have had divine guidance in what he had to say. In other words, he offered not merely his own personal opinion, but what is said appears to be inspired by the Almighty.

Job's three friends had run out of words, but such was not the case of Elihu. He declared, "I am full of matter, the spirit within me constraineth me." He had much to say, so much, in fact, that he could not keep still. His experience seems to be similar to that of Jeremiah when he was imprisoned. He wanted to keep quiet but he had to speak. He declared, "His word was in mine heart as a burning fire shut up in my bones, and I was weary with forbearing, and I could not stay" (Jeremiah 20:9). The Holy Spirit within constrained him to speak.

Should this not be the experience of every child of God? Indeed, it will be if we are walking with the Lord, for the indwelling Holy Spirit will impel us to speak about the Lord Jesus. Whenever we come in contact with a lost soul, we will find no rest until we speak out and give a witness for our Saviour. "The Spirit Himself beareth witness with our spirit, that we are the children of God" (Romans 8:16). How do we account for the fact that so few of those who profess to be followers of Christ are speaking out for Him? Is the Spirit not willing? Certainly He is. Why, then, do we not speak? Usually the matter is spiritual; Christ does not have the pre-eminence. We are more concerned about our personal interests and desires than we are for God's plan for the lost. Oh, that we could say with Elihu, "I am full of matter, the spirit within me constraineth me."

I remember reading some years ago of Dave Brougham, who was then a student in high school in Seattle, Washington. He loved to play football, but better still, he loved to talk about Jesus Christ. In speaking of Christ he would quote a dozen verses of Scripture every time. He got started studying the Bible about the time he was chosen all-city guard at Broadway High School in 1945, the year his coach presented him the coveted blocking award, with the words, "To the toughest guard in the city." Later he played football at the University of Washington and then with the Fort Lewis Engineers. Here is Dave's testimony: "The Word of God has challenged and changed my life. My philosophy has needed drastic mending since examining 1 Peter 3:15, 'But sanctify the Lord God in your hearts: and be ready always to give an answer to every man that asketh you a reason of the hope that is in you.' If someone were to ask me why I am constantly and consistently memorizing Scripture, I would quote Proverbs 7:1-3: 'My son, keep My words, and lay up My commandments with thee. Keep My commandments, and live; and My law as the apple of thine eye. Bind them upon thy fingers, write them upon the table of thine heart.' By memorizing I can speak with authority and pack a wallop. I am hoping that more of the high school gang will trust Christ, and my testimony is that 'I can do all things through Christ, which strengtheneth me.'"

Indeed, that is a radiant testimony. Would to God that it

were the testimony of every true believer in Jesus Christ. There is one thing that Dave said that I should like to re-emphasize. He did not try to witness in his own strength, but he realized, even as Elihu of old, that it was through the power of God. Elihu testified to the fact that it was "the spirit within" constraining him. Oh, that we might speak in the power of the Holy Spirit, that lost and dying men might hear of the Saviour who can give eternal life.

Further Elihu says, "Behold, my belly is as wine which hath no vent; it is ready to burst like new bottles." He felt that he was compelled to speak in answer to the arguments that had been given, likening himself to new wine which must be poured into new goatskin bottles, for it would burst the old bottles. "I will speak," he says, "that I may be refreshed: I will open my lips and answer." When a good man speaks, what he says is always refreshing to himself and those who listen. This is especially true when one speaks under the guidance of the Lord.

As the chapter closes, Elihu informs us that he will not be swayed by what he has heard. He would speak the truth, regardless of the arguments already presented. "Let me not, I pray you, accept any man's person, neither let me give flattering titles unto man. For I know not to give flattering titles in so doing my maker would soon take me away." When a man speaks the truth, rarely does he flatter anyone. The truth hurts; it often pierces deeply into one's heart. Never is this so true as when a man proclaims the Word of God, "For the word of God is quick, and powerful, and sharper than any twoedged sword, piercing even to the dividing asunder of soul and spirit, and of the joints and marrow, and is a discerner of the thoughts and intents of the heart" (Hebrews 4:12). Many there are in our pulpits offering flattery, preaching messages that please men and prompt them to exalt the speaker. On the other hand God has His faithful servants here and there who preach to present the truth, not to satisfy the whims and wishes of men

These are true servants of God who spend time on their knees listening to the voice of God. Then with hearts virtually aflame, they stand in the pulpit to preach and proclaim the truths of the Word of the Living God. Such men will not always have an easy road, for there are many in our churches who do not want the pure, unadulterated Word. But if a man is called of God to preach the Word, it is far better that he preach the message that God gives than to be guilty of high-sounding phrases that neither exalt the Lord nor help fallen men. Paul declared in 1 Corinthians 9:16, "Woe is unto me, if I preach not the gospel!" Likewise, we might say, woe unto anyone, called of the Lord to preach, who does not preach the gospel.

JOB 33:1-33

IN THE PREVIOUS CHAPTER, Elihu directed his speech toward Job's three friends. Now he speaks very pointedly to Job: "Wherefore, Job, I pray thee, hear my speeches, and hearken to all my words." He is concerned that Job listen to everything that he will say. He is even more concerned that Job will take these things to heart.

Elihu does not speak as did Job's three friends. He says, "Behold, now I have opened my mouth, my tongue hath spoken in my mouth." This implies careful consideration of the words he was about to speak. He would not ramble on with a desire to hear himself talk, but would speak with discrimination. "My words shall be of the uprightness of my heart," he says, "and my lips shall utter knowledge clearly." The word "clearly" expresses the idea of sincerely. Elihu promised that he would not let himself be influenced by passion or anger, but he would speak what he felt to be the message of God.

Elihu considered himself to be an instrument in the hands of God. "The spirit of God hath made me, and the breath of the Almighty hath given me life." The latter phrase reads, "The breath of the Almighty hath *inspired me*." He speaks as the inspired mediator between God and Job. In this respect, he is a type of Christ, the only Mediator between God and men. In 1 Timothy 2:5-6 we read of our Lord, "For there is one God, and one mediator between God and men, the man Christ Jesus; Who gave Himself a ransom for all, to be testified in due time." Though sinful mankind seeks many other ways to approach God, the Scriptures are clear: there is only one way—that is, Christ, who said, "I am the way, the truth, and the life: no man cometh unto the Father, but by Me" (John 14:6). Thus Elihu was sent by God to be a revealer of divine wisdom to the needy hearts of Job and his three friends.

The appeal is next made to Job to say anything further he desired to justify his case. "If thou canst answer me, set thy words in order before me, stand up." From the evident silence we conclude that Job had nothing more to say. Elihu continues, "Behold, I am according to thy wish in God's stead: I also am formed out of the clay." Though claiming to be God's representative, he quickly acknowledged the fact that as a man he was only frail clay, even as Job and his three friends. The good he would speak deserved to be recognized as coming from God, not from Elihu.

Job had no reason to fear what Elihu might say, for God's spokesman reminds the suffering saint that the words he was about to speak would be a help, not a hindrance. "Behold, my terror shall not make thee afraid, neither shall my hand be heavy upon thee."

From all that we have seen thus far regarding Elihu, it would seem that he was indeed a friend in need. It is wonderful to have friends to help us through times of difficulty and distress. I heard someone say one time, "If a man has one or two real friends, he is a wealthy man indeed." Friends are valuable to us. I mean by friends those we can trust, who will stay by us to help regardless of the consequences. Of course, for the believer the greatest friend is Christ. Let us not overlook our obligation in this friendship. He said in John 15:14, "Ye are My friends, if ye do whatsoever I command you." The friendship of Christ is contingent upon our obedience to His holy will. If we are living according to His Word and obeying Him, then we have the high privilege of claiming Him as the "friend that sticketh closer than a brother" (Proverbs 18:24).

Few of us really trust Christ as the Friend of friends. Some of us find it easier to look to earthly friends. What blessings we miss because we fail to trust the Lord Jesus for everything. Sometimes God must put us through myriads of trials that we might discover the friendship of the Lord Jesus. In fact, very often there is no other way to realize this friendship than through hours and hours of toil and trial.

A pastor tells of meeting a man who had lost both his wife and only child. He had been fairly wealthy, but misfortunes had used up all of his money. His friends proved to be mostly of the fair-weather variety. He was critically ill in a county home. The pastor began by saying, "You have certainly had your share of sorrow." Instantly the sick man corrected him. "Don't say that, Pastor," he responded with a smile, "say that I have had more than my share of blessings. Christ once meant little more to me than a historical character. Now He is my closest Friend. Forgiveness of sins was once a pious but meaningless thought. Now it is my most precious possession. Heaven was wishful thinking. Now it is as real to me as the fact that I shall soon die."

Have you discovered the friendship of the Lord Jesus? It may be that God has permitted you to come to the valley of the shadow of death that you might look up and find Him to be the Friend of all friends. He loves you and wants to help you. But He does not work against your will: He longs to help you, but you must let Him. Do you know Him as your Saviour and Lord? Have you definitely opened your heart to receive Him as the One who died for your sins and rose again?

After his preliminary remarks, Elihu directs his speech toward Job, charging him that, in his attempt to answer his friends' accusation of hypocrisy, Job leaned over too far. "Surely thou hast spoken in mine hearing, and I have heard the voice of thy words, saying, I am clean without transgression, I am innocent; neither is there iniquity in me." Job was upright, a man of moral integrity, but he was still a man. Indeed, he was not what his three friends had declared him to be, a vile, hypocritical sinner—though he was a sinner.

No human born into this world escapes the defilement of original sin. David said in Psalm 51:5, "Behold, I was shapen in iniquity; and in sin did my mother conceive me." There are some who would like to think of themselves as pure, without defilement, but the Word of God is clear—"The scripture hath concluded all under sin" (Galatians 3:22). No one is free from this condemnation. Job was a man of purity and high moral standards, but like all the rest of us, he had a heart that was "deceitful above all things, and desperately wicked" (Jeremiah 17:9).

Elihu informs Job that he had falsely accused God of taking advantage of him on occasion, in creating enmity and hostility against him. "Behold, He findeth occasions against me, He counteth me for His enemy, He putteth my feet in the stocks, He marketh all my paths." Elihu concludes that Job was wrong. He was not wrong in everything, as his three companions had declared, but he was definitely wrong in these statements. Elihu said, "Behold, in this thou art not just; I will answer thee, that God is greater than man."

Though Job had spoken frequently of the sovereignty of God, Elihu reminds Job again of the importance of this vital truth. Even the thought of the sovereignty of God should silence all complaints against the Lord's gracious providences. Since God is greater than man, no human has any right to say anything more than "Thy will be done." God is not our debtor. We may be assured, whatever He sends is for our good and His glory if we are His chosen possessions through Christ. Thus Elihu asks, "Why dost thou strive against Him for He giveth not account of any of His matters." No man is to strive against God, but he is to submit to Him in everything. How foolish of weak, sinful creatures to strive against the wisdom, power, and goodness of God. To complain about the providences He permits and sends is to resist His divine wisdom. To question His dealings with us is to rebel against Him. To ask God, "Why?" regarding anything, is to question His unerring care. God is not obligated to explain to us; He need not give an account of any of His matters. He is God — we are His creatures.

We need to realize that the Lord will not take advantage of us. He has His people at heart at all times. For this reason, we can rest in the fact that "All things work together for good to them that love God, to them who are the called according to His purpose" (Romans 8:28). We need not understand all His ways. In fact, it is far better that we do not understand. God makes no mistakes; His plan is the perfect plan. Why do we fear? Why do we worry? Why do we question His provision? The answer, of course, is that we are sinful, not fully committed to His unerring guidance and care.

The Apostle Paul could say, "I have learned, in whatsoever state I am, therewith to be content" (Philippians 4:11). Though imprisoned, he did not blame God for his calamity. Rather, he rested in the fact that this was part of the perfect plan permitted by His Majesty on high. Someone has said, "The Christian should never complain of his fortune while he knows that Christ is his Friend." God is always the same. He changes not. His creation will perish, but He remains. His creation may change, but He continues the same. The passing years have changed us, our friends, our homes, and our surroundings, but they have not changed our immutable Saviour and Friend. He is "the same yesterday, and to day, and for ever" (Hebrews 13:8). What a comfort to go through life with the assurance that, come what may, He remains the same and His years will not fail.

Job had declared that God had dealt with him as an enemy, that He had left him in the dark regarding his calamity. This was not so, according to Elihu. "For God speaketh once, yea twice, yet man perceiveth it not." God speaks once; if we do not hear, He speaks again. But, if there is no response still, God must send affliction. He speaks in various ways. If our ears are closed to His earnest pleadings, then He speaks through trial and chastisement.

Often God speaks to men in the quiet of the night. Elihu tells us that He speaks "in a dream, in a vision of the night, when deep sleep falleth upon men, in slumberings upon the bed; Then He openeth the ears of men, and sealeth their instruction." Man is so busy with the cares of the day that frequently the Lord chooses to speak while the mind is closed to the events of the day.

Elihu tells us further why God speaks: "That He may withdraw man from his purpose, and hide pride from man. He keepeth back his soul from the pit, and his life from perishing by the sword." God desires that all men turn from sin to follow in the Lord's way. At the same time, God is not desirous that any perish. He longs that all men escape eternal death.

Perhaps the Lord has been speaking to you lately. He speaks to all of us through His Word as we read it and study it. We should spend much time meditating on the Scriptures that we might hear the voice of God. It has been well said, "This Book will keep you from sin, but sin will keep you from this Book." Do you listen to the voice of God daily as He speaks through His Word? No book can speak to your heart like this one.

Man must give attention to the Word of God and the message of God, that he might keep "back his soul from the pit, and his life from perishing by the sword." There are many pursuing their own evil ways, living in pride, hastening to eternal destruction. God desires that all men repent and turn from the broad road that leadeth to destruction. Which road are you on —the road that leads to death or the road that leads to life? If you have never turned to Christ, I am sure that God is speaking to you and saying, "Come unto Me, all ye that labour and are heavy laden, and I will give you rest" (Matthew 11:28).

Elihu proceeds to describe the chastenings of God often experienced by humans. "He is chastened also with pain upon his bed, and the multitude of his bones with strong pain." This verse speaks of extreme suffering in the body. Oftentimes such suffering results in health for the soul. How many of us in the hour of affliction came to Christ and were born again through God's grace.

Food that once brought pleasure to Job is abhorred now in his sickness. The body wastes away and becomes thin and emaciated, "So that his life abhorreth bread, and his soul dainty meat. His flesh is consumed away, that it cannot be seen; and his bones that were not seen stick out." Growing weaker and weaker, the afflicted gets closer and closer to the grave. "Yea, his soul draweth near unto the grave, and his life to the destroyers." The "destroyers" are the death pangs which have already seized upon him. Many have laughed and joked over the subject of death, but be sure, there is no joking at a time such as Elihu described.

Elihu informs us further that the most needed man, on an occasion like this, is a man of God who can point the dying to the way of hope and assurance in the Lord. "If there be a messenger with him, an interpreter, one among a thousand, to shew unto man His uprightness." Indeed, such a man is one among a thousand. There are not many who can speak peace and comfort in the face of death. Elihu was the man God had sent to Job at this time of great need. How thankful we should be for men of God who can lift our spirits as we tread through the valley of the shadow of death.

If the dying repents of his sin and trusts in the Lord, he will be redeemed. God's grace will be sufficient. "He is gracious unto him, and saith, Deliver him from going down to the pit: I have found a ransom." The "pit" is eternal death, reserved for those who refuse to repent and turn unto the Lord. But

God will be gracious unto those who look unto Him by faith, for the Lord Himself hath provided a ransom. According to the New Testament, Christ is the ransom. He is the ransom paid for the sin of the world. Paul, in speaking of the Lord Jesus, said of Him that He "gave Himself a ransom for all, to be testified in due time" (1 Timothy 2:6). Notice here, as is often the case, when one is redeemed from sin, his body gets well. This is not always the case, but frequently it is. Rarely is there one whose body is not affected by sin. Doubtless many in our day who are suffering physically could be delivered from their affliction by getting right with God. Sin produces suffering and sorrow. In the incident which Elihu cites, he says, "His flesh shall be fresher than a child's: he shall return to the days of his youth." In the New Testament we see a similar case. Four men brought to Jesus a man on a bed, sick of the palsy. Our Lord said to him, "Thy sins be forgiven thee." Then He declared, "Take up thy bed, and go unto thine house" (Matthew 9:2,6). After his soul was healed, his body was made well again.

The healing of the soul brings about a favorable relationship between God and the believer. "He shall pray unto God, and He will be favourable unto him: and he shall see His face with joy: for He will render unto man His righteousness." Daily the ransomed child of God will walk in the mercy of the Lord, enjoying the privilege of prayer and all the blessings that ensue from this wonderful spiritual exercise.

God is no respecter of persons. "He looketh upon men, and if any say, I have sinned, and perverted that which was right, and it profited me not; He will deliver his soul from going into the pit, and his life shall see the light." Our God is willing that all come to Him and believe on His beloved Son. He is "not willing that any should perish, but that all should come to repentance" (2 Peter 3:9).

Elihu reminds Job that God uses several ways to speak to men's hearts that they might turn to God and repent. "Lo, all these things worketh God oftentimes with man, To bring back his soul from the pit, to be enlightened with the light of the living." We see from this chapter that God uses visions (verses 15-17), afflictions (verses 19-22) and His messengers (verse 23) to speak to sinful hearts. These are various operations, but God uses them all to perform His work. All this He does to keep us from the pit of everlasting darkness. We are undeserving of His grace and mercy, but keep in mind, our God is a God of boundless love. Sometimes He must speak harshly to keep us in His chosen paths, but He does it through His great love.

It may be that you are in the midst of some severe affliction. God may be speaking. Do not complain. Do not turn away from God! Turn to Him! Examine your heart; be sure it is perfect toward Him, that He has the pre-eminence in your life. Perhaps God has spoken to you once, twice, and now again. You have not listened yet. He has sought to lead you into the green pastures beside the still waters, but you have chosen the devil's field. Hear His tender and pleading voice before it is too late. "The mercy of the Lord is from everlasting to everlasting upon them that fear Him, and His righteousness unto children's children" (Psalm 103:17).

Elihu concludes the chapter by saying, "Mark well, O Job, hearken unto me: hold thy peace, and I will speak. If thou hast any thing to say, answer me: speak, for I desire to justify thee. If not, hearken unto me: hold thy peace, and I shall teach thee wisdom." Job remained silent; he had nothing to say. Doubtless he was convicted of his own evil. Who could say anything in the light of what Elihu had spoken? Before God, we are all guilty sinners, in need of the Lord's redeeming grace. If you have not experienced the Lord's redeeming grace, take Christ into your life and receive of His fullness. You will find the Lord Jesus to be sufficient for every need of life.

JOB 34:1-37

IN CHAPTER 34, Elihu continues to speak. Turning from Job to address the three friends, he respects them by recognizing them as men of wisdom and knowledge. "Hear my words, O ye wise men; and give ear unto me, ye that have knowledge." He appeals to them to act as judges on what he is about to say. "For the ear trieth words, as the mouth tasteth meat. Let us choose to us judgment: let us know among ourselves what is good." Elihu does not profess to know it all, thus he solicits the consideration of the three witnesses. He is anxious that they lay aside all prejudice and bias and give due consideration to what is about to be said. This is a fair approach. Never are we in a better position to come to right decisions than when we frankly discuss matters with the interested persons.

When accused of sin, Job affirmed his righteousness repeatedly. He further blamed God for being unfair in His dealings with him, failing to hear and help him. To those who listened, this appeared to be a reproach on God. Elihu was disturbed tremendously. Thus he lays the charge before Job. "What man is like Job, who drinketh up scorning like water? Which goeth in company with the workers of iniquity, and walketh with wicked men." Elihu puts Job in the seat of the scornful. At the same time, he has him standing in the way of sinners. This does not mean that Job actually practiced evil with wicked men, but rather that in the opinions he expressed he talked like the ungodly frequently talked.

Further Elihu argues that Job had impressed them with the thought that "It profiteth a man nothing that he should delight himself with God." Job's argument seemed to suggest that, after all, the people of the world who live in wickedness suffer; if the child of God suffers, why should he not live like the people of the world? Job was not the only one to come to this conclusion. Many in our day feel the same way. But those who hold to this view overlook a very important truth: those who walk with God and seek to obey Him do not receive their reward in this life. Man has been created for eternity. Soon our brief span of years on this earth will be completed. Then what? Those who know the Lord will go to be with Him. Those who choose sin and deny Christ must be judged in eternal perdition. In hell no man will ever say, "It profiteth a man nothing that he should delight himself with God."

The profit of walking with God does not begin when we die: it begins immediately, the moment one receives Christ into his life. The profit is realized in the transformation that takes place in the believing heart. God removes the old lusts and puts holy motives within us. Men and women who have been bound by the shackles of sin are miraculously released by trusting in the Lord Jesus. Drunkards and dope addicts have found instantaneous peace by believing on the Lord Jesus. Who would be foolish enough to declare that there is no profit in this?

Dr. P. W. Philpott used to tell of a Sunday evening service, while he was pastoring the Moody Memorial Church of Chicago, when a young man came up to him and told what happened on the previous Sunday evening.

"My Mother and I were sitting over in Lincoln Park," said the young man. "As we started to leave, my attention was arrested by the electric sign bearing the words, 'Moody Memorial Church.' I told my Mother I understood that this church had one of the largest and finest auditoriums in America and that I would like to go in and look at it. We entered and found the evening service was on. We were amazed by the tremendous crowd. We sat down to listen. You preached that sermon on 'hope.' As I sat there, you had no idea that I was a dope addict, bound by a chain I could not break, and getting more discouraged with myself all the time. Then suddenly you reached a point in your sermon where you said, 'Jesus Christ can put hope into a hopeless heart.' Then and there I opened my heart to Christ. I took Him by faith as my Saviour. When I got outside I stepped over to a drain on Clark Street and dropped my drugs and equipment down through the iron grating. As they fell out of sight, I knew that I was a new man in Christ. I have had a happy week of new life and hope."

Yes, there is profit when a man delights himself with God. Irrespective of one's background, the Lord not only forgives but provides the strength to overcome temptation and sin. He asks in Jeremiah 32:27, "Behold, I am the LORD, the God of all flesh: is there anything too hard for Me?" No, there is nothing too hard for Him. There is much we cannot do. Some have sought to overcome sinful habits through mere human strength with no apparent success; the task was too difficult for them. But nothing is too hard for God. Why not give Him a chance to prove this to you? Why not take Jesus Christ into your life and let Him show you that He is the all-sufficient One who will not fail you?

There are two sides to salvation—God's and yours. It is true that no man can save himself by anything he can possibly do. He can be saved only by personal faith in the Lord Jesus Christ. The Scriptures make this unquestionably clear. In Titus 3:5 we read, "Not by works of righteousness which we have done, but according to His mercy He saved us, by the washing of regeneration, and the renewing of the Holy Ghost." On the other hand, it is just as true that, if a man does not do something, he will never be saved at all: he must come to the place where he faces his sins and receives the Lord Jesus Christ as his own personal Saviour and Lord. Repentance toward God and faith toward our Lord Jesus Christ are inseparable.

Job's statement, "It profiteth a man nothing that he should delight himself with God," disturbed Elihu greatly. Thus he appealed to the judgment of the three witnesses by saying, "Therefore hearken unto me, ye men of understanding: far be it from God, that He should do wickedness; and from the Almighty, that He should commit iniquity." There *is* profit in walking with God, for God will never do His servants any harm. Much of the suffering we bear in life is the result of our own wrongdoing. So often we ask, "Why did God do this to me?" In reality, we bring most of our trouble on ourselves because of our own disobedience to the laws of God. It is not a case of God's doing us wrong. We read in James 1:13, "Let no man say when he is tempted, I am tempted of God: for God cannot be tempted with evil, neither tempteth He any man." Much of the misery we bear is the result of our own failures. Not all, of course. There are many things we cannot understand in life. We shall understand them better when we meet Christ face to face. But for the present we must keep our eyes fixed upon the Lord and praise Him for all things, even as David, who said in Psalm 69:30, "I will praise the name of God with a song, and will magnify Him with thanksgiving."

Elihu proceeds to tell us further why it is profitable to walk with God. "For the work of a man shall He render unto him, and cause every man to find according to his ways." Is this not in essence the same truth we find in Galatians 6:7-8? "Be not deceived; God is not mocked: for whatsoever a man soweth, that shall he also reap. For he that soweth to his flesh shall of the flesh reap corruption; but he that soweth to the Spirit shall of the Spirit reap life everlasting." It is an inexorable law of God that good works will be rewarded and evil works will be punished, if not in this life, most certainly in the next. Let no one be deceived into thinking that God will ever abrogate this law. It will stand forever, regardless of what anyone says or thinks.

Since it is impossible for God to do wrong, Elihu says, "Yea, surely God will not do wickedly, neither will the Almighty pervert judgment." God could not possibly do wrong, for He is the Lord of all. "Who hath given Him a charge over the earth? or who hath disposed the whole world?" Is not God sovereign? Is He not the Creator and the Controller of all things? It would be unreasonable to create all things good and then to oppose Himself with wickedness.

For God to do evil would be a contradiction of His purpose in the creation of man. "If he set His heart upon man, if He gather unto Himself His spirit and His breath; All flesh shall perish together, and man shall turn again unto dust." Man's purpose in life is to enjoy God and to glorify Him forever. Humans are not created to resist God and disobey Him. Nor is it God's purpose to lead man in the paths of resistance and disobedience. God longs for all to turn to Him and believe on Him. He is holy and righteous, the God of all the truth. Thus Elihu pleads, "If now thou hast understanding, hear this: hearken to the voice of my words. Shall even he that hateth right govern? and wilt thou condemn Him that is most just?" This is a special appeal to Job. Elihu endeavors to convince Job of the unreasonableness of the argument that God was not always fair in His treatment of him. If God hated the right, could He possibly govern the universe? Such a thought would be unreasonable.

One would not dare to accuse an earthly monarch of wrongdoing, for this would be a sign of deepest disrespect. "Is it fit to say to a king, Thou art wicked? and to princes, Ye are ungodly?" But how much greater the error to accuse God of wrongdoing. "How much less to Him that accepteth not the persons of princes, nor regardeth the rich more than the poor? for they all are the work of His hands." Kings and princes are God's subjects. If we would not accuse them, what right do we have to accuse the King of kings and the Lord of lords?

Judgment will come upon wicked men because God is all-righteous. "In a moment shall they die, and the people shall be troubled at midnight, and pass away: and the mighty shall be taken away without hand." God is no respecter of persons. The mighty as well as the weak will be destroyed if they know not Christ. Let no one think that he will deceive God, "For His eyes are upon the ways of man, and He seeth all his goings. There is no darkness, nor shadow of death, where the workers of iniquity may hide themselves." In Numbers 32:23 we read, "Be sure your sin will find you out." It is possible to deceive one's employer, and sometimes even the members of one's family, but no one can hide from the eye of God.

God's judgments will be righteous and just. "For He will not lay upon man more than right; that he should enter into judgment with God. He shall break in pieces mighty men without number, and set others in their stead." God shall judge with infinite wisdom. All will be equally rewarded, the righteous for his good works and the evil man for his wickedness. God will not be unjust to any. To the righteous He will say, "Come, ye blessed of My Father, inherit the kingdom prepared for you from the foundation of the world" (Matthew 25:34). But to the wicked His words will be, "Depart from Me, ye cursed, into everlasting fire, prepared for the devil and his angels" (Matthew 25:41). I wonder which He will say to you? Do you know? You can know now, and you should know. The deciding factor is whether or not you have believed on Jesus

Christ as your Saviour and Lord. Those who know Him are
prepared for eternity. Those who have not received Him into
the life are unprepared.

Elihu informs us further that God knows every evil work of
man and judges him for them. "Therefore He knoweth their
works, and He overturneth them in the night, so that they are
destroyed." Very often God judges a wicked person to provide
an example so that others living in wickedness will repent and
turn to the Lord. "He striketh them as wicked men in the open
sight of others."

How well I recall my high school years, when God reached
into our class to take one of the prominent young people in
death. All of us were made to think, but few did anything
about getting right with God. Though we were careful about
our actions for several weeks, it did not last because there was
no real repentance, and as the result, no conversions. Oftentimes God strikes that the ungodly may give attention to the
really important things of life; but even then man continues
on in his old paths of sin.

The reason God judges men is found in verse 27, "Because
they turned back from Him, and would not consider any of His
ways." The lost go to hell not because of their evil works, but
because they reject Christ and turn their backs on Him. Actually, no one can do good works apart from God. Until he knows
the Lord, he lives in his evil continually. Thus Elihu gives us
the basic reason why man must suffer the judgment of God.
"They turned back from Him, and would not consider any of
His ways."

The results of turning from God are many. One is oppression. The unsaved man will give little thought to the rights of
others. "So that they cause the cry of the poor to come unto
Him, and He heareth the cry of the afflicted."

How different it is in the life of one who has truly met the
Lord. He has experienced the peace of God that passeth all

understanding. Because of this, he is anxious that others come to know this same marvelous peace. He is vitally interested in the welfare of others. Set free from the bondage of sin and death, he is desirous that his friends know the blessed assurance of John 8:36, "If the Son therefore shall make you free, ye shall be free indeed."

Obviously, Elihu had come to know deliverance and victory through the Lord. His words evidence the fact that he speaks out of a heart of experience. He said, "When He giveth quietness, who then can make trouble? and when He hideth His face, who then can behold Him? whether it be done against a nation, or against a man only."

One of the purposes of the new life of freedom and peace is that "the hypocrite reign not, lest the people be ensnared." God is concerned that all men come to Him and live for Him, that His will be done on earth as it is in Heaven. Elihu is intimating that there was some hypocrisy in Job's speeches. Though he was not a hypocrite in the final sense, some of his statements were hypocritical. This was sin, and Elihu proceeds to instruct Job as to what he should say to God in the face of his sin and suffering. In verse 31 there is a plea for humility and repentance: "Surely it is meet to be said unto God, I have borne chastisement, I will not offend any more." We are not to complain about chastisement; we are to bear it thankfully and humbly. In it we are to discover our own failures, and after repenting, seek the will of the Lord. It is not enough for one to be sorry for sin, he must vow in the strength of the Lord to do it no more. Job is to ask for spiritual discernment to recognize his own sin, and then for grace to turn from it. Probably nothing is more difficult than seeing our sin as God sees it. Our neighbor's sin is easily recognizable; but to see our own, and to do something about it, is usually most difficult. "That which I see not teach Thou me: if I have done iniquity, I will do no more."

Further Job is to seek above all else the mind and will of God
in everything. "Should it be according to thy mind? He will recompense it, whether thou refuse, or whether thou choose; and
not I; therefore speak what thou knowest." It appears from
what Job had to say in some of his speeches that he spoke only
human wisdom. Job's thoughts were of little importance when
laid alongside of God's perfect plan. Man's wisdom is sadly
limited, but God's is perfect.

Next Elihu turns to the three friends to solicit their judgment again. "Let men of understanding tell me, and let a wise
man hearken unto me. Job hath spoken without knowledge,
and his words were without wisdom." He then gives his charge
against Job, saying, "My desire is that Job may be tried unto the
end, because of his answers for wicked men. For he addeth rebellion unto his sin, he clappeth his hands among us, and multiplieth his words against God." At their first reading, these
words would suggest that Elihu, like the three friends, was inconsiderate and harsh, saying, "My desire is that Job may be
tried unto the end." But what he meant here was that Job
should be tried until he was willing to humble himself fully in
the sight of God. For by making false statements as he had
done, he strengthened the hands of wicked men who were
heard frequently to thrust the same arguments against God.
Very often they were heard to say that God was unjust and un-
interested in the needs of His creatures. Elihu claims that this
made matters worse for Job, "he addeth rebellion unto his sin."

What Elihu has said thus far certainly has been worth while.
We should do well to ponder his words. It may be that in like
manner God has been speaking to you, that you might be humbled in His sight. There may be some lesson you need to learn
or some change you need to make. You have been too busy to
hear His voice; now He must speak by means of a severe trial.
Oh, hear Him before it is too late. Turn to Him in your anxiety; He will not fail you. Do not trust in your own self-suffi-

ciency. Surely you have learned that this is not worth while. In 2 Corinthians 3:5 Paul says, "Not that we are sufficient of ourselves to think any thing as of ourselves; but our sufficiency is of God." Let your sufficiency be of God. Surrender completely to Christ and His control.

JOB 35:1-16

ELIHU CONTINUES his speech in this chapter by reproving both Job and his three friends. He declares another charge against Job: "Thinkest thou this to be right, that thou saidst, My righteousness is more than God's?" Job did not say this in so many words, but virtually this was the essence of what he had said. Elihu is condemning Job for having expressed the thought that because of his integrity, he did not deserve what God was doing to him. He felt, as Elihu put it, "My righteousness is more than God's."

Further in his charge, Elihu claimed that Job had said, "What advantage will it be unto thee? and, What profit shall I have, if I be cleansed from my sin?" Comparing himself with the wicked and seeing the wicked prosper in his evil, Job concluded, "Why should I live righteously—the wicked are rewarded good for their evil and the righteous are rewarded by suffering." It is quite obvious that Elihu was not altogether correct in his judgment of Job. For oftentimes Job illustrated from the prosperity of the wicked merely to show that in the end the wicked would not be prospered, while the righteous on the other hand would enter his reward. But there were occasions when Job, in his lapses from depending upon God rather than on the flesh, pitied himself and strongly intimated that the righteous life was not altogether worth while.

There are few of us who are not guilty of these declining moments when we begin to pity ourselves and our plight, with the resultant discouragement and depression. How important it is that we heed the apostle's words found in Colossians 3:2, "Set your affection on things above, not on things on the earth." We must keep our eyes fixed on Christ. If we look to ourselves, we shall fail miserably. We have a mighty Lord who can never suffer defeat. Thus, even though we are plunged into despair and sorrow on occasion, we must not forget that God will not fail us. How well David knew this. He said, "Weeping may endure for a night, but joy cometh in the morning" (Psalm 30:5). Certainly we shall weep; we shall cry even as the ungodly do. But joy is on its way. "It shall come to pass, that before they call, I will answer; and while they are yet speaking, I will hear" (Isaiah 65:24). God does not forget us. He is deeply aware of our needs. Whenever the Lord permits anything, He does it with divine intelligence for our good. There are needed lessons He wants us to learn which we cannot discover in any other place quite as well as where He puts us. Or possibly there are duties to be performed in that particular place and we are His chosen ones for the tasks. At least we should be satisfied that we are never in any place by accident, but that God has placed us where we are for some good reason. Thus be assured, we are not alone; the Lord is with us. He will not fail us.

Now Elihu has a message for Job and his three companions. He begins by pointing them in the proper direction. "Look unto the heavens, and see; and behold the clouds which are higher than thou." He reminds them that their help comes from the Lord, that God is far greater than man. Elihu would have his listeners consider that they are not dealing with frail human flesh, but with the Eternal God.

We cannot always understand God's ways. We see the heavens and the clouds far above us. These are all in the control of God, far beyond human manipulation. In the same manner, trials are far above our control, as are all the ways of God. In Isaiah 55:8-9 we read: "For My thoughts are not your thoughts, neither are your ways My ways, saith the Lord. For as the heavens are higher than the earth, so are My ways higher than your ways, and My thoughts than your thoughts."

Do not try to figure out God's providences. This is impossible. As the heavens and clouds are far above us, so are the ways of God. The most miserable people in the world are those who ask, "Why? Why did God permit this to come into my life? Why must I suffer so?" The happiest people in all the world are those who lean on the Lord without reservation or fear. We must not look at the present moment but far ahead. Consider your destination. Some day you are going to meet Christ face to face. Then you will look back on your comparatively few hours of distress and discomfort and ask, "Why did I worry and fret?" With this hope in our hearts we can have peace at all times.

Dr. W. M. Taylor tells of traveling on a train on which there was a little child who romped up and down the aisle and seemed to be at home with everybody. Looking at her frolic thus, one was unable to tell to whom she belonged. She seemed to be the property of everyone. But soon the engine gave a loud shriek as they plunged into a dark tunnel, and in a moment the child flew like a bird to nestle herself on a lady's lap. There was no question about who the lady was. This child found immediate security in the closeness of her mother.

How important that we who know the Lord snuggle up closely to Him when the trials come, realizing that He is "a very present help in trouble" (Psalm 46:1). No, do not try to understand your trial. Rest in the unchangeable promises of God. Lean your whole weight on your unfailing Lord.

Things may look hazy and dark at the moment, but soon the sun will shine. God will undertake.

Elihu says further, "If thou sinnest, what doest thou against Him? or if thy transgressions be multiplied, what doest thou unto Him?" When a man sins, he hurts himself and very often others, but God is not affected by his sin. There are some who feel that they are getting even with God by committing evil. They are under the delusion that they can pay God back for their affliction by sinning against Him. Though God may be grieved by our sin, He is never affected by it, but most certainly the sinner will be. How many there are in our day who, when faced with hardships or afflictions of any kind, go out and get drunk, thinking they can drown their troubles in beer or alcohol. Nothing could be more ridiculous, for this only adds to their troubles. Sin never provides a solution to our problems, only suffering and sorrow. "The way of transgressors is hard" (Proverbs 13:15). The way of the sinner is never anything else but hard. Sin always results in misery in the life of the sinner.

Along the Sacramento River in California there is a beautiful section of country. Suddenly one comes to an area where for miles the hills and mountainsides are as barren of trees as a desert. There are practically no signs of life—only poison oak in some places. Here is the reason for the desolation: years ago two great smelters were busy in this region, caring for the copper and other ores that needed their attention. The fumes from these smelters went far and wide with the shifting winds. Trees and vegetation were blighted. They blackened and decayed, until it seemed that no growing thing could live. Farmers protested, for the fumes were reaching out into the fertile valley sections and crops were being ruined. Finally the smelters were closed, but the devastation of a great and beautiful piece of the Sacramento Canyon has remained until this day. No new trees or useful shrubs are seen struggling into life in this awful desert. The very soil is evidently poisoned. As these fumes af-

fected the vegetation of the Sacramento Valley, in like manner
sin affects the soul, destroying all beauty and producing bar-
renness. Thus, let us be sure, no one can spite God by sin. The
sinner always brings further woe upon himself.

As a counterpart to this, Elihu asks, "If thou be righteous,
what givest thou Him? or what receiveth He of thine hand?"
As sin affects one's equanimity and happiness in life, so does
righteousness. The man who obeys God receives joy and satisfaction in his own heart, but as sin does not affect God, neither
does one's righteousness. In other words, we do not help God
out by what we do. God is not dependent on any human. He
is sovereign and all-mighty. Of course, we do help ourselves
by fulfilling the commands of God. There is a confidence
and assurance in obeying God not found in disobedience. But
let us never think that God is better off as the result of how we
live or what we do for Him. Every act of service rendered for
the Lord and to the Lord benefits not only those whom we
have helped but ourselves. God's state is not changed, though
we are blessed and profited.

What is Elihu driving at? In his speeches Job had suggested
two things. He had declared that he might just as well live
like the wicked since they are rewarded, thus intimating that
possibly he could pay God back for what he considered to be
unjust affliction. On the other hand, there were occasions when
Job overemphasized his integrity, suggesting that God should
be moved to do something about his pitiful condition on the
ground of his righteous life. But God is not bound to do anything for us. Further, we do not deserve the Lord's gracious
intervention. We are sinful and wicked, worthy only of eternal
hell. God is completely independent of any incumbency to
mankind. In Psalm 50:12 He says, "If I were hungry, I would
not tell thee: for the world is Mine, and the fulness thereof."
The Lord is not in any way dependent upon us, thus there
is no reason why He should help us.

What God does, He does because of His marvelous grace.

Considering man and his wicked ways, it is amazing that God should even hear our cries. The best of us has failed the Lord time and time again. But in His mercy God says, "For all this His anger is not turned away, but His hand is stretched out still" (Isaiah 9:21). Is this not wonderful? We have been a disobedient and gainsaying people, and yet the Lord continues to love us. In Micah 7:18 the prophet says, "Who is a God like unto Thee, that pardoneth iniquity, and passeth by the transgression of the remnant of His heritage? He retaineth not His anger for ever, because He delighteth in mercy." Yes, God delights in mercy. We are undeserving of it, but He still delights in it.

Have you experienced the mercy of God in the salvation of your soul? He will not force you to come to Himself, but moment by moment He pleads that you turn to Him and live. Consider His Word found in Ezekiel 33:11, "Say unto them, As I live, saith the Lord GOD, I have no pleasure in the death of the wicked; but that the wicked turn from his way and live: turn ye, turn ye from your evil ways."

Maybe you are a child of God but you have fallen into sin, even deep sin. Had anyone told you that you would be in the condition you are in at this moment, you would have become angry and denounced him as a fool. But here you are. I have good news for you: the grace of God is sufficient. If you are willing to confess, God will forgive your sin and you will be restored to fellowship with Him again. He is still the same. You have not affected Him, but only yourself by your sin. It is as Elihu says, "Thy wickedness may hurt a man as thou art; and thy righteousness may profit the son of man." But God is still the same: He loves you. We hurt only ourselves when we sin. We help others when we do kind things for them. But God remains the same. He is unchangeable in His goodness and grace. He will forgive you if you will ask Him.

Beginning with verse 9 of this chapter, Elihu infers that he felt Job was somewhat critical of God's mercy and goodness.

"By reason of the multitude of oppressions they make the oppressed to cry: they cry out by reason of the arm of the mighty." Doubtless Elihu has in mind Job's words as recorded in chapter 24, verse 12, "Men groan from out of the city, and the soul of the wounded crieth out: yet God layeth not folly to them." That is, God would not help them, even though they cried unto Him in the midst of their needs. Job would have us believe that if God is a righteous God, then He ought to help those who have needs when they cry unto Him.

The reason Elihu gives that God does not help them is that they do not look to Him to help. "But none saith, Where is God my maker, who giveth songs in the night?" Though they cry unto God, it appears to be merely complaining and bitterness rather than repentance and dependence. Many people who cry aloud in their calamity to God are not really interested in Him but in themselves, seeking to find quick alleviation from their suffering. James suggests this: "Ye ask, and receive not, because ye ask amiss, that ye may consume it upon your lusts" (James 4:3). Selfish praying avails nothing.

Oftentimes afflictions are sent that we might turn to the Lord in complete dependence on Him. It is hard for sinful man to realize that he has no resources of his own. Rather than go to the Lord in complete reliance, he feels that he needs only a little emergency help, but beyond this he is sufficient within himself. He overlooks the fact that God is his Maker, that the God who made him can certainly keep him and sustain him, if he will permit himself to be kept.

Frequently trials are for the purpose of opening areas to our hearts that hitherto have not been opened to God. Many of us can look back on hours of affliction as being turning points in our spiritual lives. In these seasons of distress we found the Lord in a way in which we had never known Him before.

It may be that your present trial is for the very purpose that you might surrender completely to the Lord's control. You may say, I do not know of any unsurrendered portion of my heart.

Ask God! His analysis may differ from yours. Ask Him to show you wherein you have failed to lean on Him as you should; then commit everything to Him. Remember, He is the One "who giveth songs in the night." When the trial is at its worst and all around seems the darkest, even then God can put a song in the heart because there is a way with Him. David said in Psalm 62:8, "Trust in Him at all times; ye people, pour out your heart before Him: God is a refuge for us." How true! He certainly is. He "giveth songs in the night."

Even more than this, Elihu tells us that He "teacheth us more than the beasts of the earth, and maketh us wiser than the fowls of heaven." God has created us in such a manner that we can receive His communications. He has given us the reasoning powers and the faculties to understand His truth as it is presented in the Scriptures. We are not like the beasts of the earth who lack in spiritual discernment and understanding. In Christ we can know even as we are known. Job needed to be reminded that God is gracious, that He does hear the cry of the oppressed and the afflicted if they are sincerely concerned about the will of God rather than selfish interests.

Elihu declares that unless one cries unto the Lord in humility, he might just as well not call on the Lord. "There they cry, but none giveth answer, because of the pride of evil men. Surely God will not hear vanity, neither will the Almighty regard it." When proud men pray, their prayers go unheard and unanswered because God will not give attention to a proud heart. In Proverbs 6:17-19 the inspired man of wisdom tells us of six things that God hates: "Yea, seven are an abomination unto Him: A proud look, a lying tongue, and hands that shed innocent blood, An heart that deviseth wicked imaginations, feet that be swift in running to mischief, A false witness that speaketh lies, and he that soweth discord among brethren." What is first on the list? "A proud look." Pride is an abomination to God. Thus the basic requisite to be realized, if anyone is to be heard by God, is humility, which in the strict sense is discipline and submission to the Lord's control.

As we draw to the close of the chapter, we find Elihu picking up another statement made by Job, "Although thou sayest thou shalt not see Him, yet judgment is before Him; therefore trust thou in Him." In the valley of despair Job had felt so forsaken that he doubted he would ever see the Lord. But Elihu assures Job that judgment is before him. No one need worry about seeing the Lord. If we have met Him on His terms, there is no doubt about it—we shall see Him. God's Word is not contingent on our varying concepts. Thus Elihu says, "Trust thou in Him." This is good advice. One's faith may waver, but God's promises never change. For this reason, we must fully believe Him.

Elihu feels that not only is mercy being shown Job, but because of Job's attitude of complaint there is judgment in the Lord's actions. "But now, because it is not so, He hath visited in His anger; yet he knoweth it not in great extremity." Elihu would have Job see that, because he failed to humble himself completely in God's sight and because he refused to depend upon Him for all things, judgment was being visited upon him.

Elihu concludes, "Therefore doth Job open his mouth in vain; he multiplieth words without knowledge." He is not as severe as Job's friends in his accusation. They had declared that Job was a hypocrite; Elihu feels that Job had spoken, when he would have done well to humble himself in the sight of the Lord and listen. Have not all of us been guilty of this same evil? How important that we examine our hearts at this moment. Is there any trace of pride or self-dependence? If so, let us yield ourselves fully to the control of Christ, and then trust Him for all things.

JOB 36:1-33

IN HIS FOURTH SPEECH, Elihu pleads with his audience to be
patient and listen a little longer, for he has yet more to say
which he feels is divinely given. "Suffer me a little, and I will
shew thee that I have yet to speak on God's behalf." Elihu does
not take credit for what he is saying, but he tells us that this is
"knowledge from afar." He honors the Lord as his Maker and
strongly declares that God is righteous in all of His dealings
with men, and that God can never be unrighteous. Job had
intimated in his speeches that God had been unrighteous on
occasion because He did not help the needy when He could
have.

Elihu vows to speak the truth. "For truly my words shall not
be false." Because he speaks the truth he can say, "He that is
perfect in knowledge is with thee." He was "perfect in knowledge" in the sense that he was a man of integrity, seeking to
present the truth as God had given it to him.

In verse 5, Elihu begins this particular speech on behalf of
his Maker by stating, "Behold, God is mighty, and despiseth

not any: He is mighty in strength and wisdom." Job felt that he had been ignored by God because of the lack of immediate divine intervention on his behalf. Elihu disagreed. He would have us to see that God ignores no one. His grace is sufficient for all.

Job argued further that God takes care of the wicked, while often overlooking the needs of the righteous. Elihu informed him that it was not so. "He preserveth not the life of the wicked: but giveth right to the poor." The wicked live all the days of their appointed time, but theirs is a hard life. God tells us this in Proverbs 13:15, "The way of transgressors is hard." Then, of course, following the death of the wicked, judgment must be faced. Indeed, there is nothing attractive about this kind of living. But on the other hand, God takes care of the poor, that is, the poor in spirit, those who have humbled themselves in the sight of the Lord and acknowledged Him as their Saviour. In Psalm 5:12 we read, "For Thou, LORD, wilt bless the righteous; with favour wilt Thou compass him as with a shield." How wonderfully He undertakes for those who love Him, for those who have believed on His beloved Son as Lord. To them He says in Psalm 32:8, "I will instruct thee and teach thee in the way which thou shalt go: I will guide thee with Mine eye." No, God will not forsake the righteous. He promises to undertake for His own. Elihu is certainly correct in what he is saying here.

Notice further what Elihu has to say about God. "He withdraweth not His eyes from the righteous: but with kings are they on the throne; yea, He doth establish them for ever, and they are exalted." Not only does He focus His eyes on His beloved ones; He never removes His eyes from them. "He withdraweth not His eyes from the righteous." It may seem on occasion that providence has been withdrawn from us, but this is impossible. David says in Psalm 48:14, "For this God is our God for ever and ever: He will be our guide even unto death." God's redeemed ones are the Lord's eternal possession. Thus

He promises to care for them, even to the extent of exalting them. As subjects respect and honor their king, so the Lord is gracious to His born-again children, and expresses His favor toward them as the subject toward the king. Oh, what grace is manifested here, that we who are so deserving of eternal perdition are honored and exalted in such a manner by our Maker. Such an attitude on the part of God, however, is no promise of escape from affliction. Nor is affliction a proof of hypocrisy, as Job's friends had stated. On the other hand, neither is it an evidence of God's neglect, as Job had declared. Affliction is for the purpose of discipline and instruction, as Elihu has said, "And if they be bound in fetters, and be holden in cords of affliction; Then He sheweth them their work, and their transgressions that they have exceeded." The word "work" here has to do with one's transgressions. Sin is always the work of the human heart. If there is any good in us, it is because of God at work in us.

In affliction, God makes us conscious of our sinfulness that we might yield to His lordship. "He openeth also their ear to discipline, and commandeth that they return from iniquity." When God chastens us, He teaches us. Oftentimes He makes us conscious of sins we would not normally recognize. With the affliction comes the call to "return from iniquity." The wise man will heed the call of God and turn from his wicked way, that he might enjoy the blessing of the Lord. The foolish man will continue in sin, but in so doing he will bring further judgment upon himself. "If they obey and serve Him, they shall spend their days in prosperity, and their years in pleasures. But if they obey not, they shall perish by the sword, and they shall die without knowledge."

Obedience to God is the only sure way to prosperity and peace. Those who walk with the Lord day by day enjoy His abundant provision materially, physically, and spiritually. But those who refuse to repent, if not killed by their affliction, will die by ultimate judgment. For the sword of the Lord will come upon them when they least expect it, and they will die without further notice, or as Elihu says, "without knowledge." God speaks to us in affliction, that we might yield to His will and follow and obey Him.

It is very possible that God is speaking to you through financial trouble, domestic problems, sickness, or some other method of divine chastisement. What is the message He would have you hear? Open your ears to His voice. Do not be deceived by your pride. Bow to your Maker and respect Him as Lord of lords. Acknowledge Christ as the One who died for your sins and rose again. Should you be a Christian, confess all known sin, that you might walk in fellowship with the Lord.

Elihu now speaks of a particular kind of sinner, those who are "hypocrites in heart." Of them he says, they "heap up wrath: they cry not when He bindeth them."

There are many who appear to be Christians outwardly. That is, they attend church, they pray, some even take an active part in the work of the Lord; but inwardly they are an abomination to God because they are hypocrites at heart. They have never been born again. All they do is but a sham. Of these Jesus said in Matthew 15:8, "This people draweth nigh unto Me with their mouth, and honoureth Me with their lips; but their heart is far from Me." Because they are unrepentant at heart, they are heaping up wrath. They are bringing the judgment of God upon themselves. They think they are heaping up treasures by what they are doing, but actually they are provoking God's wrath because of the evil nature of their sinful hearts. Of them God says in Romans 2:5, "But after thy hardness and impenitent heart, treasurest up unto thyself wrath against the day of wrath and revelation of the righteous judgment of God."

God's wrath is often executed upon the wicked prematurely because of their sins. "They die in youth, and their life is among the unclean." They had hoped to live to a ripe old age but suddenly the judgment of God comes upon them. Then they are confined to hell to spend eternity with the vilest of men, adulterers, thieves, murderers, drunkards, yea, all who have rejected the grace of God and spurned the offer of salvation. They will be in hell because of the hardness of their hearts. God has spoken to them many times in life by way of affliction, but they refused to listen. Elihu says in verse 13, "They cry not when He bindeth them." That is, when God afflicted them, they refused to repent and seek His mercy. Thus they must suffer the consequences. For as God says in Ezekiel 18:20, "The soul that sinneth, it shall die."

Notice what the Lord does for those who humble themselves in His sight during their affliction: "He delivereth the poor in his affliction, and openeth their ears in oppression." God is always ready to help those who are poor in spirit and of a broken and contrite heart. He draws near to them in tenderness during their severest affliction, and He speaks to them in words of comfort and hope as they faithfully trust Him until His chastening ends.

In verse 16, Elihu addresses himself in particular to Job, saying, "Even so would He have removed thee out of the strait into a broad place, where there is no straitness; and that which should be set on thy table should be full of fatness." Job might have enjoyed God's richest blessing even in his severest affliction had he refused to complain against God's providence and care, and had he humbled himself in full and complete dependence on the gracious hand of God's mercy. The Lord promises in Luke 14:11, "For whosoever exalteth himself shall be abased; and he that humbleth himself shall be exalted." Yes, God always cares for those who are willing to humble themselves in His sight.

Elihu condemned Job by accusing him of acting like the wicked when they are tried. "But thou hast fulfilled the judgment of the wicked: judgment and justice take hold on thee." In trial, the wicked complain and murmur against God rather than rest in the holiness of His providence. Thus because God is all-righteous and just, Job should expect further suffering as the result of his disobedience.

Elihu pleads with Job to repent of his evil in the light of the wrath of God. "Because there is wrath, beware lest He take thee away with His stroke: then a great ransom cannot deliver thee." Job is warned here that he might suffer physical death as the climax of God's chastisement because of his failure to repent. There is no escape from the wrath of God without repentance. Money, wisdom, friends are all to no avail when the anger of God is kindled against an unrepentant soul.

Elihu says further, "Will He esteem thy riches? no, not gold, nor all the forces of strength." How many there are in our day trusting in their money as a means to security. Money cannot possibly enable one to escape from the wrath of God. Man must be judged for his sin unless it is put under the blood of Christ, who died for all sin at Calvary. "Forasmuch as ye know that ye were not redeemed with corruptible things, as silver and gold, from your vain conversation received by tradition from your fathers; But with the precious blood of Christ, as of a lamb without blemish and without spot" (1 Peter 1:18-19). Christ will freely forgive on the ground of His shed blood if only sinful man will turn to Him and repent.

Elihu continues by saying to Job, "Desire not the night, when people are cut off in their place." It would seem that 'night" as used here refers to death. Job had pleaded to die as an escape from his calamity. But Elihu would have him understand that death is not always an escape. Oftentimes it produces even more misery because of an unrepentant heart. Truly a man who complains against God and resists His divine counsels is not ready to die. Rather than die, Elihu informs Job, he should do something about his sin. "Take heed, regard not iniquity: for this hast thou chosen rather than affliction." This is certainly a worth-while plea, for only as a man is willing to face up to his own sin and do something about it, is he ready to die. Of course, there is only one thing he can do about his sin, and that is to confess it to Christ and acknowledge Christ as Saviour and Lord of his life. When Jesus Christ died on the cross, He did not die for His own sin, for He had none. He died for your sin and for mine. Thus what Elihu said to Job might be said to each one of us, that we may examine our hearts before God: "Take heed, regard not iniquity: for this hast thou chosen rather than affliction." Is this true of you? Have you chosen sin rather than respond to the love of God? If so, give attention to the words of Isaiah 55:7, "Let the wicked forsake his way, and the unrighteous man his thoughts: and let him return unto the LORD, and He will have mercy upon him; and to our God, for He will abundantly pardon."

OUR REFUGE

Are you drifting on life's ocean?
  Ere you sink beneath the wave
Anchor to the Rock of Ages:
  He will rescue, He will save.
There's no other Friend like Jesus,
  For He died to set us free,
If we will believe the record
  Of His death and victory.
Then love the Lord with all your heart.
  Love and lift your fellow men.
Turn from sin, and follow Jesus;
  For you must be born again.
All have sinned. Not one is righteous:
  All, like sheep, have gone astray.
Only Christ can save the lost one,
  He's the Truth, the Life, the Way.

—Selected

Let Christ become all that He wants to be to you—your Saviour, your Provider, your Guide, your Friend.

Elihu continues by drawing attention to the greatness and majesty of God. Because of who He is and what He is, God should be respected and honored by everyone. He is sovereign no one has any right to tell God what to do or how to do it. "Behold, God exalteth by His power: who teacheth like Him?" God has the right to exalt or humble those He pleases. He need not take orders nor instructions from any. His teachings are final. For this reason His Word, the Bible, is the only infallible rule of faith and practice. No one could ever teach God, for He is the Fountain of all truth. Thus we are to respect His Word as truth. "All scripture is given by inspiration of God" (2 Timothy 3:16). It is not to be questioned or criticized. It is to be received as the authoritative truth of God.

As God's Word is truth, so His providences are without error. "Who hath enjoined Him His way? or who can say, Thou hast wrought iniquity?" Who would be brazen enough or fool enough to declare that God is a sinner? He who is all-righteous has never known anything but righteousness. For this reason we are to acknowledge Him as the only true and holy Deity.

"Remember that thou magnify His work, which men behold." God has given evidence of "His work" wherever we look. Thus no one is excused, for every human has some association with the handiwork of God. The trees, the grass, the shrubs, the heavens with the stars, the sun, the moon, all evidence the work of God. Everyone may see it, Elihu declares. Paul tells us in Romans 1:20, "For the invisible things of Him from the creation of the world are clearly seen, being understood by the things that are made, even His eternal power and Godhead; so that they are without excuse." Man is without excuse because God's works of creation are clearly seen, bespeaking the fact of God's greatness and power. Every man, even those who do not have the benefit of the Word of God, may see God's handiwork. For, "There is no speech nor language, where their voice is not heard" (Psalm 19:3).

"Behold, God is great," declares Elihu. Indeed, He is great in power, great in wisdom, and great in wealth. But in our present limited state, "we know Him not." From His revealed knowledge we know that He is, but not what He is. In this life we know of Him only in part. Some day, praise God, we shall know Him as He is.

God cannot be limited to years, for He is eternal. Elihu tells us further, "Neither can the number of His years be searched out." He is without beginning and without ending—the eternal "I Am."

Not only does Elihu tell us of God's greatness but also of His providential works. "For He maketh small the drops of water: they pour down rain according to the vapour thereof; Which the clouds do drop and distil upon man abundantly." Here is one of God's many miraculous phenomena, the sending of rain for the welfare of man. Elihu asks, "Can any understand the spreadings of the clouds, or the noise of His tabernacle?" He is referring to the thick clouds that seem to cover the heavens at the time of storm. The "noise of His tabernacle" is literally "the crashing," that is, the thunder. In verse 30 he refers to the lightning, which in its great light penetrates to the bottom of the ocean, laying even the darkness of the ocean bare. "Behold, He spreadeth His light upon it, and covereth the bottom of the sea."

Notice the twofold effect of rain storms. "For by them judgeth He the people; He giveth meat in abundance." Oftentimes God sends judgment through severe storms, reminding men and women of His mighty power and of the need of worshiping Him. On the other hand, by the sending of the rains He nourishes the crops that feed our bodies.

God does not send storms upon us without warning. "With clouds He covereth the light; and commandeth it not to shine by the cloud that cometh betwixt." Usually before the storm strikes, the clouds cover the skies. Often the lightning precedes the rains. Elihu says, "The noise thereof sheweth concerning it." Further he says, "the cattle also concerning the vapour." With the warning signals of a storm, cattle usually seek shelter.

What is God telling us in these verses? Before judgment,

warning is given, so that man is without excuse. As storms are preceded by warnings, so throughout the Word of God we find scores of warnings to hardened sinners to repent before it is too late. Have you turned from your sins to the living God? Do you know Christ as your Saviour and Lord? Oh, if not, turn to Him immediately. If you are a Christian, has God been speaking to you about some sin in your life? You would do well to hear His voice before it is too late. The Apostle Paul declares, "I beseech you as strangers and pilgrims, abstain from fleshly lusts, which war against the soul" (1 Peter 2:11). Claim victory over your sin through the power of Christ. Not only has life been given to all who believe, but divine power has been given to live to the glory of God and the good of our fellow men. We have the Holy Spirit, the Holy Scriptures, the fellowship of the saints, and the blessed hope of the Lord's return. What possible excuse has a Christian for not living the victorious life? The Christian life is the one and only full life for time and eternity. If there is sin hindering your walk with the Lord, confess it and ask God to enable you to be more than a conqueror through Christ. He will hear your prayer and answer if you are sincere and repentant.

JOB 37:1-24

ELIHU CONTINUES his informative speech by reminding Job of
the mighty power of God as evidenced in the changes of the
weather. As weather changes are controlled by God, Elihu
would have us realize that every change in any of the circumstances of life are also prompted by God's will and purpose.

Elihu begins by speaking of the thunder and lightning.
He says, "At this also my heart trembleth, and is moved out of
his place." Doubtless the storms had already begun out of
which God was to speak to Job. Hearing the thunder and seeing the lightning probably induced Elihu to speak as he did,
for they had exerted a profound influence on him.

Recognizing the thunder as the voice of God, Elihu's heart
trembled, so much so that it seemed that it would jump out
of its place. Thus he pleads with Job to "Hear attentively the
noise of His voice, and the sound that goeth out of His mouth."
In Psalm 29:3 thunder is spoken of as "the voice of the Lord."
Indeed, we are reminded in the sound of thunder of the greatness and splendor of our omnipotent God.

It should be understood that whatever course the lightning may take, or however great or small the sound of thunder, every detail of these phenomena is directed and ordered by God. "He directeth it under the whole heaven, and His lightning unto the ends of the earth." The lightning flashes, and "after it a voice roareth," says Elihu. Because light travels faster than sound, first the lightning is seen and after a brief interval the thunder is heard. The thunder is termed "the voice of His excellency" probably because it reminds us of God's greatness and power. Lightning and thunder always go together. We may be too distant to hear the thunder, but somewhere it is heard.

Elihu says further, "He will not stay them when His voice is heard." God will not prevent the lightning nor the winds and rain. Usually the thunder is an evidence that more of the storm is to follow. In the storm which follows, God speaks to the people of the world, reminding them of His majesty.

Elihu makes an application of what he has already said, declaring, "God thundereth marvellously with His voice; great things doeth He, which we cannot comprehend." As God speaks in the thunder, so He speaks in many ways. In fact, His works are so great that we could not begin to comprehend their greatness. Some people, because they cannot comprehend everything, refuse to believe that God exists. Because their finite minds cannot fully understand the infinite, they decline to acknowledge the fact of God.

I am reminded of the atheist who met a farmer friend on his way to church. A friendly argument about God followed. The atheist asked if God were a great God or a little God. The farmer replied, "Both."

"How can He be both?"

The answer came, "He is so great that the heavens cannot contain Him, and so little that He dwells in my poor heart." Indeed, our God is a great God, and who by searching can find Him out?

The most remarkable thing of all is that this transcendent,

almighty God, who created the universe and all that is therein, has condescended to reveal Himself to sinful man. Not only is He a great God but He is a loving God. For this reason He sent His beloved Son into the world to die for the sins of all who believe on Him. As God created the universe and as daily He directs every phase of nature, so He has provided an eternal plan of salvation, that man may have more than mere animal life. God provided man with a soul and, at the same time, He offers eternal salvation to every human on the ground of faith in Jesus Christ. The God who speaks in the sounds of the thunder and the flashes of lightning also speaks in the person of His Son. We read in Hebrews 1:2, "God . . . hath in these last days spoken unto us by His Son." The words He would have everyone hear are found in Matthew 11:28, "Come unto Me, all ye that labour and are heavy laden, and I will give you rest."

It seems almost unreasonable that a God who is as great as our God would have so much interest in sinful man. But as He orders every particular of nature by His divine wisdom, He is concerned about every aspect of our lives. He longs that all men come to Him to receive eternal salvation by believing on His Son. Jesus Christ is the only substitute for sin. In 2 Corinthians 5:21 we read, "God . . . hath made Him to be sin for us, who knew no sin; that we might be made the righteousness of God in Him."

A man and his wife were visited by two missionaries and were invited to their open-air meetings. The couple attended and both trusted the Saviour. The man told one of the missionaries that, earlier that morning, as he had wandered around the streets looking for a job, he had looked up into the sky and said, "Oh, God, if You are there and can give me a sign that You are interested in me, please do."

"Seven hours later," said the missionary, "I was leading him to the Lord to whom he had prayed."

Maybe you have wondered if there is a God. You have

heard His voice in the thunder and seen His evidence in the lightning, but you are not quite convinced. Do you want to find out? Let me tell you how. Believe in your heart that Christ died for your sins and that He rose again. Ask Him to come into your life. You may be sure that He will. At the same time, He will make things plain to you. He can remove the doubts and give assured understanding. As you faithfully read His Word day by day, you will be thoroughly convinced that there is a God and that His Son, Jesus Christ, is the only Saviour.

Elihu had declared, "God thundereth marvellously with His voice; great things doeth He, which we cannot comprehend." He proceeds to tell us about some of these great things. "For He saith to the snow, Be thou on the earth; likewise to the small rain, and to the great rain of His strength." According to His will, God speaks and the snow falls. As to how much or how little, this again is under the control of the Lord of all. There have been numerous times when God has revealed His mighty power through a snowfall. Is it not amazing that an entire city or state can be completely incapacitated in just a few hours by a severe snowstorm?

I recall one time, while I was living in New York City, when in just one short night everything in that great city was completely curtailed by a heavy snowfall. Indeed, all theorists, speculators, philosophers, dictators, armies, must bow to God's power. For God's weakness is infinitely superior to man's puny strength.

Before the mighty conqueror Napoleon invaded Russia, he informed the Russian ambassador that the empire would be destroyed. The ambassador's reply was, "Man proposes, but God disposes."

"Tell your master," thundered the arrogant Napoleon, "that I am he that proposes and I am he that disposes."

This was a direct challenge to the living God to show who was ruler of the world, and God accepted this challenge. He moved not from His august throne, but He sent one of His most humble messengers, the crystal snowflake, to punish the audacious boaster. In his retreat from Moscow, Napoleon left on the frozen plains the bulk of his vast army, and the official returns of the Russian authorities reported 213,516 dead Frenchmen and 95,816 dead horses.

Would that the present-day rulers in Russia were prepared to recognize the sovereignty and supremacy of God as did their predecessors a century and a half ago. But whether or not men bow to God Almighty, the fact remains that God is sovereign, and nations, like individuals, flout His authority to their own peril and ruin. Indeed, it is true as Elihu says, "He sealeth up the hand of every man; that all men may know His work." Foolish men resist the counsel of God. They overlook His providences in nature. But frequently He so confounds them that they are hindered and hampered from doing their work. By the snowfall, the heavy rains, or the flood God stops the activities of men.

Oftentimes God seals up the hands of men so that their hearts might be opened to Him. I am sure you will agree that there have been many times in your life when you were help-less, certain that there was absolutely nothing you could do about your perplexities. You were driven to your knees to de-pend upon the Lord God Almighty. He did not fail. Even though your hands were sealed, the hands of God continued to work. Oh, that we might depend upon Him more and trust Him for all things. How we need to reaffirm with Jeremiah, "Ah Lord GOD! behold, Thou hast made the heaven and the earth by Thy great power and stretched out arm, and there is nothing too hard for Thee" (Jeremiah 32:17). What a foolish lot we are to worry when we have such a God as ours.

Not only does God care for His people but He cares for all of His creation. Elihu says, "Then the beasts go into dens, and remain in their places." By God-given instinct the animals know to search out a shelter. God provides for them and cares for them. Animals seem to have more dependence on the Creator than many humans. I am reminded of Matthew 6:26, "Behold the fowls of the air: for they sow not, neither do they reap, nor gather into barns; yet your heavenly Father feedeth them. Are ye not much better than they?" The God who cares for the birds in the air and the animals in the forest will care for you, if you will let Him.

What is your particular need at this moment? Is God not sufficient? Have you gone to Him in prayer and told Him that you believe He can do all things? Indeed, He can. What is your need — physical, material, mental; or is it spiritual? Whatever it may be, turn to the Lord God. Look to Christ! He will prove Himself to be abundantly sufficient.

In speaking further of the handiwork of God, Elihu mentions the winds, the frost, and the clouds, which are all under the Lord's constant control. "Out of the south cometh the whirlwind: and cold out of the north. By the breath of God frost is given: and the breadth of the waters is straitened. Also by watering He wearieth the thick cloud: He scattereth His bright cloud." In verse 12 he tells us that the clouds, like the lightning, are guided by God's wisdom and power. "And it is turned round about by His counsels: that they may do whatsoever He commandeth them upon the face of the world in the earth." Never are the elements without purpose. "He causeth it to come, whether for correction, or for His land, or for mercy." God may use the elements to bring about judgment. On the other hand, He may use them for productivity. Whatever the case, all is according to His wise counsel.

We need to remind ourselves constantly of the grace of God in the sending of the rain and the sunshine to produce the crops that sustain life. How frequently we take things for granted. Suddenly a drought comes and we begin to complain of the lack of supply. But how little praise is given to God for His constant provision. In Philippians 4:19 the Apostle Paul makes a tremendous statement, "But my God shall supply all your need according to His riches in glory by Christ Jesus." Our great

God supplies all the needs of the universe, but He also supplies all the needs of His people.

There is one word in Philippians 4:19 that must not be overlooked if one is to claim this promise. It is the personal pronoun "my," "But *my* God." Many believe in *a* God, or even in *the* God; but that is not enough. It would be the same as saying, "There is *a* bank." There may be many banks, but you may be miserably poor. If you can say, "*My* bank," it is obvious that you have an investment in that bank. Indeed, there is *a* God, but until you can claim Him as your own personal God, He will be of no great comfort to you. How can you know Him personally? Through His Son, Jesus Christ! Jesus declared in John 14:6, "No man cometh unto the Father but by Me." Is the eternal God your God? Oh, if not, let the Lord Jesus come into your heart. Then you will be able to say, "But *my* God shall supply all my need."

Elihu now urges Job to give heed to what he has just said. "Hearken unto this, O Job: stand still, and consider the wondrous works of God." This is worth-while advice for all of us. How needful that we stop occasionally to consider who God is and how wonderful He is. As we pause to behold the marvelous works of nature all about us, we should fall before the Majesty on High to give thanks for His provision and goodness. It is easy to overlook the source of the many joys and blessings we receive. We need to remind ourselves frequently that all these wonderful things come from the hand of God. David knew the source of his provision, for in Psalm 68:19 he declared, "Blessed be the Lord, who daily loadeth us with benefits, even the God of our salvation." How important that we "stand still, and consider the wondrous works of God."

Next Elihu considers the gross inadequacy of finite knowledge as contrasted to the infinite. Speaking of God's wondrous works Elihu asks, "Dost thou know when God disposed them, and caused the light of His cloud to shine? Dost thou know the balancings of the clouds, the wondrous works of Him which is perfect in knowledge?" We can see the handiwork of God, but who of us knows the counsels and purposes behind all this? We know some things about the changing of the seasons, but consider how much we do not know. For example, do you know, as Elihu asks, "How thy garments are warm, when He quieteth the earth by the south wind?" All we know is that our winter clothes suddenly become too warm when the season changes, and we must seek lighter garments. Man in his conquest of space has gained some knowledge of the skies, but how inferior, compared to the knowledge possessed by Him who created the skies. "Hast thou with Him spread out the sky, which is strong, and as a molten looking glass?" Indeed, the sky is as a great mirror, reflecting the glory of God. Ironically, Elihu appeals to Job to explain these things regarding nature if he can, for as yet man had not been able to give any adequate explanation. "Teach us what we shall say unto Him; for we cannot order our speech by reason of darkness." After thousands of years we are still in the dark as to the explanations. Even if we were to offer explanations for much that is unknown in nature, later discoveries would probably prove our ignorance. "Shall it be told Him that I speak? if a man speak, surely he shall be swallowed up."

Who can begin to fathom the wonders of God's creation? For example, swallows can fly 7,000 miles without chart, compass, or radio beam, and land at the place they left six months before. Spiders can make a silken rope, creating the materials in their own chemical laboratory, very fine but strong enough for their own transport through the air. Beavers are engineers, without aid of tools, cement, or precision instruments; they can construct bridges, tunnels, roadways, canals, and dams that last for years.

Bees, wasps, and ants solve their housing problems by building well-ventilated, weatherproofed, well-designed, and practical apartment houses. A young squid travels by jet propulsion; he swims by pumping water through a tube along his thin, streamlined body. When pursued, he can gather great speed, and he always jets backwards. When he gets going fast enough, he can set his fins at an angle and take off into the air. He has been seen to fly as far as sixty yards at one take off, leaving his foes far behind.

A group of scientists in Chicago were experimenting. A female moth of a rare species was placed in a room. Four miles away a male moth of the same species was released. In spite of the din and smoke of the city, in spite of the distance and the fact that the female was in a closed room, in a few hours the male moth was found beating his wings against the windows of the room in which the female moth was confined.

Who could begin to explain these miracles of nature? The only answer we can give is that God made it so.

Next Elihu says, "And now men see not the bright light which is in the clouds: but the wind passeth, and cleanseth them." This, of course, refers to the sun shining above the clouds. God sends the winds, the clouds are dispersed, and then the light is seen.

Many times believers become disturbed because they feel that God has forsaken them. Covered over with the clouds of sorrow and sadness, they cannot see the light. But soon the clouds are dispersed and the glory of the Lord is revealed clearly. Thus the true believer need not despair, for God promises, "I will never leave thee, nor forsake thee" (Hebrews 13:5).

Elihu assures Job that even though the storm clouds may be over us, "Fair weather cometh out of the north: with God is terrible majesty." That is, God in His splendor always overwhelms His adversary. Even as He dispels the storms by the clearing winds from the north, so He will produce relief in the midst of our trials. He promises in 1 Corinthians 10:13, "There hath no temptation taken you but such as is common to man: but God is faithful, who will not suffer you to be tempted above that ye are able; but will with the temptation also make a way to escape, that ye may be able to bear it." God will never fail if only we lean upon Him.

God's ways are unfathomable. "Touching the Almighty, we cannot find Him out: He is excellent in power, and in judgment, and in plenty of justice: He will not afflict." Man by searching with his human ingenuity cannot find God out, nor can he understand His ways. It would be ridiculous for man to try, for he is but human. God is divine. "Men do therefore fear Him," Elihu says. This is what we should do — respect God, bow before Him, and acknowledge Him as Lord of all.

Further Elihu says, "He respecteth not any that are wise of heart." God cannot help those who refuse to bow to His beloved Son, Jesus Christ. "The preaching of the cross is to them that perish foolishness; but unto us which are saved it is the power of God. For it is written, I will destroy the wisdom of the wise, and will bring to nothing the understanding of the prudent" (1 Corinthians 1:18-19). Possibly you have been trying to figure out all the knowledge you have received concerning God. Stop trying! Maybe you have said you will not believe until you can understand it all. If you really mean this, then you will never believe. As you cannot understand the billions of intricacies of nature, so you cannot figure out salvation. Thank God that we need not figure it out. The Bible simply says, "Whosoever shall call upon the name of the Lord shall be saved" (Romans 10:13). Have you called upon His Name?

JOB 38:1-41

HAVING LISTENED to the theories of Job's three friends and then to the arguments of Elihu, the next voice we hear is that of the Master. "Then the LORD answered Job out of the whirlwind, and said, Who is this that darkeneth counsel by words without knowledge?" The Lord Jehovah appears unexpectedly in a whirlwind, and as His voice was heard by Moses on Mount Sinai, so He is heard by Job, his three friends, and Elihu. God speaks of Job as the one "that darkeneth counsel by words without knowledge." Job is about to discover how limited human wisdom is apart from divine revelation.

The Lord begins by saying to Job, "Gird up now thy loins like a man; for I will demand of thee, and answer thou Me." In facing the counsels and providences of God, one must be brave and courageous as a soldier going to war. Paul writes in 1 Corinthians 16:13, "Watch ye, stand fast in the faith, quit you like men, be strong." Thus the Lord calls upon Job to be valiant and bold as the truth of his case is revealed.

Job had expressed perplexity and even doubt as he pon-

dered the purpose for his extreme suffering, but God reminds
him that there are many things man cannot know because of
his lack of knowledge. Thus God begins a series of questions
to reveal man's natural ignorance of divine chastening on the
grounds of limited wisdom.

"Where wast thou when I laid the foundations of the earth?
declare, if thou hast understanding." Job, as well as his friends,
had argued with each other on the basis of mere human intelligence. How limited they were! Though they knew something
of the effect, they knew little of the cause. They were not with
God at the creation of the world to know why He did things
as He did. If man is fully to understand the ways of the universe, he must know far more than he can see. Next, several
questions are asked concerning the creation of the world. "Who
hath laid the measures thereof, if thou knowest? or who hath
stretched the line upon it? Whereupon are the foundations
thereof fastened? or who laid the corner stone thereof?" Of
course, the answer to these questions is, "God." There can be
no other answer. This being the case, what right do we have
to question divine providence? He who created all things has
the perfect right to control all things.

In speaking of the establishment of daytime as opposed to
night, God continues by asking, "When the morning stars sang
together, and all the sons of God shouted for joy?" "Sons of
God" refers to the angels who rejoice in the power and the
works of the Almighty. Further revelations of God's creative
power are revealed as He asks, "Or who shut up the sea with
doors, when it brake forth, as if it had issued out of the womb?"
Not only did Jehovah create the waters; He controls them. Even
the clouds of the sky are all of divine composition. "When I
made the cloud the garment thereof, and thick darkness a swad-
dlingband for it." The seas are lined by the shores containing
cliffs and rocks, broken up according to the purposes of God.
"And brake up for it My decreed place, and set bars and doors."
The sea and all within are under the control of the Almighty

hand. "Hitherto shalt thou come, but no further: and here shall thy proud waves be stayed?"

Turning from creation to the marvels of the present world, God asks, "Hast thou commanded the morning since thy days; and caused the dayspring to know his place; That it might take hold of the ends of the earth, that the wicked might be shaken out of it?" The answer is obvious: Job had not caused the days to appear, nor had he been responsible for light covering the universe at its appointed time. God says further, "It is turned as clay to the seal; and they stand as a garment. And from the wicked their light is withholden, and the high arm shall be broken." As clay responds to an object rolled over it, leaving its impression, so the earth which appeared to be without form and void, responded to light, giving evidence of its hills, mountains, and valleys. But as the light of the sun reveals the hidden things of the earth, so the eternal light of the knowledge of God reveals sin. No man shall be able to escape the judgment of God. Hebrews 9:27 is clear, "It is appointed unto men once to die, but after this the judgment."

Job had complained of unjust treatment from the hand of the Almighty, but he must be reminded afresh that God sees all and knows all; not only is He the Creator, He is also the Provider. Job had not been forsaken as he thought—the Eternal God was close at hand. It may be at this moment that you need to realize this. You may feel forsaken and forlorn, but be of good cheer: "The eternal God is thy refuge, and underneath are the everlasting arms" (Deuteronomy 33:27).

A friend tells how his father taught him as a seven-year-old to fish for bass in a beautiful lake in Maine. The father gave the boy a hand line, and when the child hooked a fish, he got so excited he tangled the line as he pulled it in. Finally he handed it over to his father, and the well-experienced father managed as always to straighten out the line. Years have passed, and this boy, now a man, says, "I have been reminded that, if I will only

turn over my problems to my Heavenly Father and trust Him
fully, He can undo the tangles."

Yes, He can. As far as you are concerned, life may appear to
be a tangled mess. Turn everything over to the eternal Christ;
He will not fail you. Cast upon Him the weight of your care;
He will provide comfort and help.

"Hast thou entered into the springs of the sea? or hast thou
walked in the search of the depth?" Here reference is made to
the knowledge that comes from a careful and detailed study of
the deepest recesses and caverns of the ocean. Man may make
such a study, but even then his knowledge is limited when
compared to that of the Creator.

The next two questions can have nothing but a "no" answer.
"Have the gates of death been opened unto thee? or hast thou
seen the doors of the shadow of death?" The living know very
little about death. God, on the other hand, knows all about
death. In the same manner, man is extremely limited in his
knowledge of the earth. "Hast thou perceived the breadth of
the earth? declare if thou knowest it all." Surely man has determined much about the earth, but there are so many unan-
swerable questions. The Creator has all the answers.

From earth, our attention is now turned toward Heaven
as the Lord Jehovah reveals man's ignorance of the knowledge
of Heaven. "Where is the way where light dwelleth? and as
for darkness, where is the place thereof, That thou shouldest
take it to the bound thereof, and that thou shouldest know the
paths to the house thereof? Knowest thou it, because thou wast
then born? or because the number of thy days is great?" Certainly man cannot control the sun. Over the years of time he has
been able to peer into many of the mysteries of the sun, but
there are still many puzzling questions.

Consider the snow; how little we know about this amazing
phenomenon that has confounded the greatest of minds. "Hast
thou entered into the treasures of the snow? or hast thou seen

the treasures of the hail, Which I reserved against the time of trouble, against the day of battle and war?" God has used snow and hail most opportunely in defeating the enemies of the children of God. An entire nation may be brought to a standstill when blanketed by a heavy snowfall. How limited is the strength of man.

The diffusion of light is another remarkable fact. "By what way is the light parted, which scattereth the eastwind upon the earth?" Though seeming to come from one point, light is equally diffused when it appears on the earth.

Further, we see the sovereignty of God evidenced in the control of the rain, directing its course as well as controlling its intensity. "Who hath divided a watercourse for the overflowing of waters, or a way for the lightning of thunder; To cause it to rain on the earth, where no man is; on the wilderness, wherein there is no man; To satisfy the desolate and waste ground; and to cause the bud of the tender herb to spring forth? Hath the rain a father? or who hath begotten the drops of dew?" The lightning and the thunder are controlled by the providence of God. No one should ever fear lightning, for it does not pierce the skies as blind bullets. Every charge of lightning is perfectly controlled by divine providence. Likewise, God knows when to send rain and when to withhold the rain. But someone asks, "Have there not been periods of drought?" Yes, but oftentimes God speaks through the withholding of the elements, that we might be reminded of our dependence upon Him. Indeed, God is the "Father" of the rain. He sends it according to His knowledge of the need.

Consider the ice and the frost. God asks, "Out of whose womb came the ice? and the hoary frost of heaven, who hath gendered it?" Furthermore He says, "The waters are hid as with a stone, and the face of the deep is frozen." Most of these elements are so common that we fail to recognize their greatness. Is it not wonderful to know the God who personally controls the earth, sun, waters, rain, frost, ice, and all the other elements? We worry and fret over the "little things" that, in comparison to the "great things" of the universe, seem infinitely small. And yet, the God who undertakes for all of the providences of the universe has promised to care for our every need. How tragic it is that most of us are prone to acknowledge the fact that God can control the universe, but we seem to doubt that He can provide for our immediate needs. Is it not foolish that we of such little faith fail to rely upon His grace and care? In Psalm 24:1 we read, "The earth is the LORD's, and the fulness thereof; the world, and they that dwell therein." Do not forget it — not only is the earth the Lord's, but they that dwell therein. If you have received Jesus Christ into your heart, you belong to God. You are His possession. Further we read in Psalm 34:15, "The eyes of the LORD are upon the righteous, and His ears are open unto their cry." God knows all about your trials and heartaches. Cast the weight of your care upon Him.

A Christian mother tells of a service she attended in a home in which several young mothers were present with their children. The children were put to sleep in a remote room in the house. As the service proceeded, the sudden cry of a baby was heard. Do you think all the mothers hastened to respond to the baby's cry? No, only one mother rose and left the room to quiet the child. She knew the voice of her baby. The Lord, who distinguishes perfectly, knows the voice of each of His children. He delights to respond to their cries. Call on Him; He will hear your voice. He will provide for your present necessity. Our God is the unfailing God. Do not worry, but trust. Rest in the everlasting promises of the Word of God.

The Lord reminds His servant next of the inability of man to control the stars. "Canst thou bind the sweet influences of Pleiades, or loose the bands of Orion? Canst thou bring forth Mazzaroth in his season? or canst thou guide Arcturus with his sons?" As humans are powerless in controlling the course of the stars, likewise they are in ignorance concerning the ordinances of Heaven. "Knowest thou the ordinances of heaven? canst thou set the dominion thereof in the earth?" If man is so limited in his intelligence regarding the ordinances of Heaven, how can he expect to understand fully the providences of God? For this reason we must trust the Lord for all things. He who controls the stars and the heavens above can certainly undertake for every care and need in the life of the believer. My, how this chapter evidences the utter weakness of man in comparison with the unlimited and almighty power of our great God!

Can man lift up his voice and command rain, or can he by a word control the lightning? Of course he cannot. "Canst thou lift up thy voice to the clouds, that abundance of waters may cover thee? Canst thou send lightnings, that they may go, and say unto thee, Here we are?" Humans may pray for rain but they cannot demand it. The rain and the lightning are controlled by the divine wisdom and counsel of God.

The Lord asks further, "Who hath put wisdom in the inward parts? or who hath given understanding to the heart?" How needful that we recognize that all knowledge comes from Him who is omniscient. Man boasts of his learning, but were it not for the grace of God in revealing wisdom, we should know nothing. It is wonderful to realize also that God never learns of our cares and needs; He knows all about them. For this reason we need not fear, but simply rest in His unchangeable promises. How wonderful that whatever our needs, God promises to supply. Are you perplexed, in utter despair? Do you need wisdom at this moment? How do you get it? Listen to James 1:5: "If any of you lack wisdom, let him ask of God, that giveth to all men liberally, and upbraideth not; and it shall be given him." Claim your possessions in Christ! Ask great things of God; expect great things from God!

Consider man's inability to control the rains that provide the needed moisture for the earth. "Who can number the clouds in wisdom? or who can stay the bottles of heaven, When the dust groweth into hardness, and the clods cleave fast together?" It is God who has the clouds and the vapor in His cognizance and control. Many have been the times when man desired to draw rain to the earth, but he was helpless. This, of course, is just another proof of man's dependence upon the God of Glory.

Beginning with verse 39 of this chapter and running through all of the next chapter, the Lord Jehovah reminds His servant of the divine care and providence for the animal kingdom. Though we may be certain that the clouds above have no dependence upon us, God assures us that even the inferior creatures on the earth need not look to humans for their supply. "Wilt thou hunt the prey for the lion? or fill the appetite of the young lions, When they couch in their dens, and abide in the covert to lie in wait? Who provideth for the raven his food? when his young ones cry unto God, they wander for lack of meat." These closing words in this chapter remind me of what our Lord said in Matthew 6:26-29: "Behold the fowls of the air: for they sow not, neither do they reap, nor gather into barns; yet your heavenly Father feedeth them. Are ye not much better than they? Which of you by taking thought can add one cubit unto his stature? And why take ye thought for raiment? Consider the lilies of the field, how they grow; they toil not, neither do they spin: And yet I say unto you, That even Solomon in all his glory was not arrayed like one of these." What is the lesson God is conveying to Job? The same lesson you and I need to learn, not once, but many times: that it is God who provides and cares for every phase of the universe, even to the feeding of the birds and the animals. In a similar manner He will care for you and for me, if we will trust Him to do it. But so often we neglect to walk by faith! Reaching out and rushing off in every direction, we overlook the path of faith. Where might we be today had we trusted God implicitly for all things, rather than fret and worry so?

Following His remarks about His unerring provision for the fowls of the air and the lilies of the field, our Lord says, "Wherefore, if God so clothe the grass of the field, which to day is, and to morrow is cast into the oven, shall He not much more clothe you, O ye of little faith? Therefore take no thought, saying, What shall we eat? or, What shall we drink? or, Wherewithal shall we be clothed? (For after all these things do the Gentiles seek:) for your heavenly Father knoweth that ye have need of all these things" (Matthew 6:30-32). Let those words penetrate deeply into your heart: "Your heavenly Father knoweth." Is anything else necessary? If your Heavenly Father knows about your need, what have you to fear? If for some reason He were uninformed or limited in understanding, we might fear. But, child of God, never forget it: "He knoweth." Because "He knoweth," He will provide for you.

Daddy Hall, known to many in bygone years as a man of reliant faith in the Lord, used to tell the story about "Try — T-R-Y." He used to say that the trouble was that it used up only three fingers and left two for the devil to use. In his characteristic way he gave illustrations of how the thumb and first finger should be used also. He would tell his listeners to use the word "Trust — T-R-U-S-T" and use up all five fingers.

A man told Daddy Hall that, after hearing his message, he went out and tried to trust; however, it did not work with him. He said, "I found that the devil gets hold of the fingers of my other hand. What am I to do with them?" Daddy Hall had an immediate reply.

"Do this," he said. "Yield — Y-I-E-L-D." The Christian brother did that very thing. He yielded and began trusting, and all of life was different. Why not try the same for your life? Have you been disturbed by needless care? Yield to Christ's control; then fully trust Him.

JOB 39:1-30

GOD CONTINUES TO SPEAK to His servant relative to the mysteries of nature unsolved by human minds. Notice how wonderfully God provides for the wild animals. "Knowest thou the time when the wild goats of the rock bring forth? or canst thou mark when the hinds do calve? Canst thou number the months that they fulfill? or knowest thou the time when they bring forth?" The undomesticated are not dependent upon man for help even in childbearing. God undertakes for them.

But will not the God who cares for the most insignificant beast care for your problems? Are you not the possessor of an eternal soul, which is of far greater worth than an animal that will soon die and go back to dust? Most certainly! Oh, that we might learn the secret of taking all our cares to Him who is in a position to help. For this reason we can say with confidence, "Let us therefore come boldly unto the throne of grace, that we may obtain mercy, and find grace to help in time of need" (Hebrews 4:16). Lift your troubled heart to the Lord in prayer. Lay your requests at Jesus' feet. He will not fail.

Think about God's providence for the animals in childbearing. "They bow themselves, they bring forth their young ones, they cast out their sorrows. Their young ones are in good liking, they grow up with corn; they go forth, and return not unto them." How astounding is God's provision! Though animals may bring forth their young with difficulty and sorrow, yet they are not alone. The hand of providence brings their young into the world. In addition to this, the God of all grace nurtures these little ones, feeds them, and enables them to grow. Later He helps them break away from motherly care. Who can explain all this? There is only one explanation — the sovereignty of God. He who created animal life provides for His creation.

Job had complained because of his sad lot. The burdens and cares of his affliction weighed heavily upon him. But God explained to Job that man is not promised an easy way in this life. Animals may have an easy way, but not man.

Next our Lord speaks of the freedom He has given to the wild ass. "Who hath sent out the wild ass free? or who hath loosed the bands of the wild ass? Whose house I have made the wilderness, and the barren land his dwellings. He scorneth the multitude of the city, neither regardeth he the crying of the driver. The range of the mountains is his pasture, and he searcheth after every green thing." So often the donkey is pictured in the Scriptures as untamable. Well, be sure God made him that way. His God-given instincts motivate him to seek a life of ease rather than labor.

Man, on the other hand, was created differently. God made him to work and produce. After the Fall, his responsibility became even greater. God declared in Genesis 3:19, "In the sweat of thy face shalt thou eat bread, till thou return unto the ground; for out of it wast thou taken: for dust thou art, and unto dust shalt thou return." We must not look for an easy path. Hard work, sorrow, and suffering will be our lot. But if we know the Lord Jesus Christ in our heart, God will make the hard way easy and the burden light. As He has revealed His care repeatedly throughout Job 38-39 for all of His works of creation, we may be absolutely certain that He will undertake for us.

God continues by speaking of the unicorn. Some think this to be the buffalo with his mighty strength in his head and shoulders. "Will the unicorn be willing to serve thee, or abide by thy crib? Canst thou bind the unicorn with his band in the furrow? or will he harrow the valleys after thee? Wilt thou trust him, because his strength is great? or wilt thou leave thy labour to him? Wilt thou believe him, that he will bring home thy seed, and gather it into thy barn?" Job thought his life should be ordered as he wanted it. But God makes it clear that we cannot expect things to fall in line as we desire them. Thus He illustrates from the unicorn, which was not created to be harnessed to a plow. God made some animals for this purpose but not the unicorn. Though he possesses great strength, this strength cannot be utilized as man thinks it should.

Life is somewhat the same. All of us know how we would like to see things work out. Yet God declares in Isaiah 55:8-9: "For My thoughts are not your thoughts, neither are your ways My ways, saith the LORD. For as the heavens are higher than the earth, so are My ways higher than your ways, and My thoughts than your thoughts." God's plan is the better one. It is far more worth while for us to trust in the providences of God for all things than to seek to order our lives according to our own desires and concerns. How much better to submit to the control of the Lord and receive whatever comes as the gift of His grace. How important that we surrender completely to the Lord's perfect control.

There are times when outwardly we appear to be nonchalant in the face of adversity and trials, but inwardly we are chafing against the perfect providences of God. These so-called disappointments are not accidents; they are incidents in God's indefectible plan for our lives. The road may get difficult at times;

but this has been promised. God declares in 2 Timothy 3:12, "Yea, and all that will live godly in Christ Jesus shall suffer persecution." There are no exceptions to this rule. Whatever comes, realize the truth of 2 Corinthians 3:5, "Our sufficiency is of God." Keep in mind that every individual believer is precious in the sight of the Lord. A shepherd would not lose one sheep, nor a jeweler one diamond, nor a mother one child, nor a man one limb of his body. The Lord would not lose one of His redeemed people. However insignificant or unimportant you may seem to be, never forget that if you are in Christ, you are the Lord's. You are kept and preserved by Christ Jesus, our wonderful Saviour. Rest in Him, child of God! Believe Him! He who cares for every animal of the forest and field will most certainly care for you.

"Gavest thou the goodly wings unto the peacocks? or wings and feathers unto the ostrich?" Both the peacock and the ostrich possess beautiful feathers. Could anyone by human skill produce such a work of art? Of course not! Such beauty demands the touch of the divine hand. But though one may marvel at the beauties of the feathers, yet the ostrich has certain deficiencies unexplainable by human minds. One of the deficiencies, we are told, is that she "leaveth her eggs in the earth, and warmeth them in dust." Unlike many birds, the ostrich fails to provide constant care for her eggs. Normally she buries them about a foot below the ground and hatches them as other birds do. But in hot countries, where the eggs do not need the constant incubation, she simply lays them on the surface and very often she leaves them throughout the day. God says to Job, she "forgetteth that the foot may crush them, or that the wild beast may break them." Thus the ostrich has been known as the foolish bird, devoid of wisdom in caring for her young.

Further it is stated of the ostrich, "She is hardened against her young ones, as though they were not hers: her labour is in vain without fear." Yet in spite of her carelessness, God provides the heat of the sun and soon the young break forth from the eggs. Thus we are to understand that the failures of the ostrich do not frustrate the plans of providence.

Oftentimes we humans become extremely disturbed because of the perplexing events that surround us. But as God provides for the eggs of the careless ostrich, He will undertake for the trials of His beloved children, if we trust and obey Him.

Notice how detailed God is in the care of His creatures as He speaks further regarding the ostrich. "Because God hath deprived her of wisdom, neither hath He imparted to her understanding." How revealing! Even the want of wisdom in the ostrich is not without divine providence. "Every good gift and every perfect gift is from above, and cometh down from the Father of lights, with whom is no variableness, neither shadow of turning," the Apostle James tells us (James 1:17). Sometimes we look at others and regret that we cannot duplicate their abilities. God made us as we are. We should be content with such gifts as we possess.

But though the ostrich is lacking in some gifts, she excels in others. "What time she lifteth up herself on high, she scorneth the horse and his rider." She cannot mount up into the air and fly, but her strong wings enable her to excel in her running speed. She runs so fast that even a horse and its rider cannot overtake her. Thus what appears to be bad is not entirely bad. There is always something for which to give thanks.

Before leaving the ostrich, we might proffer this word of warning: as the ostrich is careless in the care of its young, many humans are careless in the care of their souls. The Lord Jesus said in Matthew 4:4, "Man shall not live by bread alone, but by every word that proceedeth out of the mouth of God." It is important that each one think about the welfare of his soul. Have you settled the most important matter of life? Are you certain that you will spend eternity with God? There need be no doubt about this, for the Bible is unquestionably clear. In I John 5:12 God declares, "He that hath the Son hath life; and he that hath not the Son of God hath not life." Have you received Jesus Christ into your heart? If you have, then you are the possessor of eternal life. But if you have not received Christ, you are still a stranger to God. How important that you do not delay in receiving Christ. Many there are who have good intentions. They are not opposed to God or the church, but they are too busy. Constantly putting God off, they are waiting for a more convenient day. What a tragic mistake it is to postpone one's soul salvation.

One day an earnest Christian doctor called to see an elderly man, whom he had visited before on many occasions. Frequently the doctor had spoken faithfully to old John and his wife about their soul's salvation, but apparently without any result. The aged man listened attentively and practically agreed to the truths set before him, but seemed always to avoid coming to the point. John was suffering from an attack of bronchitis. His life was not in danger but he felt painfully weak and ill. The doctor made the necessary inquiries, and after promising to get some medicine ready, was about to say good-by when the wife of the sick man inquired, "When must John take the medicine?"

"I will put the directions on the label," replied the doctor. Then with a smile he turned to his patient and said, "Let me see. You are not very ill. Suppose you begin taking the medicine in a month."

"In a month?" cried both at once in astonishment.

"Yes, why not? Is that too soon?"

"Too soon? Why, I may be dead by then," said John.

"That is true. But you must remember, you really are not very bad yet. Still, perhaps you had better begin to take it in a week."

"But I beg your pardon, Sir. I may not live a week," cried John in great perplexity.

"Of course you may not, John, but very likely you will. And the medicine will be in the house. It will keep, and if you find yourself getting worse you can take some. I shall not charge anything for it. If you should feel worse tomorrow, you might even begin then."

"Sir, I may be dead tomorrow."

"When would you propose to begin, John?"

"Well, Sir, I thought you would tell me to begin today."

"Begin today, by all means," said the doctor kindly. "I only wanted to show you how false your reasoning is when you put off taking the medicine which the Great Physician has provided for your sin-sick soul. Just think how long you have neglected the remedy He has provided. For years you have turned away from the Lord Jesus."

What was true of John may be true of you. Carelessly you may have neglected to receive the Son of God into your life. He wants to become your Saviour at this moment. You need Him, for without Him you are lost forever.

God speaks next of the horse as He asks Job, "Hast thou given the horse strength? hast thou clothed his neck with thunder? Canst thou make him afraid as a grasshopper? the glory of his nostrils is terrible." In Job's day the horse was used primarily for warfare, being quite adaptable to the demands of the battlefield. Though possessing great strength, the horse was tamable by man. Thus in this sense he is "afraid as a grasshopper." Though mighty in strength, he is made willing to obey his rider.

Notice the description God gives of the fearlessness of the horse as he carries his rider into the heat of the battle. "He paweth in the valley, and rejoiceth in his strength: he goeth on to meet the armed men. He mocketh at fear, and is not affrighted; neither turneth he back from the sword. The quiver rattleth against him, the glittering spear and the shield. He swalloweth the ground with fierceness and rage: neither believeth he that it is the sound of the trumpet. He saith among the trumpets, Ha, ha; and he smelleth the battle afar off, the thunder of the captains, and the shouting." Consider the question again, as we have of the other creatures described in these chapters: who made the horse this way? Of course, the answer is clear: God did. How different the horse is from the ostrich, described in the earlier part of this chapter.

What God does for animal life, He does also for humans. He has not made us alike. Sometimes we look at others and wish we were like them. A Sunday school teacher longs to teach like another. A preacher desires to preach and teach like a gifted Bible teacher he has heard. Never forget it, God has endowed us with specific gifts. Some have more than others. Theirs is the greater responsibility to God; for the greater the gift, the greater the responsibility.

The important thing is to be yourself. Live daily in harmonious fellowship with God your Saviour. Seek to discover what your gifts are, then develop them through the Holy Spirit' guidance and leading. Remember, God made you as you are. In the parable of the talents recorded in Matthew 25, each servant was given a different amount "according to his several ability." I have known students in school to become greatly disturbed because they could not make all "A's." Not every young person is an "A" student. Thus I say, discover what gifts God has bestowed upon you, then use every possible means to develop those gifts for the glory of your Saviour, to whom you belong. When we stand before our Lord at the Judgment Seat of Christ we shall not be judged on the basis of the number of our gifts but how we used them. Many who call themselves Christian are wasting their God-given talents. They are failing to use them for the glory of the Lord. This is a tragedy which can produce not only misery in one's life in the present, but greater sorrow in the days to come.

In further illustrating His providence and care over all of creation, God reminds Job of the hawk and the eagle. The fowl of the air, like the creatures on earth, are likewise kept and controlled by the power and wisdom of God. "Doth the hawk fly by thy wisdom, and stretch her wings toward the south? How does the hawk know to leave the cold country in the winter to follow the sun to the warmer climate? Again, there is only one answer. God gave the hawk this wisdom; this is instinctive. God reminds Job that it is not man that trains the birds to do this; rather, it is a God-given instinct.

Likewise the Lord asks, "Doth the eagle mount up at thy command, and make her nest on high?" Is the eagle dependent upon training to be received from man? Of course not. It is the natural power and instinct God has given. Notice how she builds her nest: "She dwelleth and abideth on the rock, upon the crag of the rock, and the strong place. From thence she seeketh the prey, and her eyes behold afar off." With her all-seeing eyes she watches for her prey from her lofty observatory. She leads her young to the prey also, that they, too, might feed on the dead. "Her young ones also suck up blood: and where the slain are, there is she." Here again we see God creating the eagle in a manner peculiar only to itself, different from every other form of fowl in its habits and traits.

Surely Job had no answer for his complaining. Indeed, he had to realize that his circumstances were ordered of the Lord. It is true that when one knows the Lord and follows the Lord, whatever befalls him may be received and respected as God's will. God makes no mistakes; man does, but God never does. He is almighty, He is sovereign. Six times in the stirring forty-fifth chapter of Isaiah God declares, "I am the LORD, and there is none else." Oh, that you and I might fully realize this. Were we to do so, we should worry no more. How ridiculous that believers fret and worry. Our God created the heavens and the earth and all that is within the scope of the universe. In addition, He offers to provide every one of our needs. How foolish that we fail to trust in His grace and providence.

Repeatedly in these various illustrations from creation, God has declared the truth of His mighty power and all-sufficient providence, that not only Job but also you and I might realize the privilege that is ours to lean on the everlasting arms of God.

It may be at this moment that you are going through a season of disturbing trial. Perhaps this is the most sorrowful event you have ever experienced in life. Do not forget the lesson God has given in telling of the eagle, the hawk, and the horse. As our Father in Heaven cares for the beasts and the fowl, you may be sure He will care for you. Look up! Look into the face of the Lord Jesus and see Him as the One who will direct you through your period of adversity!

JOB 40:1-24

IT WOULD SEEM that God concluded His instructive message to Job after chapter 39 and waited for a reply. But since Job remained silent, God spoke again. "Moreover the LORD answered Job, and said, Shall he that contendeth with the Almighty instruct Him? he that reproveth God, let him answer it." Actually, by his many complaints, Job had been contending against God. As far as the believer is concerned, every complaint is contention against the Lord. If we really believe that all things are ordained of God and that we are His people, then whatever comes our way is of divine appointment. To rebel against circumstances is to strive against divine providence.

Someone might raise the question as to how God could answer Job if Job did not say anything. Remember that we are dealing with Deity here. God knew Job's thoughts, and the Lord answered not only what Job had said, but what he was thinking. How important it is that believers permit the Holy Spirit to control their thoughts. We read of our Lord Jesus Christ, in John 2:25, that He "needed not that any should testify of man; for

He knew what was in man." Christ knows every thought that enters the mind. It is for this reason that we should do as the Apostle Paul said in 2 Corinthians 10:5: bring "into captivity every thought to the obedience of Christ." Even more important than words and actions is the control of our thoughts, for what we think precedes what we say and do.

The question God put before Job was heart-searching indeed. "Shall he that contendeth with the Almighty instruct Him?" In other words, will the complainer be so presumptuous as to think that he could improve upon the wisdom and counsel of God? Sometimes we become very critical of the circumstances in which we find ourselves. Never forget that all things are purposeful. Could you and I do a better job in caring for our needs than God does? How ridiculous that we do not rest in the marvelous providences of our all-sufficient Lord. We need to obey the truth of Hebrews 13:5: "Be content with such things as ye have: for He hath said, I will never leave thee, nor forsake thee."

After this humiliating and heart-searching question, God demanded an answer from Job. What was his reply? "Then Job answered the LORD, and said, Behold, I am vile; what shall I answer Thee? I will lay mine hand upon my mouth. Once have I spoken; but I will not answer; yea, twice; but I will proceed no further." It is obvious from these words that Job fell before the Lord in humble repentance. When his friends spoke to him and sought to reprove him, he became incensed with their arguments. But Job, realizing the truth of all that God had said, was brought face to face with himself before his Lord. Most of us have a pretty good estimation of ourselves; but when face to face with the Lord and His Word, our attitude changes. Like Job, we confess, "I am vile; what shall I answer Thee?" This was the case of Simon Peter, you will recall, when he fell down at the feet of the living Christ and cried out, "Depart from me; for I am a sinful man, O Lord" (Luke 5:8). When ever we see Christ as He is, we see ourselves as we really are. Sometimes we are proud and egotistical, but getting a glimpse of Christ in His perfection and holiness, we recognize our utter worthlessness. How important that we take time daily to go before the Lord and permit Him to examine our hearts, that we may be purged from unknown as well as known sin.

Job was silenced as he realized his own sinfulness. He was brought in humble contrition to the feet of God. Formerly he was quick to retaliate in self-justification, but he had nothing more to say. "What shall I answer Thee? I will lay mine hand upon my mouth." He was speechless now before the Lord, although he did confess that he had spoken out of turn, not only once, but many times. The word "twice" as used in verse 5 means "many more times than one."

It would seem that Job's great problem was the one common to many of us—uncontrolled speech. How much sorrow and misery we have brought into our lives because of words we have spoken. Ponder 1 Peter 2:23, where we read of Christ, "Who, when He was reviled, reviled not again; when He suffered, He threatened not; but committed Himself to Him that judgeth righteously." Oh, how necessary that we take these words to heart.

Never permit yourself to answer back when you are blamed for anything. Do not try to defend yourself. Be willing to accept the abuse or rebuke others might give in private or in public. Let them revile you; it shall be a great victory for you. Let them say the unkind things about you. If you remain silent, it can be an excellent oil which shall anoint your head.

A great saint of God has said, "It is the mark of deepest and truest humility to see ourselves condemned without cause and to be silent under it. To be silent under insult and wrong is a very noble imitation of our Lord. 'Oh, my Lord, when I remember in how many ways Thou didst suffer, who in no way deserved it, I know not where my senses are when I am in such haste to defend and excuse myself. Is it possible I should desire anyone to speak any good of me or to think it, when so many ill things were thought and spoken of Thee?' "

Are you a child of God? Have you received Jesus Christ into your life? If you have, do you permit Him to control your tongue at all times? In Colossians 4:6 we read, "Let your speech be alway with grace, seasoned with salt." Does your speech manifest the grace of God, or is it a reproach to Him whose name you bear? Maybe some of us ought to get on our knees and tell God as Job did, "I will lay my hand upon my mouth." The Lord can control your tongue. Ask Him to do it.

Job was brought low, but evidently not low enough. For God continues to deal with him on the ground of his proud claim of righteousness. It is not enough for one to get rid of some of his pride or some of his self-righteousness; to be usable he must claim a complete victory. God refuses to stop at anything less than full submission. Thus the Lord continues to set before Job certain important facts, with a design to provoke repentance from His erring servant.

Job had accused God of overlooking his pathetic calamity. The Lord proceeds to inform Job that divine providence must never be questioned. "Then answered the LORD unto Job out of the whirlwind, and said, Gird up thy loins now like a man: I will demand of thee, and declare thou unto Me. Wilt thou also disannul My judgment? wilt thou condemn Me, that thou mayest be righteous?" Because one cannot understand the acts of providence is no reason to accuse God of neglect. Such faulty reasoning only makes matters worse.

Actually, when we question the providence of God, we place ourselves in a position of trying to become greater than God. Those who claim to be God's people should never in any measure complain about His actions. Thus, because Job was assuming the position of God's judge, Jehovah asked, "Hast thou an arm like God? or canst thou thunder with a voice like Him?" Those who would criticize God must prove their right o such action by producing the mighty works of Deity. The Lord Jehovah is omnipotent. His "hand is not shortened, that it cannot save" (Isaiah 59:1). If one is to be critical of God, he must display this same degree of omnipotence.

The eternal God upholds all things by the word of His power. Could such be said of any human? Are not all of us feeble and tottering? No man is sufficient in himself. We were created to be dependent upon the Lord Jehovah. We can do nothing without Him, and at the same time, He can do all things without us. God is not in the slightest measure dependent upon any of us, but we are wholly dependent upon Him. Have you realized this? Have you submitted to the Lord's rulership? Is your life being lived to the glory of God? In 1 Corinthians 10:31 we read, "Whether therefore ye eat, or drink, or whatsoever ye do, do all to the glory of God." Have you recognized the need of moment-by-moment dependence upon the Lord?

It may be that you have never come to Christ for salvation. You may feel that you are sufficient within yourself. But no man is sufficient within himself. He needs the constant guidance and help of God in his life. It is only possible to know God as you know His beloved Son, who died for your sins. Jesus declared in John 14:6, "No man cometh unto the Father, but by Me." Commit your life to the Lord Jesus Christ and let Him direct your steps. He can do a far better job of running your life than you can.

The Lord continues to humiliate Job by challenging him to produce divine glory and beauty if he can. "Deck thyself now with majesty and excellency; and array thyself with glory and beauty." It is true that man has produced some great works of art, but have not all these been mere copies of some phase of God's creation? In His majesty and excellency, God provides the originals, but man with his frail limitations produces only copies.

Next God questions Job's ability to put down the proud. God

suggests that if it were in the power of Job to abase defiant humans for their sins, then Job would be a rightful competitor for God's authority. "Cast abroad the rage of thy wrath: and behold every one that is proud, and abase him. Look on every one that is proud, and bring him low; and tread down the wicked in their place. Hide them in the dust together; and bind their faces in secret. Then will I also confess unto thee that thine own right hand can save thee." We read in James 4:6 "God resisteth the proud, but giveth grace unto the humble" and in Daniel 4:37, "Those that walk in pride He is able to abase."

Have you ever wondered why God chose the particular sin of pride in testing Job's right to criticize God? It seems very reasonable, for can it not be said that pride was Job's chief sin? It was something he had been battling for years. Thus God reminds His servant how weak his attempts have been in combating this evil.

Will you not agree that not only was pride Job's chief sin but it is one of the common evils of all mankind? Think of the damage done in our lives by the sin of pride. God say in Proverbs 29:23, "A man's pride shall bring him low." How many times we have been brought low because of this sorrowful evil. But is there no hope? Not in us as humans; but there is in God our Saviour. We read in 1 Corinthians 15:57 "Thanks be to God, which giveth us the victory through our Lord Jesus Christ." There is a way of escape through Him. If you have been plagued by this destructive sin, go to your knees immediately. Claim God's forgiveness and power through Jesus Christ and find deliverance which only He can give.

In further reminding Job of the power of God as revealed in creation, the Almighty describes another of His mighty works "Behold now behemoth, which I made with thee." Several ideas are offered by various commentators as to the meaning of "behemoth." In general, the word means "beast." In particular it is thought by some to be a bull; others associate it with the river horse, or the hippopotamus; still others believe it to be the elephant. The description God gives fits any of these in part but none in its entirety.

Consider the description. First we are told that "he eateth grass as an ox." That is, he dwells on the land as well as in the water. Next God says, "Lo now, his strength is in his loins, and his force is in the navel of his belly." More literally, "navel" as used here means the muscles of his belly. This suggests the hippopotamus, whose stomach is covered with extremely thick skin as opposed to the elephant's thin skin. Further, "He moveth his tail like a cedar." In straightness, the hippopotamus's tail would resemble "a cedar," but certainly not in its length. Also, we are told, "The sinews of his stones are wrapped together"; literally, "his thighs are wrapped together," reminding us of the Herculean strength in the legs of the hippopotamus. "Wrapped together" implies a rope that is twisted for strength. And then, "His bones are as strong pieces of brass; his bones are like bars of iron." This suggests the unexcelled strength of this powerful beast. Notice, too, that "he is the chief of the ways of God: He that made him can make his sword to approach unto him." God has provided this animal with its own cutting instrument, its sickle-like teeth which are used primarily to cut down the grain.

How interesting that "behemoth" is termed by God as "the chief of the ways of God." Doubtless this means that there is no creature in all of creation, with the exception of man, that would excel this beast in its uniqueness of creation.

God says further, "Surely the mountains bring him forth food, where all the beasts of the field play." This would strongly indicate that the animal being described is the hippopotamus, because he is very often found in the mountains. Also, he does not attack the other animals but rather feeds on grass. "He lieth under the shady trees, in the covert of the reed, and fens. The shady trees cover him with their shadow; the willows of the brook compass him about." We gather from this that the beast lives an inactive life, spending much of his time in relaxation, but choosing to relax in protected areas where he might guard against the attacks of other wild animals. "Behold, he drinketh up a river, and hasteth not: he trusteth that he can draw up Jordan into his mouth." We understand from this that he can live in water as well as on land. Though the Jordan rises up to his mouth, he has no fear of the overflowing river. "He taketh it with his eyes: his nose pierceth through snares." The idea expressed here is, can the hunter overwhelm the hippopotamus when the beast is aware of the hunter's presence? Or can the hunter pierce the nose of the hippopotamus and put a cord through his nose to lead him at will? This was a very common method of taming animals in the East. Of course, the answer is, "No." The animal was too ferocious for that.

This great beast of the mountains and the waters provides us with another conclusive evidence of the sovereignty and power of the Creator. What we are seeing in these studies is that God does not make any two creatures alike. Some are created with unexcelled strength, while others are pitifully weak. It must be remembered also that in God's creation there are no two humans who are alike. Recognizing our individuality, it is important to consider that the Lord has a specific plan for each one of us. The plan may not be according to our choice, but who of us could improve upon God's plan?

I am sure Joseph would not have chosen the unkind treatment he received when he was sold into Egypt. Yet how comforting it is to know that God's plans are never frustrated. Even though Joseph's brothers were unmerciful to him, everything dovetailed together for good, as God's perfect plan was fulfilled. We have Joseph's own confession, after he revealed himself to his brothers many months later: "So now it was not you that sent me hither, but God: and He hath made me a father to Pharaoh, and lord of all his house, and a ruler throughout all the land of Egypt" (Genesis 45:8). Oh, how important it is for the child of God that he rest in the providences of God. Maybe you are sick in body, or possibly you are going through a time of severe mental distress. Never forget, "It is God which worketh in you both to will and to do of His good pleasure" (Philippians 2:13). Do not resist the all-wise hand of providence. God has something better for you up ahead. You cannot see all things, but remember, He can see the end from the beginning. Thus, take hold of the great truth embodied in 1 Timothy 6:6, "Godliness with contentment is great gain." Do not complain! Be content! Rest in God's plan and purpose, saying, "I know, Lord, that You will not fail." It may be that your friends have failed you. Even dearest loved ones may have neglected you in your hour of great need. But God declares in Hebrews 13:5, "I will never leave thee, nor forsake thee." No, you cannot see your way clear. As you look ahead, it looks like a confusing, bewildering maze. Take courage, child of God. Go to your knees and boldly claim, as did David in Psalm 27:1, "The Lord is my light and my salvation; whom shall I fear? the Lord is the strength of my life; of whom shall I be afraid?" You may be confident that there is a way out with God. There always is. There are no dead-end streets in God's providence. Trust Him for all things!

JOB 41:1-34

THE LORD TELLS us of another of His unique creatures by the name of "leviathan," which means a serpent, or more explicitly in this case, a crocodile or some other large sea monster. Some even think the reference is to a whale, but it seems more probable that it was a large crocodile.

God asks, "Canst thou put an hook into his nose? or bore his jaw through with a thorn?" This mighty beast of the sea could not be caught in the usual manner of catching fish. Of course, once again God is reminding Job that all of His creatures were made with various characteristics and abilities. The crocodile seems to be quite different from any other inhabitant of the sea. Wild beasts, later domesticated, had a hook put through the nose, by which they were led about. But certainly this could not be done to a crocodile. After fish were caught, a rope was run through their jaws and they were put in the water to keep fresh. Likewise, such could not be the case in preserving the crocodile.

The crocodile is untamable. God made him this way. "Will

he make many supplications unto thee? will he speak soft words unto thee?" That is, when being caught, will the crocodile plead with his pursuer to spare him? No, he is too mighty and strong for that. "Will he make a covenant with thee? wilt thou take him for a servant forever?" Can one domesticate the crocodile? Of course not! The crocodile was not created to be a pet. "Wilt thou play with him as with a bird? or wilt thou bind him for thy maidens?" Could the crocodile be put into a cage as a bird and kept in the home? Or would it be possible to tie a rope about one of his feet that little girls might play with him, as they often did with birds?

The crocodile was of little monetary value in Job's day; he was not desired for food, nor for trade. Indeed it is remarkable to see how detailed and correct the Word of God is. "Shall the companions make a banquet of him? shall they part him among the merchants?" Furthermore, the skin of the crocodile is impenetrable. He is not like many of the other creatures of the sea, in that spears will easily pierce their bodies. God asks, "Canst thou fill his skin with barbed irons? or his head with fish spears?"

It would seem from the next few verses that God is making a very pointed application to Job. "Lay thine hand upon him, remember the battle, do no more. Behold, the hope of him is in vain: shall not one be cast down even at the sight of him? None is so fierce that dare stir him up: who then is able to stand before Me?" It is foolish for man to attempt to resist or fight against the mighty crocodile, but it is even more foolish for man to rebel against the Almighty God. God asks the question, "Who then is able to stand before Me?" It is obvious from this question that, though Job was a righteous man and one of moral integrity, there was rebellion in his heart. He was revolting against his circumstances. Can there be any peace of heart in such a state? Matthew 6:24 provides us with a conclusive answer: "No man can serve two masters: for either he will hate the one, and love the other; or else he will hold to the one, and despise the other." As long as there is rebellion of any kind in the heart, even though we may be followers of Christ, we are serving two masters, self and Christ. Rather, we are trying to serve two masters. The Bible declares that it is impossible to serve two masters, for we are committed either to one or to the other.

Let us pray that God will remove from us every trace of rebellion to His holy will. If we would know peace and blessing, there must be absolute and full submission to Christ's control. Jesus made this clear when He said in John 12:24, "Verily, verily, I say unto you, Except a corn of wheat fall into the ground and die, it abideth alone: but if it die, it bringeth forth much fruit." We must die to self and the personal ambitions that stand between us and the Lord. We are only as near to God as we are far from ourselves.

You and I live in a world cursed by selfishness. On every hand there are wars and rumors of wars. Nations are coveting and seeking the territory of other nations because of selfishness. Men and women think only of their personal comfort and sustenance while millions perish with hunger and cold. Selfishness is at the root of nearly all of our national and social conflicts. Indeed, because of this evil, we are yet far away from political and social observance of the truths of Scripture. In the midst of this national turmoil we need a generation of young people who will take a stand for Christ, who will be willing to deny themselves to take up the cross to follow the Lord Jesus. The only hope for the future is that millions of our youth will come to Christ and submit to His Lordship in lives of willing obedience.

But as we consider others, what about you today? Are you totally committed to the will of God? Is there any trace of rebellion in your heart? Are you a Christian? Can you say, "Yes, I know the Lord; I am sure I am saved"? If you cannot, you are rebelling against the grace of God, revealed and made possible at Calvary. You need Christ.

In all of these lessons from Creation, God has intended that Job might see that, since God is sovereign and Master of all, it is never in order to rebel against His providence and grace. What God chooses to do is always best. He is the Creator; we are the creatures. He is not obligated in any way to us, for as He says, "Who hath prevented Me, that I should repay him? whatsoever is under the whole heaven is Mine." The word "prevented" as used here means to do a favor for one, in the sense of putting him under obligation. Is God obligated to any of us for the few things we have done? Indeed, we are obligated to Him for the many things we have left undone. We owe Him everything; He owes us nothing. God is not indebted to us for anything we have. Everything within our possession is but a heavenly trust. All things belong to Him, even those which we think are ours. In Psalm 50:10 He says, "For every beast of the forest is Mine, and the cattle upon a thousand hills." In verse 12 we read, "If I were hungry, I would not tell thee: for the world is Mine, and the fulness thereof." "Fulness" has to do with everything in the world. Thus it would be impossible to put God under obligation to any human, for all humans are entirely obligated to Him.

The description of the mighty leviathan is resumed after the worth-while digression. God says, "I will not conceal his parts, nor his power, nor his comely proportion." At this point, the Lord proceeds to give us a detailed view of the greatness of the crocodile. Though large and bulky and not too pleasing to the human eye, yet God declares that he is comely in his proportions.

Notice how utterly inaccessible the crocodile is to humans: "Who can discover the face of his garment? or who can come to him with his double bridle? Who can open the doors of his face? his teeth are terrible round about." Would anyone dare to get close enough to the crocodile to attempt to remove his outer covering from the lower layer of his skin? Or would anyone attempt to put a bridle in his mouth, as we put a bridle in a horse's mouth? Just one glance at that gaping mouth with its jagged teeth would be enough to cause any human to keep his distance.

How remarkable is the protection that God has given the crocodile: "His scales are his pride, shut up together as with a close seal." The word "scales" is really "shields." He has seventeen rows of scales which appear to be shields, as a mighty armor protecting him from any enemy. God describes them further, saying, "One is so near to another, that no air can come between them. They are joined one to another, they stick together, that they cannot be sundered."

Notice something else extremely interesting regarding the crocodile. "By his sneezings a light doth shine, and his eyes are like the eyelids of the morning." After remaining under water for some time, he comes to the surface and expels his breath as though he were sneezing. At the same time, it is said, that the warmth of his breath when expelled in the sunshine appears to be as fire. "Out of his mouth go burning lamps, and sparks of fire leap out. Out of his nostrils goeth smoke, as out of a seething pot or caldron. His breath kindleth coals, and a flame goeth out of his mouth."

Again we have reference to the crocodile's unexcelled strength. "In his neck remaineth strength, and sorrow is turned into joy before him." The "sorrow being turned into joy" in the path of the crocodile is because of his great strength; practically everything in his path suffers defeat. He is made joyful by his many victories. The enemy is helpless because of the crocodile's mighty armor. "The flakes of his flesh are joined together: they are firm in themselves; they cannot be moved." The crocodile possesses a God-given protection unknown by many of the other creatures of divine creation.

Most important of all is his courage and fearlessness, as suggested by verse 24, "His heart is as firm as a stone; yea, as hard as a piece of the nether millstone." The nether millstone, upon which the upper turns, is extremely hard. This indicates the dauntless courage of the crocodile.

Let me pause a minute to reflect a lesson we might learn from what God has said about the crocodile. We should not forget that God created this beast with massive strength. The God who gave the crocodile his strength is a God of great and mighty power. The more I read about the crocodile in this chapter, the more I am reminded that our God is not only a God of love, but He is a just God. He is a God who hates sin and who judges sin. In this age of frivolity and looseness of morals, even Christians are known to give little regard to the awfulness of sin. God is a God of grace; He showers us with His grace. But grace is never given with the intention of liberty and license for evil. Consider the Word of God, as found in Titus 2:11-13, "For the grace of God that bringeth salvation hath appeared to all men, Teaching us that, denying ungodliness and worldly lusts, we should live soberly, righteously, and godly, in this present world; Looking for that blessed hope, and the glorious appearing of the great God and our Saviour Jesus Christ." What does the grace of God teach us? That we should deny "ungodliness and worldly lusts"; even more, that we should live for God. Our lives should be holy, in anticipation of the return of Christ. Oh, how important it is that those who name Christ's Name honor Him with lives that will attract the unsaved to Him.

Never forget it, if the believer persists in sin, God will judge him and humble him. Maybe there is sin in your life, known sin that has been shutting out the blessing and power of God. Confess it immediately! We read in Proverbs 28:13, "He that covereth his sins shall not prosper: but whoso confesseth and forsaketh them shall have mercy." Our God is a mighty God. He is a God of love, but He is also a just God, demanding holiness and righteousness.

Notice how fearful humans are before leviathan. "When he

raiseth up himself, the mighty are afraid: by reason of break-ings they purify themselves." The last phrase concerning the purification of themselves should really be read, "They flee away bewildered." There was such fear and consternation in those who were confronted with the crocodile that they simply took to their feet and ran.

Because of his extremely hard skin, even weapons of war-fare had little effect on the crocodile. God says, "The sword of him that layeth at him cannot hold; the spear, the dart, nor the habergeon. He esteemeth iron as straw, and brass as rotten wood. The arrow cannot make him flee: slingstones are turned with him into stubble. Darts are counted as stubble: he laugh-eth at the shaking of a spear." The Lord equipped the crocodile with a coat of armor that afforded him certain protection against his would-be captors.

Whenever I read this forty-first chapter of Job, I am reminded repeatedly of the sovereignty of our great God. We read of His beloved Son in 1 Corinthians 15:25, "For He must reign, till He hath put all enemies under His feet." As we look about us in the world in which we live today, it would seem that God's sovereignty has been broken. Dictators laugh and mock at the oracles of God. But the day is coming when Almighty God will "put all enemies under His feet." At that time, "The wicked shall be turned into hell, and all the nations that forget God" (Psalm 9:17). How foolish of any mortal soul to reject the claims of the living Christ.

May I ask, which will it be for you — Heaven or hell? Where you will go after death depends upon what you believe before you die. Jesus said in John 3:36: "He that believeth on the Son hath everlasting life: and he that believeth not the Son shall not see life; but the wrath of God abideth on him." Do not be deceived into thinking that you are not lost until you choose to be lost. The Bible teaches that if you have not believed on Jesus Christ, the wrath of God abides on you at this moment.

You are lost until you are saved. Because of Adam's transgression, you are under the condemnation of God. For this reason, you are responsible to Him for your soul. What will you do with the Lord Jesus, who died for you on the cross? Will you respond to His grace and mercy? Or will you refuse Him, choosing to suffer judgment for your sins? Maybe you have your own philosophy: you may refuse to believe what I am telling you from the Word of God. Many people have their own ideas of conversion, but the Bible declares in Proverbs 14:12, "There is a way which seemeth right unto a man, but the end thereof are the ways of death."

Adolph Eichmann, according to a minister who talked to him before his execution, had a religion. He claimed to believe in a personal god who "did not judge sin" and "would not condemn anyone." The man who exterminated six million Jews was trying, as others have tried before him, to build his own religion.

There are many religions in the world, but only one Christianity. Christianity centers in the substitution of God for man. World religions embody the attempts of mankind to reach up to God. Christianity is God reaching down to man. The Bible shows very clearly how God's hand has moved through the ages in carrying out His plan of redemption. The story is told in words as short and simple as those of a third-grade reader. I plead with you not to miss God's best. Receive Jesus Christ into your heart and know the blessedness of the certainty of salvation.

Do not plan to convince God that your way is right. There is only one right way and that is His way. This is the way that leadeth unto life. Learn the lesson of the mighty crocodile, for it speaks of the power and might of the Eternal God. But unlike the crocodile He created, God is not only powerful and mighty, He is gracious and loving. He will receive you if only you will come to Him.

Notice something else about the crocodile: "Sharp stones are under him: he spreadeth sharp pointed things upon the mire." Because of his thick protective skin, he can rest on the jagged rocks as well as in the soft mire. God has equipped the crocodile to endure all circumstances. But can we not say that the Lord has also equipped each one of us who believe to "endure hardness, as a good soldier of Jesus Christ" (2 Timothy 2:3)? The believer's enjoyment should not be dependent upon his circumstances. He may rest in the most difficult of circumstances because of the peace of Christ within. No one but God can accomplish this in us, but He can do it for us only if we permit Him.

The crocodile does not always lie on the rocks or in the mire basking in the sun! Like a flash, at times, in pursuit of his prey, he makes the waters to appear to be boiling as he sneezes and turns, stirring up the water. "He maketh the deep to boil like a pot: he maketh the sea like a pot of ointment. He maketh a path to shine after him, one would think the deep to be hoary." One may trace the crocodile under the water by the foam and the bubbles on top of the water. That is what God means when He says, "He maketh a path to shine after him."

Having given us this detailed description of the crocodile, God concludes by stating four facts concerning this mighty beast. First, as to his strength and terror, he is in a class by himself: "Upon earth there is not his like." Secondly, of all the beasts, the crocodile is the most fearless: God tells us that he "is made without fear." Thirdly, because of his powerful strength he is extremely proud: "He beholdeth all high things." And finally, he excels the animal creation: "He is a king over all the children of pride."

Thus God concludes His instruction about the crocodile, but I wonder if the last phrase of the chapter is not significant: "He is a king over all the children of pride." Is this not the message God sought to convey to Job and his friends? God is over all. Humans are proud and unworthy of the grace of God. Oh, how important that we fall upon our faces before Him, yielding to His Lordship, that He might truly be the Master of everything having any bearing on our individual lives.

JOB 42:1-17

GOD HAD FINISHED His discourse. "Then Job answered the LORD, and said, I know that Thou canst do every thing, and that no thought can be withholden from Thee." Job has nothing to say for himself after listening to God. In the past, Job was quick to respond to the arguments of his friends, but he refuses to argue with the Lord. Rather than justify himself, he speaks with humility and complete self-abasement. Furthermore, he reaffirms his faith in the omnipotence of God. He had always known that God could do everything, but as the result of his afflictions, doubts had crept in. There are no more doubts, for he is convinced that the God who could create and control behemoth and leviathan is able to do all things.

Job stated a marvelous truth most of us know but few of us realize fully. "I know that Thou canst do every thing." God *can* do all things! On one occasion Jeremiah said, "Ah Lord GOD! behold, Thou hast made the heaven and the earth by Thy great power and stretched out arm, and there is nothing too hard for Thee" (Jeremiah 32:17). Never forget this! What is that perplexing problem disturbing your heart at this moment? Fear not! God is able. David said in Psalm 42:11, "Why art thou cast down, O my soul? and why art thou disquieted within me? hope thou in God: for I shall yet praise Him, who is the health of my countenance, and my God." Consider these words: "Hope thou in God." He will not fail you.

Job confessed further to God that "No thought can be withholden from Thee." The word "thought" is really the word for "purpose." It is usually applied to evil devices. What Job means is, though the affliction and suffering he had endured seemed unwise to him, he is confident now that it was not unwise to God. He is certain that, though his sorrow had brought only misery into his life, yet somehow God would bring good out of it all. This, of course, is one of the comforting truths presented repeatedly in the Word of God from Genesis to Revelation. No believer need ever worry or fear, for "no thought can be withholden" from God.

When the Lord began His discourse to Job, He asked the question, "Who is this that darkeneth counsel by words without knowledge?" Job found it difficult to get away from that question. Therefore with humble penitence he says, "Who is he that hideth counsel without knowledge? therefore have I uttered that I understood not; things too wonderful for me, which I knew not." He freely acknowledged the fact that he is the one who sought to hide counsel without knowledge. He realized that he overlooked the counsels of God in his affliction simply because of human ignorance of the divine plan of God. As the result, he criticized God's providence by uttering things he did not understand and, as he says, "things too wonderful for me, which I knew not."

Are we not all like Job in this respect? The plans and purposes of God are wonderful. But who of us is not guilty of complaining and rebelling against the perfect plan of God? Maybe our greatest need at this moment is to come to the place of complete submission to the Lord and His divine will.

Job further said, "Hear, I beseech Thee, and I will speak: I will demand of Thee, and declare Thou unto me." Job was made ready to speak, not as a defendant, but as one humbled by the mighty hand of God. He desired to speak, not to teach, but only to learn. He quoted God again, saying, "I will demand of Thee, and declare Thou unto me." Job realized that his words in the past had been strong demands rather than humble petitions. All changed, however, so that now he realizes that only God has the right to demand. Thus Job was willing to retract his statements and submit to divine providence. He declared, "I have heard of Thee by the hearing of the ear; but now mine eye seeth Thee." He saw God in the sense that he understood Him. Prior to this he had much knowledge about God, but lacked spiritual discernment. From childhood he had been taught the truth, but like many, he had never fully submitted to God's control, permitting its practical application. Of course, the more one knows about God, the greater is his responsibility to obey Him. But so often we glory in knowledge rather than faithfully applying the truth to our hearts.

Job then experienced a complete breakdown before God, crying out, "Wherefore I abhor myself, and repent in dust and ashes." It took a long time for God's servant to come to this place of complete yieldedness to God's plan. But what about us? We must not be too hard on Job. Some of us have not come yet. We are still struggling under the bondage of care, bound by the chains of despair and self-pity. Oh, hear the voice of the Lord at this moment, "Humble yourselves in the sight of the Lord, and He shall lift you up" (James 4:10). Have you been questioning certain events in your life, harboring rebellion in your heart for what God has permitted to cross your path? Oh foolish man, foolish woman, how long will it be before you realize that God makes no mistakes? His ways are always best. The present may seem dismal and dark, but you need only trust Him. Up ahead, along the way, you may be sure He will provide.

The story is told of the little girl who was unaccustomed to traveling. It was her first trip on a train. During the course of the day the train had to cross two branches of a river and several wide streams. The water, which could be seen before reaching the stream, awakened doubts in the mind of the little child. She did not understand how it could be crossed in safety. As they drew near the river, however, a bridge appeared and furnished a way over. Two or three times the experience was repeated. Finally the child leaned back with a sigh of relief and said, "Somebody has put bridges for us all along the way."

God has done the same for you and for me. Regardless of the trial, we will always discover that there is a way with God. Thus let us turn from our vain complaining and rely upon the unchangeable, inerrant Word of the living God.

To read what God spoke to Job from the whirlwind, one might conclude that Job was in the wrong. But such was not the case. For, after speaking to Job, God turned His attention to Eliphaz and his two friends, and what He had to say proves who was to blame: "And it was so, that after the LORD had spoken these words unto Job, the LORD said to Eliphaz the Temanite, My wrath is kindled against thee, and against thy two friends: for ye have not spoken of Me the thing that is right, as my servant Job hath." You will recall that repeatedly Job had called upon God to come to his aid in resistance to the false arguments of his friends. In His own time, God responded to these pleas. Now He condemns the three men and justifies Job. Elihu was not censored, for he was God's spokesman, having remained neutral in his attitude. He sought to divorce himself from both sides, acting simply as a divinely-sent messenger.

Perhaps you have wondered why Eliphaz was named rather than either of the other two friends. God spoke to him because he was the foremost speaker of the three. The others merely voiced Eliphaz's arguments in their own words. But in speaking to Eliphaz, God's rebuke was for all three men because they had ignored the truth to advance their humanistic theories. Job, on the other hand, was commended for speaking properly. He was perfectly in order when he denied the theory of his three friends, who had stated that he suffered because of his hypocrisy. At the same time, Job was out of order in going to the other extreme of practically denying all guilt whatsoever. But in comparison to the three men and their arguments, God declared Job to be right.

How careful we must be in judging others. We have seen Eliphaz, Bildad, and Zophar judging merely from outward appearance. They knew nothing of Job's heart and God's dealings with him. Theirs was hasty judgment, like most human judgments are. You and I must beware of this evil. Remember, the Lord is the only true Judge. If your friends appear to be wrong in your sight, it is far better to be faithful in committing them to the Lord in prayer than to harp on their shortcomings. What Jesus said in Matthew 7:1 should be kept in mind constantly, "Judge not, that ye be not judged." Job's three friends had judged God's servant severely; now God is judging them. To be sure, no one can stand before the judgment of God.

Have you been guilty of unjust criticism? Realize that when you criticize someone, not only do you harm the one you criticize, but you harm yourself as well. Have nothing to do with this destructive evil. Criticism and slander are of the devil and there is no need for any of us to assist him in his wicked practices.

A godly minister was approached by one of his church members, who wanted to repeat to him some of the wrongdoings of another. The pastor said, "Does anybody else know about this but you?"

"No, Sir."

"Have you told it to anybody else?"

"No."

"Then," said the man of God, "go home and hide it away at the feet of Jesus and never speak of it again unless God leads you to speak to the man himself. If the Lord wants to bring scandal upon His church, let Him do it. But don't you be the instrument to cause it."

This is excellent advice. Let God do the judging; don't you be guilty. There is no easier way to ruin your prayer life and to hinder your spiritual growth than by the sin of criticism.

Because of their failure, God said to the three friends of Job, "Therefore take unto you now seven bullocks and seven rams, and go to My servant Job, and offer up for yourselves a burnt offering; and My servant Job shall pray for you: for him will I accept: lest I deal with you after your folly, in that ye have not spoken of Me the thing which is right, like My servant Job." The three men had been proud, thinking that eventually God would reward them. But just the opposite was the case. God told them that each one of them must offer up seven bullocks and seven rams as a burnt offering. What a humiliating experience for three men who were so proud and vain.

Further we note that the man they had condemned for hypocrisy was told to pray for them. The one they had so bitterly criticized was chosen by God to be their priest to intercede for them. Indeed, Job was on praying ground. He had humbled himself in God's sight, and being completely forgiven, he was in a position to reach into God's presence in prayer. He had repented of all his sin. Thus he was in a position to pray.

Sometimes when one is extremely proud, he will refuse to humble himself in the sight of God. But this was not the case with Job's friends. "So Eliphaz the Temanite and Bildad the Shuhite and Zophar the Naamathite went, and did according as the LORD commanded them: the LORD also accepted Job."

There is something not said in this verse, but it need not be said, because what is written proves that it took place. Nothing is said here about Job forgiving the three men for their unkindness, but it is quite obvious that he did. First of all, the three friends did what God told them to do. They were not rebellious or hardened. They responded to the call of God and humbled themselves in His sight. As the verse closes, we read that "the Lord also accepted Job." Why did God accept Job? Because he did what he should have done; he forgave these men and he prayed for them. It would be ridiculous for one to try to pray for someone he had not personally forgiven for a wrongdoing. Thus a happy reunion was effected. Indeed, this verse is a grand commentary on God's words about Job in the first chapter of the book: "There is none like him in the earth, a perfect and an upright man, one that feareth God, and escheweth evil."

How important that we search out our hearts before the Lord. Is there any trace of an unforgiving spirit? Do not try to pray until you go to your brother and forgive him completely, making all things right. For let us be reminded of the words of our Lord Jesus, as found in Matthew 6:14-15: "For if ye forgive men their trespasses, your heavenly Father will also forgive you: But if ye forgive not men their trespasses, neither will your Father forgive your trespasses."

Having gotten right with God and having offered prayer for his friends at the command of God, Job was in a position to receive the Lord's blessing. Thus we read that "the LORD turned the captivity of Job, when he prayed for his friends: also the LORD gave Job twice as much as he had before." It would seem that the phrase, "the Lord turned the captivity of Job," means that in a miraculous way the Lord touched the body of Job and healed him completely. At the same time, Satan who had buffeted God's servant so severely was now subdued, no longer able to plague Job. In addition to this, "the Lord gave Job twice as much as he had before."

Oh, the mercy and the grace of God! He is certainly faithful. His promises are ever true. In Psalm 34:15 we are told that "The eyes of the LORD are upon the righteous, and His ears are open unto their cry." God never fails His own. So often we look at our present status and become fretful and fearful. But never forget it, we have a mighty God who does not once remove His eyes from His people. It may be that at this moment you are suffering severely. It may seem that God has forsaken you. "The Lord turned the captivity of Job." He can turn your captivity if you will fully trust Him by faith and believe that He is able to do all things.

In Proverbs 16:7 God says, "When a man's ways please the LORD, He maketh even his enemies to be at peace with him." This was certainly true regarding Job. "Then came there unto him all his brethren, and all his sisters, and all they that had been of his acquaintance before, and did eat bread with him in his house: and they bemoaned him, and comforted him over all the evil that the LORD had brought upon him: every man also gave him a piece of money, and every one an earring of gold." After Job got right with God, the Lord put it in the hearts of his friends and relatives to be kind to him. During his affliction they had abused him and judged him as a hypocrite. But later they flocked about him, giving him money and gold, with the marvelous result that "the LORD blessed the latter end of Job more than his beginning." Through the gifts that were presented to him, Job was able to become re-established in life. "He had fourteen thousand sheep, and six thousand camels, and a thousand yoke of oxen, and a thousand she asses." It was not necessary that all of this come about instantaneously; probably this vast increase took place over a period of time.

Not only was Job blessed with possessions, but with that which had been so dear to his heart, a family. "He had also seven sons and three daughters. And he called the name of the first, Jemima; and the name of the second, Kezia; and the name of the third, Kerenhappuch." Possibly these were children of Job's second wife, for it would seem that his first wife had died. The question has been raised that if the Lord gave Job twice as much as he had before, why were there only ten children, the same number he had before? The answer, of course, is that the first ten children were not really lost. They were in Heaven, very much alive. Job would see them again.

It would seem that the daughters' names were given for a

purpose. Jemima means "daylight," perhaps to remind everyone
that Job's night of suffering was past and the daylight of blessing had come. Kezia meant "cassia," an herb of pleasing fra-
grance; God had healed Job's ulcers, which had been offensive
to all who came near him. Kerenhappuch means "plenty restored," another evidence of God's abundant mercy manifested
in Job's life.

Further we read of the three daughters that "in all the land
were no women found so fair as the daughters of Job."
Throughout this chapter we see the exceeding greatness of
God's provision for His humble saint. Truly the beauty He bestowed upon these daughters was another evidence of His great
love for Job. Job rewarded the girls with an inheritance, he
"gave them inheritance among their brethren." This was a further proof of the love God had shed abroad in Job's heart, for
in the East it was rare for a father to honor his daughters in
this manner while his sons were still living.

As a climactic blessing poured out on Job, God gave him a
long life. "After this lived Job an hundred and forty years, and
saw his sons, and his sons' sons, even four generations. So Job
died, being old and full of days." It would seem that God dou-
bled the years of his life as another sign of great blessing.

We conclude the study of the book of Job with a helpful
lesson to be learned. David expressed it well in Psalm 30:5:
"Weeping may endure for a night, but joy cometh in the morning." Trouble, sorrow, and care may be our lot. But God will
never fail His own. The apostle has written in 2 Corinthians
4:17, "For our light affliction, which is but for a moment, worketh for us a far more exceeding and eternal weight of glory."
We may rest assured that the believer's future will be far more
wonderful than his past or present. We may not see the same
prosperity and provision Job realized in his latter years, but
when we see the Lord Jesus face to face, our provision will far
exceed Job's, for we shall have all things. God says in James
1:12, "Blessed is the man that endureth temptation: for when

he is tried, he shall receive the crown of life, which the Lord hath promised to them that love Him."

Do you love Christ? Do you know Him as your Saviour and Lord? Then keep looking up, for the best is yet to come. Keep going on, living patiently, trusting Him daily for all things. If you do not know Him, receive Him into your heart, that you might be eternally saved and ready to meet Him when He calls. Life without Christ is empty and hopeless. With Him, it is filled with abundant joy and happiness. Fully trust Christ and see for yourself.